THE
REFERENCE
SHELF

AMERICAN INDUSTRY

edited by VERNON WHITFORD

THE REFERENCE SHELF

Volume 55 Number 6

THE H. W. WILSON COMPANY

New York   1984

THE REFERENCE SHELF

The books in this series contain reprints of articles, excerpts from books, and addresses on current issues and social trends in the United States and other countries. There are six separately bound numbers in each volume, all of which are generally published in the same calendar year. One number is a collection of recent speeches; each of the others is devoted to a single subject and gives background information and discussion from various points of view, concluding with a comprehensive bibliography. Books in the series may be purchased individually or on subscription.

Library of Congress Cataloging in Publication Data

Main entry under title:

American industry.

    (The Reference shelf ; v. 55, no. 6)
    Bibliography: p.
    1. United States—Industries—Addresses, essays lectures. 2. Industrial productivity—United States—Addresses, essays, lectures. 3. Industry and state—United States—Addresses, essays, lectures. I. Whitford, Vernon, 1947- . II. Series.
HC106.8.A445   1984   338.0973   84-2319
ISBN 0-8242-0687-8

Printed in the United States of America

CONTENTS

PREFACE

One of the most serious problems facing the United States today is the condition of the national economy, whose weaknesses are attributed to a decline in American industrial strength. Since the 1960s the United States has been steadily losing ground both as an exporter of manufactured goods and as a supplier of its own domestic market for such commodities as steel, automobiles, textiles, and electric appliances. American products are being challenged by manufacturers who produce cheaper, often higher quality goods, and as other nations increase their share of both foreign and domestic markets, so the gross national product stops rising and fewer resources are devoted to building new plants or expanding producing capacity.

The United States still produces more than any other nation, but the gap is rapidly closing, and when the gross national product is divided by the number of American workers it appears that there has been virtually no growth in productivity per worker since the early 1970s. This decline in manufacturing has had an effect on American society, and the hardship has been felt most severely in those areas—chiefly the North and Midwest—where heavy manufacturing industries are concentrated. The closing of plants that once housed busy production lines, and the movement of many industries to the so-called "sunbelt" areas have tended to create distinct areas of poverty and affluence.

But not all American industries are in trouble, and the U.S. economy as a whole remains the largest and most diverse in the world. Many commentators believe that current difficulties can be overcome provided that the structure of many industries is overhauled, and that the business community—both management and unions—face up to the stringent competitive demands of the world market. It is sometimes argued that Americans, accustomed to believe that the future will bring higher and higher standards of living, have become complacent and have failed to match their economic expectations with higher productivity. This has occurred at a time when other industrialized nations, notably West

Germany and Japan, have adopted the means to create consumer goods and export them aggressively in the markets once dominated by the United States. The goal of American industrialists, as all agree, is to improve the productivity of the American worker and restore the United States to a competitive position in the world market.

This compilation offers a selection of opinions on what is wrong with American industry, why the economic decline has taken place, and what can best be done about it. Section I contains three reviews of the general state of American capitalism, its historical foundation and its present condition, two of which predict that government will in future take a larger hand in the accumulation of capital necessary for industrial expansion. Section II presents varying opinions on the need for a national "industrial policy" to rejuvenate industry. Section III gathers reports on the present state of American industry, showing that the business scene is too complex and too various to be summarized as either hopeful or discouraging. The articles in this section also seem to suggest that American business people still place great confidence in their ability to overcome difficulties through sheer entrepreneurial energy. Section IV is a selection of viewpoints on how industry will affect the society of the future.

The editor wishes to thank the authors and publishers who have kindly granted permission to reprint the material in this compilation.

Vernon Whitford

February 1984

I. THE STATE OF AMERICAN CAPITALISM

EDITOR'S INTRODUCTION

It is generally believed that the underlying cause of America's economic problems is declining productivity. If industries stagnate or disappear and are not replaced by other revenue-producing sources, recessions will occur with increasing severity and frequency, and may even become a permanent condition. Since 1979 the United States has enjoyed two "recoveries," but the latest (1983), achieved at the expense of a greatly increased national debt and high unemployment, could be followed by yet another downturn. On one point, and only one, economists will agree: American productivity must be increased. But the question of how to stimulate the economy while holding down inflation and maintaining a high level of employment is one that no one has yet been able to solve.

In this section two eminent economists offer explanations for this decline. Robert L. Heilbroner's *New York Times Magazine* article takes a historical view of the rise and fall of giant corporations, coming to the conclusion that western capitalism is undergoing a crisis from which it will emerge radically changed, probably as a form of "state capitalism." Both he and Robert B. Reich, writing in *Atlantic Monthly,* foresee state control of the means of production, and Reich finds this prospect especially favorable because of his animus against the current practices of large corporations, whom he regards as cumbersome, prone to seek short-term profit at the expense of long-range goals, and misled by the temptations of paper entrepreneurialism. Whereas Heilbroner regards present economic troubles as the outcome of inexorable global trends, Reich is convinced that U.S. corporations should shoulder much of the blame. Arthur Burck, a company president, supports Reich's case against the large corporations, whose very size and strength, he believes, has stifled the competitive instinct and left the U.S. vulnerable to more nimble, energetic foreign companies. Unlike the two professional economists, he thinks that any attempt to encourage state capitalism should be resisted. American industry will prosper, he believes, if the entrepreneur is allowed to thrive and a spirit of competitive diversity prevails.

DOES CAPITALISM HAVE A FUTURE[1]

What lies ahead for capitalism? That's a question that makes people nervous. It conjures up visions and specters. It paralyzes thought.

Nevertheless, it is a question that ought to be thought about now, while most of us are concentrating only on the present and the immediate future, worrying about the depression and whether it will get worse. For I believe we are not only in a depression but also in a crisis—a period of change for capitalism. Hence to the question "Does capitalism have a future?" my answer would be, "Yes, but not the future most people expect." Sooner or later, the depression will mend and we will be back to where we were, more or less. But the crisis will not mend in the same way. When it has run its course, we will be on new ground, in unfamiliar territory.

Thinking about long-term change rather than short-term prospects requires that we forget for the moment about tight money and unmanageable deficits and the other well-known reasons for our economic troubles. Instead, we must look back over the history of capitalism's fortunes and misfortunes for the last century or so. Then we can see that capitalism has more than once gone through a period like our own—a period in which a depression or a panic has masked farreaching, but often ill-perceived restructurings. Only later did people realize that they had not only gone through an economic trauma, but a historical one—a period in which familiar institutions were replaced by unfamiliar ones, accustomed ideas by unaccustomed ones. If I am right, that is what we are experiencing today.

[1]Reprint of an article by Robert L. Heilbroner. *New York Times Magazine* p20+. Ag. 15, '82. © 1982 by The New York Times Company. Reprinted by permission.

What is the nature of our present historic crisis? That question requires that we take a moment to reflect on the nature of capitalism itself. Volumes have been written on what capitalism "is"—a market system, a system of economic and political freedom, a system of wage labor and exploitation. But all these different interpretations have one central area of agreement: It is that the life of capitalism is its incessant and insatiable drive to accumulate wealth. Ask Adam Smith and Karl Marx to name the first necessity of the system they both analyzed, and they would answer from widely different perspectives that it was *accumulation*—using the capital created by the system to build more capital. Ask any businessman, and his answer will be the same: The first necessity is expansion, growth. Capitalism is a system that cannot stand still.

But what determines the pace of what Smith and Marx called accumulation, or what we today call "investment" or "capital formation"? The economist and labor historian David Gordon has developed an original and fruitful way of approaching this question. In "Segmented Work, Divided Workers," written with Richard Edwards and Michael Reich, Gordon stresses the importance of the milieu of institutions and attitudes within which accumulation takes place. That milieu begins at the immediate locus of production itself, on the factory floor where the capitalist must equip and organize and discipline his work force. Needless to say, workfloor conditions may be propitious for expansion or not. But the milieu extends beyond the frictions of the work-place to the critical interface between Government and business, and then still further out into the social climate itself. Both of these may or may not be conducive to the process of accumulation. Then, finally, there is the setting, benign or otherwise, of the larger world order within which capitalist nations coexist and compete, and extend their networks of trade and production into noncapitalist regions.

Gordon calls the entire complex set of influences that bears on the pace of investment the "social structure of accumulation." The phrase clarifies the meaning of a crisis period, such as our own, that is larger than just another business downturn. A crisis occurs, Gordon suggests, when an existing social structure of institutions and attitudes loses its capacity to impart momentum to the system, and becomes a drag on its performance. When these junctures arise, the propulsive energy of the system slackens, and business and Government leaders alike engage in a frantic, although usually uncoordinated, search for a new structure that will permit the process of growth to start up once again.

Two periods in American (and European) history within the last century dramatically illustrate this interpretation. The first began in the 1870's, when the capitalist process was becoming seriously imperiled by its inability to cope with the effects of the emerging technology of mass production. As a labor historian, Gordon pays special heed to the difficulties of reconciling this technology with the necessary control over labor, still organized in semi-independent craftlike groupings. I would place equal emphasis on the effect of mass production in bringing about business instability, as torrential flows of production forced firms into cut-throat competitive tactics.

Much has been written about this turbulent period, with its robber-baron tactics, its business atmosphere of "panic and pain," its social unrest. But the period has not been much analyzed from Gordon's perspective as a crisis brought on by the failure of an adequate social structure of accumulation. Yet, looking back, we can see that an institutional framework of small business—with a virtual absence of Government regulation, a suspicious view of "monopolists" and a defensive attitude toward foreign trade—could not possibly cope with the massive disruptions of technology. The necessary adaptation came finally from a few bold business leaders who were determined to mitigate the destructive, competitive wars of mass production. Their means was the formation of giant companies or cartels to control production, first by illegal and not very effective voluntary "pools," then by the legal but cumbersome method of "trusts," ultimately by the highly efficacious legal invention of "mergers."

The resulting big businesses were certainly not popular. Trusts and monopolies, as they were called, were the favorite target of cartoonists and politicians, and not least of small businessmen who found themselves undersold or shouldered aside by the giant companies. But there was no stopping the rise of Carnegie's or Rockefeller's or McCormick's enterprises. There was no stopping them because big business succeeded in minimizing its exposure to the vagaries of the market. It did so partly by encompassing more and more phases of production within its own operations, and partly by each huge firm dominating its own industry. Thus, United States Steel mined its own ore, shipped it on its own barges and rail lines, smelted it in its own furnaces, and fabricated the steel in its own plants, out of which finally emerged two-thirds of the nation's entire output of steel. As Alfred Chandler, our foremost business historian, has put it, the rise of big business replaced the invisible hand of the market with the visible hand of management.

Accompanying this radical reorganization of business came a no less far-reaching change in the relation of business to Government. Leaders like Theodore Roosevelt vigorously endorsed the creative powers of what he called the "good" trusts, while simultaneously supporting regulations to modify the behavior of the "bad" trusts. Actually, the regulations themselves, by enforcing minimum standards of performance, also served to mitigate the destructive effects of competition. Meanwhile a complementary change in foreign policy further strengthened the new structure of accumulation by openly adopting a probusiness, imperialist stance. And not least, the suspicious view of monopolists was gradually supplanted by a public attitude of admiration for, even adulation of, the heroic captains of industry.

Thus, the social structure of accumulation—the milieu of institutions and attitudes within which capital formation took place—underwent a sea change between Lincoln's time and the first Roosevelt's, a sea change whose effectiveness is evidenced by the fact that the capitalism of big business industrialized the Western world.

Why, then, did it all end in the Great Depression of the 1930's? The answer is that the changes that imparted thrust to capitalism at the end of the 19th century slowly lost their vitality and relevance during the first quarter of the 20th century. The trusts and monopolies, for instance, temporarily lessened but could not eliminate competition, so that as time went on the great giants watched the unruly forces of the market once again invade their precincts. Within the giant firms, a new mode of organizing the work process—semiskilled labor working under the supervision of driving foremen—was also not an unqualified success. It broke the old craft bottlenecks, but laid the basis for the troubles of an incipient industrial union movement.

Meanwhile, the initial euphoria and triumphs of the age of imperialism were followed by political and economic frictions. Even the climate of adulation soured as the captains of industry came to be seen as malefactors of great wealth.

But at the center of the eventual failure of the structure was a problem brought into being by the very emergence of big business itself. This was a new instability introduced into the economic framework—not the instability of markets upset by mass production, but the instability of an entire structure threatened by mass collapse. The downturns of earlier periods were painful enough, but they were not marked by the devastations of huge toppling structures, simply because there were very few such structures in the system. Early 20th century capitalism was another affair entirely. Interlocked into a grid of national scale, the economic system resembled a vast scaffolding where the displacement of a single beam could destabilize the whole. The shutting down of a steel plant in Pennsylvania could paralyze an entire region; a decline in the order books maintained in Schenectady could throw men out of work in Sacramento; the fortunes of the Ford Motor Company not only reflected but directly affected the fortunes of the national economy.

Thus, the economic structure created by massive enterprise was inherently more dangerous than that of small business. When adversity struck, it was capable of spreading fearful wreckage throughout the system. This is essentially what happened in the 1930's. The Great Crash triggered a self-feeding, self-worsening collapse of the interconnected but unsupported scaffolding. An initial fall of 13 percent in national output from 1929 to 1930 brought a further fall of 17 percent the next year, and that in turn resulted in a 22 percent fall the following year. By 1933, almost half of 1929's production had vanished and a quarter of the nation's work force had lost its jobs. To compound the tragedy, the unemployment appeared in an age when most families had only one, not two, members at work, and when the Government's attitude of enthusiastic support for business did not extend to, and indeed seemed incompatible with, support for the casualties of business failure.

The economy entered a period of free fall—a period that lasted for four seemingly interminable years and that brought the capitalist system to what seemed to many the end of its days. But it was not the end of its days, and the next part of the story has special relevance for the conditions in which we find ourselves today.

Working with no predetermined objective in mind, seeking to do no more than clear away the wreckage, maintain social order and start up the stalled engines of growth, business and Government leaders began to construct a new basis for expansion. Rudimentary floors were laid under the household economy, first as "work relief," then as the initial timid measures of Social Security and the cautious insuring of bank deposits, both violently assailed as unworkable and Communistic. An array of legislative measures sought to restore order to disorganized markets by creating Government marketing agencies in agriculture and by allowing industry for a while to regulate its own competition. Perhaps most important, there gradually emerged the entirely new idea of a *managed* economy, first from the writings of John Maynard Keynes, then from the work of his American disciples.

And so, without the faintest intention of creating a new "social structure of accumulation," the New Deal did create just that. Or rather, it began its creation. The structure was not completed until after World War II, when it received its legitimation from the conservative Governments of Dwight Eisenhower and Konrad Adenauer and Winston Churchill and Charles de Gaulle. Only then did it become widely recognized that a new form of capitalism had come into being—"people's capitalism," Eisenhower liked to call it. The mixed economy or the welfare state (as economists soon named it) openly admitted its reliance on Government support, both as a reserve engine for economic growth and as the main source of personal security against unemployment and the penury of old age. It was widely hailed as the purified descendant of the "bad" capitalism that had led us into the Great Depression, which would never be allowed to happen again.

Fulsome as it was, the praise had a core of truth. The new system did propel capitalism into the most remarkable and extended period of growth it had ever known. The previous burst of growth, under the regime of "bad" capitalism, had industrialized the West. The new burst of growth, under the regime of "good" capitalism, sought to industrialize the world. However, even with the powerful stabilizing influence of a global American hegemony, it did not succeed in that ambition. But it did create an unprecedented degree of widely shared affluence within its own core nations. This was the social structure of accumulation that supported most of us very comfortably until the depression of the 1980's.

Then what happened?

As we come down to the present, we have to disentangle historic trends from current events. Unquestionably, much of our immediate economic distress is the consequence of Government policies combining overoptimism with strategies that work at cross purposes. The ills of tight money and ballooning deficits have not been visited on us by history, but have been put there by the Reagan Administration.

But it would be quite wrong to attribute our woes solely to Government policy. Whether his remedies are effective or not, Presient Reagan is right when he says that he inherited an economy that was already in trouble. And from our historic perspective it now becomes possible to describe that trouble as the gradual loss of effectiveness of the very institutions that initially gave us our long postwar boom.

In complex ways, the mixed economy and the welfare state, mighty engines of growth in the 1950's, became mighty engines of inflation 20 years later. The American hegemony that assured a stable world in the 1950's lost its efficacy as European nations began to challenge us, and as the underdeveloped world proved unexpectedly resistant to easy industrialization. The social peace that had been achieved by the welfare state ended in a restive and rebellious mood—a taste of social justice had whetted appetites, not satisfied them.

Not least, technology once again posed challenges that exceeded the grasp of existing institutions. The jet plane and the computer—the two great triumphs of the new capitalism—made it possible to transplant high technology around the world in a manner unimaginable in the 1930's. Assembly lines manned by workers barely out of the paddy fields began to mount competitive attacks against the citadels of capitalism itself. Nowhere was this new capacity to raise up an industrial structure of terrific penetrative power more startlingly evidenced than in the conversion of Japan from a maker of Christmas tree ornaments and shoddy textiles into a power capable of leveling the American auto and steel industries, all in a mere 25 years.

This is not, of course, a complete or systematic account of the roots or the extent of our present crisis. I have not mentioned the long steady upward climb in unemployment until it has now surpassed the unemployment rate in 1930. I have not discussed the sagging performance of American productivity, a 10-year source of concern. And then there is the superstructure of shaky credit that looms over the system, all too reminiscent of the rickety scaffolding of the 1930's. Most important of all, I have not drawn attention to the global aspect of our time of troubles.

For virtually the entire capitalist world is experiencing ills similar to ours. There are 30 million without jobs in the Western countries, a virtual nation of the unemployed. In France, Britain, West Germany, even in Japan (which had achieved unsustainably high rates of productivity growth), the pace of productivity has been falling during the last decade—in Japan, by more than half. And the Damoclean sword of a financial debacle hangs over the whole world, not just over America. The international debts of the underdeveloped world are more than a half-trillion dollars. What will happen when they are not paid? All these deep, persisting and farflung evidences of disarray suggest that we are going through more than a "mere" depression that will cure itself at least partially, as depressions do. In the light of history, it is plausible that the pattern of capitalist development is again at work, and that the institutions and policies that led to expansion in one period have again become ineffective and even detrimental, to expansion in another.

Is President Reagan correct, then, when he says that the mixed economy and the welfare state are the root causes of our difficulties—that what we thought was "good" capitalism is "bad" capitalism, and that we must go back to a simpler way of organizing the economy? I think he is half right. The mixed economy and the welfare state *are* responsible for many of our problems. Where I think he is completely wrong is in asserting that we should therefore rid ourselves of these encumbrances to the maximum possible extent.

The institutions needed to create a viable system in one period cannot simply be discarded in another, unless we are willing to accept the return of the problems to which those institutions were addressed. The rise of big business assuredly gave us an economy much more vulnerable to cumulative depressions than in the past, but that did not mean that we could therefore get rid of big business. Liberal reformers who have dreamed of doing so have not asked themselves how a reinstated world of small business would control and contain a technology even more destabilizing today than when big business arose to make it manageable. So, too, conservatives who dream of dismantling the welfare state and the mixed economy do not reflect on what will then provide the personal security or the collective underpinning on which we all depend. Indeed, we have already seen from the effects of the Reagan Administration's retrenchments that the answer is—nothing.

So it is futile to think of social evolution as permitting a return to the "simpler" ways of the past. History is a cumulative process that permits no such retreats. If a social structure of accumulation no longer serves its original purpose, it cannot simply be ripped out. Another, better suited to the times, must be built.

Indeed, just as big business steadily strengthened its strategic place within the American economy *after* the mixed economy and the welfare state were put into place, so I imagine that the welfare state and the mixed economy will steadily strengthen their places within the system after new structures have been added to it. The logical extension of the mixed economy lies in the deliberate encouragement and guidance of investment, the key to economic planning. The natural growth of the welfare state lies in the provision of permanent public employment for those unable to find private employment, in particular for the victims of the robotization that is cutting into factory and office work. Similarly, we can expect more Federal support for our older cities if urban decay is not to become a source of dangerous social infection.

So I do not think the existing structure will shrink, despite the efforts of the present Administration. Rather, I would expect that over the long run these governmental elements of our structure would increase until they reach at least the proportions found in most capitalist countries abroad. Very roughly speaking, a third of our economy is cycled through the Government in the form of welfare payments (including Social Security) and the actual purchases of output, from arms to public education. In Europe, that percentage is considerably higher: In West Germany, for example, between 40 and 50 percent of the total.

With all their difficulties and inefficiencies, Government activities will remain and grow because they still provide the necessary underpinning and the essential economic security required for a workable capitalism. But their growth will by no means create a new milieu for capitalist expansion, any more than the continued growth of big business after the New Deal constituted the foundation of the new structure within which the postwar boom took place. Something will have to be added to the present, inadequately functioning system, if accumulation is to find a new basis for vitality.

Is it possible to speculate about what such additions might be? With all the risks that such a prognosis entails, I shall try.

Let me first deal briefly with two possible directions of evolution, fervently espoused by their supporters, that seem unlikely to lead very far. One I have already mentioned. It is the vision of the Reagan Administration (and to a lesser degree of Mrs. Thatcher's Government in England)—of a born-again capitalism, stripped down to its natural, lean, aggressive fighting weight, once more undertaking its accumulative mission with assurance and pride. Whether this is a realistic vision or a fantasy we should discover fairly soon. My own views must be clear. I only hope that if the Reagan program fails, we do not move on a dangerous course, preaching the gospel of freedom and enterprise, but practicing the economics of military capitalism.

A second vision, entertained much more strongly in Europe than in the United States, sees this period as the forcing ground for a new attempt to create socialism—not the sclerotic socialism of the centrally planned systems, such as the Soviet Union, but a socialism of intensified democratic participation, of widespread workers' management of enterprises and of the gradual elimination of capitalist privileges and waste. Whether this is a fantasy or not may take a little longer to find out. My guess is that the main threat to such democratic socialistic efforts is not the likelihood of clear-cut failure, but of disappointment. High, perhaps even heady, expectations are needed to create socialism. Thus, disappointment can lead easily to disillusion. That is likely to be the greatest challenge that socialism will have to face.

This brings me to the third direction of evolution, to my mind the most probable. It is an effort to restructure things in ways that will once again encourage capital accumulation.

Here I would imagine that the first order of business would be to deal with the chronic ailment of the present structure— inflation. I do not see how this can be done without the introduction of various kinds of ceilings and restraints—price and wage and dividend controls of one kind or another—that will serve as counterparts of the floors and supports that underpin the system today.

It is because of these floors and supports that our present depression, for all its severity, is not likely to repeat the nearly fatal self-feeding contractions of the 1930's. The next structure of accumulation will require ceilings and anti-inflationary controls at least as effective as these floors—not removing the inflationary propensity of the system, but limiting the harm it can do. W. David Slawson, who has perceptively described the upward-ratcheting tendencies of our modern markets, writes in his book *The New Inflation* that we will eventually require an anti-inflationary administrative structure as pervasive in our economic life as that of the Internal Revenue Service. It is a disconcerting image, but I think it is a correct one. Nothing else will match the power of the inflationary process that is now part of the normal workings of the system. And so we will learn to live with ceilings and be grateful to them, as we have learned to live with floors, and have become grateful to them.

Next, I believe there will be a marked lessening in the distinction we now make between the private and public sectors. The idea that growth only originates in the activities of the business

world and that the activities of government are essentially inimical
to expansion is one that cannot survive the realities of the coming
century. To put it boldly, just as the strategic vehicle of accumulation in Adam Smith's day was the pin factory, in Henry Ford's
time the national corporation, and in our own day the multinational enterprises, I think tomorrow's vehicle will be the state corporation.

We have already seen the first examples of such a linking of
Government's powers of finance and diplomacy with business's
capabilities of management in the Japanese system, or in the public-private consortium that builds the European Airbus, or in the
Volkswagen company or British Petroleum. These public-private
enterprises have considerable advantages over purely private companies in the jockeying that goes on for shares in the global markets. American businessmen who protest the "dumping" and
"export subsidies" and "unfair tactics" of these formidable state
corporations remind me of nothing so much as the small businessmen of a century ago who railed against the practices of the emerging trusts and monopolies.

To be sure, there is no guarantee that all such state enterprises
will succeed. There are plenty of examples of failures in putting
together the power of the public treasury and the efforts of private
management—Renault, Fiat, not to mention our own Lockheed
(on an unacknowledged basis). But that is like saying that the
emergence of big business was a failure because most of the trusts
eventually lost control over their markets or because some big
business did not make the grade. The giant enterprise arose to
cope with the problems of production on a national scale. The
state enterprise will arise to cope with the problems of production
on a global scale. And it will arise because business as well as Government will come to see that it is the only possible means of
amassing the finance, exerting the political pressure, and supply-
ing the entrepreneurial zeal needed to establish our place in the
new arena of global competition.

And so I expect that 20 years from now, General Motors and
Boeing and I.B.M. will have Government officials on their boards
and access to Government financing; they will no longer clearly
know whether they are part of the private or the public undertak-

ings of the economy. They *will* know, however, that they are able
to carry on the business of capital accumulation and growth much
better than they could in the old-fashioned days of the 1980's.

I have left to the end a wrenching change that I foresee as a
precondition for erecting a new structure of accumulation. This
is the abandonment of the idea of a unified world market as the
global basis for accumulation, and its replacement with a system
of regional blocs, each securing a reasonably protected market for
its favored producers, and regulating its intercourse with other
large blocs.

The reason for this change again lies in the power of modern
technology to outflank and bypass established centers of production, as the German tanks in 1940 penetrated the old Maginot line
and reduced its great outposts to impotence. The pressures of international competition are largely determined by the technology
of transportation and information and communication. As long as
these pressures were bearable, a worldwide free market could be
held up as the ideal by which the greatest welfare could be
achieved for all. In fact, that was not the way the free market
worked, so far as the underdeveloped countries were concerned,
but unquestionably free trade and the associated free market in
currencies served the interests of the industrial countries very well.

Today, though, things have changed. Cities that were Ki-
plingesque tourist attractions a decade or two ago are now centers
of low-wage, high-technology manufacture and assembly. The
jobs of German, French, British and American workers are being
performed by Taiwanese, South Koreans, Thais—perhaps soon
by Chinese. This is all very well for the consumer, but it is not
so well for the producer. A successful social structure of accumulation must ultimately support its producers over its consumers, and
that includes its working force as well as its capitalists. I believe
that the flag of free trade will be hauled down in the coming restructuring of things, as the flag of laissez-faire was hauled down
in the last restructuring.

Of course, this is not intended to be an inventory of prospective
alterations. I have done no more than sketch the general kinds of
changes I think will be needed to set a successful new structure
of growth in place. I suppose it can be succinctly described as a

movement toward state capitalism or, perhaps more accurately, as a movement toward a capitalism in which the line that divides the economy from the polity is redrawn in favor of the polity. No doubt such a movement will be regarded by many as "socialistic" by others as "fascistic." I think that its political coloration could be as varied—as authoritarian or as liberal—as other forms of capitalism have shown themselves to be.

Two last thoughts seem necessary. First, the period of change will last a long time. The passage from the world of small-scale capitalism to that of big business took more than two decades. The creation of the mixed economy and the welfare state required roughly as long. So it seems altogether possible that the next transformation will also last more than a decade—an extended period during which we can expect all the unease and dissension characteristic of times that have not discovered a consensus, or concluded a social contract, or forged a viable social structure of accumulation.

Second, the change will not necessarily be welcomed. Indeed, it is likely to be greeted as totally incompatible with capitalism, denounced in the names of liberty and freedom, and proclaimed both unworkable and un-American.

But that has been the reception accorded to all major restructurings of the system. Change has come nevertheless, because it has been brought by the efforts of business and political leaders who were more concerned about finding ways past the obstacles that were blocking capitalism's expansion than about ideological purity. Just as capitalism does not grow by blueprint, so I do not think its adaptation can be easily stymied by sentiment. Capitalism is powered by something stronger than that—the drive for survival. When capitalism can no longer find effective new means for carrying on its task of accumulation, its life energies will have ebbed and its historic career will be finished. For better or worse, I do not think that time is yet at hand.

THE NEXT AMERICAN FRONTIER[2]

The worldwide recession that began in 1981 will end eventually. Some say it already has ended. But the underlying problems of the American economy will not come to an end with the next upturn in the business cycle, unless American industry undertakes some basic changes in its organization of production. Unemployment will remain high. Millions of jobs in the nation's basic industries will never return. And the American standard of living will continue to decline.

Between 1920 and 1970, business, labor, and government hewed to a set of organizing principles—originally called "scientific management"—in which tasks were simplified, ordered according to pre-established rules, and carefully monitored. These principles were put into effect by a new class of professional managers. High volume, scientifically managed industry, producing standardized goods, generated vast economies of scale and levels of wealth unparalleled in history.

The management era ended for America around 1970. Its decline began, ironically, just as many Europeans were coming to view the mastery of high-volume production as the "American challenge," which Europe had either to emulate or to succumb to. Gradually the economic cycles began to follow a downward trend, and over the next decade America's industry was progressively idled.

The proportion of U.S. manufacturing capacity employed in production, which had reached 86 percent in 1965, averaged around 80 percent during the 1970s, and fell to less than 70 percent by 1982. Only 3.5 percent of the labor force was jobless in 1969, but thereafter unemployment climbed persistently, reaching almost 11 percent last year. By the 1980s, the core industries of the management era—steel, automobiles, petrochemicals, textiles,

[2]Reprint of a magazine article by Robert B. Reich, a professor of business and public policy at the Kennedy School of Government, Harvard University, *Atlantic* 251:43 –56+ Mr '83. From *The Next American Frontier* by Robert B. Reich. Copyright © 1983 by Robert B. Reich. Reprinted by permission of Times Books.

consumer electronics, electrical machinery, metal-forming machinery—were in trouble.

Productivity growth slowed from an average yearly increase of 3.2 percent between 1948 and 1965 to an average of 2.4 percent between 1965 and 1973. The rate of growth then dropped to 1.1 percent between 1973 and 1978, and in 1979 American productivity began actually to decline. Meanwhile, productivity growth in Japan and several Western European nations stayed relatively high. After 1965, American real incomes slowed their long climb. Between 1965 and 1981, the average U.S. worker's real wages declined by one fifth. The American engine of prosperity had stalled.

Standardized production had brought America unparalleled wealth. True, our national well-being was interrupted by a depression and by periodic recessions. But these were interruptions, nothing more. Standardized production always restored prosperity, consistently exceeding previous levels, consistently achieving more efficiency and greater volume.

As the trusted formula has ceased to work, America has been ready to embrace any explanation but the most obvious: the same factor that once brought prosperity—the way the nation organizes itself for production—now threatens decline. Everywhere America has looked, it has seen the symptoms of its economic impasse, but it has been unable to recognize the actual causes because the roots of the problem are so deeply embedded in our business enterprises, labor unions, and government institutions.

Government regulation served as a convenient rhetorical scapegoat in the 1980 presidential election, but offers no real explanation. Environmental laws indeed require firms to invest in new equipment, but those requirements have imposed only modest costs. During the 1970s, the U.S. steel industry spent an average of $365 million annually to reduce pollution and improve worker safety—about 17 percent of its annual capital investment during the decade. Of this cost, 48 percent was subsidized by state and local governments through industrial-development bonds. Spending by European steelmakers was of an equal magnitude. During the same period, Japanese steel manufacturers spent substantially more for these purposes.

Safety regulations also add some costs to operations, but the reduction in accidents has meant savings in time and expense that go far to offset these extra costs. Overall, capital expenditures on pollution control and safety combined have never exceeded 6 percent of industrial investment, and can be blamed for at most around a tenth of the slowdown in productivity.

Nor do government deficits explain any major part of the problem. There is no evidence that deficits have been nearly large enough to discourage private investment and economic growth substantially. Indeed, through much of the 1970s, the governments of West Germany, Japan, and France maintained a much larger public debt in proportion to the national economy than did the U.S. government.

Inadequate capital formation has not been the problem either. Between 1965 and 1980, even in the face of inflation, the country continued to invest about 10 percent of its gross national product in plant and equipment; for the period between 1977 and the present, the rate is more than 11 percent, and early last year it reached 11.7 percent—its highest level since 1928. Indeed, investment in *manufacturing* as a percent of the total output of goods increased substantially—from 10.8 percent between 1960 and 1964 to 14.8 percent between 1973 and 1978. This level of manufacturing investment was not significantly below that of America's foreign competitors.

Other proposed explanations also have failed. U.S. investment in research and development declined from 3 percent of gross national product at the start of the 1970s to 2 percent at the start of the 1980s. But this decline stemmed mostly from the slowdown in publicly financed defense and space programs, which affected American industry only indirectly. In any event, the decline in America's productive growth actually began in the late 1960s, well before any cutback in research expenditures. Nor can responsibility be placed on escalating energy prices. The oil shock affected all nations, many of which, including Germany and Japan, were much more dependent on imported energy resources than was America. Even more to the point, America's economic decline pre-dated the oil embargo, in 1973.

Nor can the blame be put on the inevitable drop in output from America's mines, on the slowdown in the movement of American labor out of agriculture, on the entrance of women and young people into the labor force, or on unfair trade practices by foreign manufacturers. Even taken together, these explain only a small part of our gradual, steady economic decline relative to other leading industrial nations. They overlook the worldwide reorganization of production and America's failure to adapt to it.

The central problem of America's economic future is that the nation is not moving quickly enough out of high-volume, standardized production. The extraordinary success of the half-century of the management era has left the United States a legacy of economic inflexibility. Thus our institutional heritage now imperils our future.

America's relative decline has been rooted in changes in the world market. Prior to the mid 1960s, foreign trade did not figure significantly in our economy. Only a small proportion of American-made goods were traded internationally; an equally small amount of foreign production entered the United States. This situation changed dramatically.

In 1980, 19 percent of the goods Americans made were exported (up from 9.3 percent in 1970), and more than 22 percent of the goods Americans used were imported (also up from 9.3 percent in 1970). But even those figures understate the new importance of foreign competition. The most telling statistic is this: By 1980, more than 70 percent of all the goods produced in the United States were actively competing with foreign-made goods. America has become part of the world market.

American producers have not fared well in this new contest. Beginning in the mid-1960s, foreign imports have claimed an increasing share of the American market. By 1981, the United States was importing almost 26 percent of its cars, 17 percent of its steel, 60 percent of its televisions, radios, tape recorders, and phonographs, 43 percent of its calculators, 27 percent of its metal-forming machine tools, 35 percent of its textile machinery, and 53 percent of its computerized machine tools. Twenty years before, imports had accounted for less than 10 percent of the American market for each of these products.

America's declining share of the world market has been particularly dramatic in capital-intensive, high-volume industries. Since 1963, America's share of the world market has declined in a number of important areas: automobiles, by almost one third; industrial machinery, by 33 percent; agricultural machinery, by 40 percent; telecommunications machinery, by 50 percent; metalworking machinery, by 55 percent.

The globe is fast becoming a single marketplace. Goods are being made wherever they can be made the cheapest, regardless of national boundaries. And the most efficient places for much mass production are coming to be Third World countries.

The International Labor Office estimates that every year between 1980 and 2000, 36 million people will enter the world labor force, and 85 percent of them will be from developing nations. The newly integrated world market will put many of them to work at America's old specialty of high-volume, standardized production.

Over a period of only fifteen years, many of the world's developing countries have begun to specialize in capital-intensive production. Their production costs are lower than those of the United States, both because their workers are content with lower real wages and because some of these countries have better access to cheap materials. Moreover, the demand for many standardized commodities has been growing faster in developing nations than in industrialized nations, whose citizens already possess these products; and it is often more profitable to manufacture them within these growing markets than it is to ship them there.

One important trend is often overlooked: the hourly output of workers in these newly industrialized nations is catching up to the output of American workers, simply because they are beginning to use many of the same machines. Developing countries have been able to buy (from international engineering and capital-equipment firms) the world's most modern steel-rolling mills, paper machines, and computerized machine tools. The growth of large-scale retail outlets in industrialized nations has given developing countries an efficient way to distribute their wares. Korean television manufacturers, for example, have gained a sizable share of the U.S. television market by selling to no more than a dozen large American department-store chains.

By the mid-1960s, Korea, Hong Kong, Taiwan, Singapore, Brazil, and Spain were specializing in simple products—clothing, footwear, toys, and basic electronic assemblies—that required substanital amounts of unskilled labor but little capital investment or technology. Between 1970 and 1975, Korea's exports of textiles increased by 436 percent, Taiwan's by 347 percent, and Hong Kong's by 191 percent.

Japan's response was to shift out of these simple products into processing industries, such as steel and synthetic fibers, that required substantial capital investment and raw materials, but used mostly unskilled and semiskilled labor and incorporated relatively mature technologies that were not subject to major innovations. Between 1966 and 1972, the Japanese steel industry increased its steelmaking assets by more than 23 percent a year. As its own steel needs began to level off in the early 1970s, Japan increased its exports of raw steel. It invested in more than fifty finishing facilities in developing countries in order to expand its market share.

By the mid-1970s, Korea, Hong Kong, Taiwan, Singapore, Brazil, Spain, and Mexico had followed Japan—shifting their export mix toward the basic capital-intensive processing industries. All told, these developing countries increased their share of world steelmaking capacity from 9 percent in 1974 to 15 percent by 1980.

As less-developed countries moved into steel production, Japan reduced its domestic steelmaking capacity and became a major exporter of steel technology—engineering services and equipment. Japan moved its industrial base into more complex products, such as automobiles, color televisions, small appliances, consumer electronics, and ships—industries requiring considerable investment in plant and equipment as well as sophisticated new technologies.

At the same time, Malaysia, Thailand, the Philippines, Sri Lanka, India, and other poorer countries were taking over the production of clothing, footwear, toys, and simple electronic assemblies. Workers in these countries earned, on average, no more than $25 a month.

By 1980, Korea, Hong Kong, Singapore, Brazil, Spain, and Mexico had increased their production of complex products such as automobiles, color televisions, tape recorders, CB transceivers, microwave ovens, small computers, and ships. Korea already has the largest single shipyard in the world; and with its salary rates averaging only one third those of major Japanese shipyards, Korea may surpass Japanese tonnage in five years.

Almost all of the world's production of small appliances (whether Panasonic, Philips, General Electric, Sony, Zenith, or an obscure brand) is now centered in Hong Kong, Korea, and Singapore. Components and product designs are bought from major companies; financing is arranged through Japanese, U.S., and European banks; and distribution is handled through large retailers, such as Sears, Roebuck, or through the established distribution channels of large Japanese or American consumer-electronics companies.

The trend is becoming clear enough. First, America's basic steel, textile, automobile, consumer-electronics, rubber, and petrochemical industries (and the other high-volume industries that depend on them) are becoming uncompetitive in the world. Second, now that production can be fragmented into separate, globally scattered operations, whole segments of other American industries are becoming uncompetitive. Whatever the final product, those parts of its production requiring high-volume machinery and unsophisticated workers can be accomplished more cheaply in developing nations.

Automation, far from halting this trend, has accelerated it. Sophisticated machinery is readily moved to low-wage countries. Robots and computerized machines further reduce the need for semiskilled workers in high-volume production (except for workers with easily learned maintenance and programming skills). For example, robots in the automobile industry are replacing workers at more semiskilled jobs, such as welding and spot welding, than unskilled jobs. Meanwhile, automated inspection machines are reducing the cost of screening out poor-quality components—thereby encouraging firms in industrialized nations to farm out the production of standardized parts to developing nations.

What began in the 1960s as a gradual shift became by the late 1970s a major structural change in the world economy. Assembly operations were being established in developing countries at a rapid clip, and America's manufacturing base was eroding precipitously. The recession of the past two years has stalled growth around the globe and plunged several developing nations into near bankruptcy. But it is important to distinguish these short-term phenomena—brought on by a temporary oil glut and high interest rates—from long-term trends that have been growing for two decades and surely will resume.

Other industrialized nations have faced the same competitive threat. Since the mid-1960s, European industries have faced an ever-greater challenge from low-wage production in developing countries. And since the late 1970s, Japan has been challenged as well. Japan is no longer a low-wage nation—the real earnings of Japanese workers are approaching those of their European and American counterparts.

Japan, West Germany, France, and other industrialized countries have sought to meet this challenge by shifting their industrial bases toward products and processes that require skilled workers. Skilled labor is the only dimension of production where these countries retain an advantage. Technological innovations can be bought or imitated by anyone. High-volume, standardized-production facilities can be established anywhere. But production processes that depend on skilled labor must stay where the skilled labor is.

The fate of British industry over the past twenty-five years illustrates this new reality. Britain has consistently led the world in major technological breakthroughs, such as continuous casting for steel, monoclonal antibodies, and CAT-scan devices. But because British businesses lacked the organization and their workers lacked the skills necessary to incorporate these inventions into production processes quickly enough, the British have reaped no real competitive advantage from them. These inventions were commercialized in Japan and the United States.

Industrialized countries are therefore moving into precision castings, specialty steel, special chemicals, and sensor devices, as well as the design and manufacture of fiberoptic cable, fine ceramics, lasers, large-scale integrated circuits, and advanced aircraft engines. Emerging industries such as these hold promise of generating new wealth and employment as their markets expand.

Some of these products or processes require precision engineering, complex testing, and sophisticated maintenance. Others are custom-tailored to the special needs of customers. The remainder involve technologies that are changing rapidly. All three are relatively secure against low-wage competition.

These product categories—precision-manufactured, custom-tailored, and technology-driven—have a great deal in common. They all depend on the sophisticated skills of their employees, skills that are often developed within teams. And they all require that traditionally separate business functions (design, engineering, purchasing, manufacturing, distribution, marketing, sales) be merged into a highly integrated system that can respond quickly to new opportunities. In short, they are premised on *flexible systems* of production.

Flexible-system production has an advantage over high-volume, standardized production whenever solving new problems is more important than routinizing the solution of old ones. The unit costs of producing simple, standardized products such as cotton textiles, basic steel, or rubber tires generally decline more with long production runs than with improvements in the production process. Manufacturers of these products therefore do well to emphasize large capacity, cheap labor, and cheap raw materials rather than flexible systems.

This does not mean that industrialized countries must abandon their older industries—steel, chemicals, textiles, and automobiles. These industries are the gateways through which new products and processes emerge. Rather than abandoning these older industries, other industrialized countries are seeking to restructure them toward higher-valued and technologically more sophisticated businesses—specialty steel, special chemicals, synthetic fibers, and precision-engineered automobiles and auto components. As this adjustment occurs, they can allow the lowest-skilled standardized segments of their production to migrate to developing countries.

Of all industrialized countries, Japan has made the most rapid shift from standardized production to flexible-system production, and rather than forsaking its older industries has accelerated their evolution. Japanese auto makers are experimenting with a variety of fuel-saving materials. They are developing complex manufacturing systems, and have reduced to eighty-four hours the amount of labor required to produce each car (in contrast to 145 hours per car in America). By the same token, Japan's production of high-quality polyester-filament fabrics, requiring complex technologies and skilled labor, now accounts for 40 percent of its textile exports. Japan has substantially reduced its capacity to produce basic steel, basic petrochemicals, small appliances, ships, and simple fibers, while dramatically expanding its capacity in the higher-valued, more specialized segments of these industries. To accomplish this transformation, it has applied such innovations as process-control devices, fiber-optic cable, complex polymer materials, and very large-scale integrated circuits. Japanese companies are also packaging some standard products—copiers and typewriters, for instance—within technologically complex product systems, such as office communications and computer-aided manufacturing, which require custom design and servicing. In Japan's flexible-system enterprises, the distinction between goods and services is becoming blurred.

Japan has reduced its capacity in the capital-intensive, high-volume segments of its basic industries by scrapping plant and equipment, by simultaneously investing in new high-volume capacity in Korea, Taiwan, Singapore, and Brazil, and by retraining workers for higher-skilled jobs.

West Germany and France are having more difficulty shifting their economies, but each country is making progress. Although the current recession has slowed industrial adjustment in both nations, Germany nevertheless has reduced its basic steel, chemical, and automobile-making capacity somewhat, and has shifted more of its production into specialty steel, pharmaceuticals, and precision machinery.

Even Taiwan and Korea are seeking to shift into flexible-system industries. Korea is now establishing a semi-conductor research-and-development association, jointly funded by government and industry. Taiwan is building a science-based industrial park at Hsinchu.

For the United States, however, the shift has been slow and painful. The country has been far less successful than other industrialized nations in increasing its manufacturing exports to cover its increasing import bill. Recently Japan and the nations of Western Europe have been selling America more manufactured goods than America has been selling back to them.

Sales of grain and coal and revenues from services have helped ease America's trade imbalance. But these enterprises alone cannot guarantee our economic future. The most accessible coal will have been mined within the next few years; additional coal will be more costly to retrieve, not only in terms of machinery and equipment but also in damage to the environment and injuries to workers. Nor can grain exports be relied upon indefinitely; improvements in agricultural production will spread to the areas of the globe with favorable climate and soil conditions, and our soil will gradually become depleted.

Nor can we rely on services. The nation's service exports depend on the vigor of its future manufacturing base. Approximately 90 percent of America's income from services consists of the investment income of its manufacturing firms and, to a lesser extent, of individuals. But this income has declined significantly since the mid-1960s. In 1965, America received 3.6 times as much investment income as it paid out to foreign firms and individuals in dividends and royalties, but by 1978 the ratio of investment income to payments was 1.8 to 1. As foreign firms continue to gain strength relative to their American counterparts in merchandise businesses, this pattern will continue.

These trends pose a troubling question. If it is true that the economic future of countries lies in technically advanced, skill-intensive industries, why have American firms failed to respond by adopting the new products and processes?

The answer is that the transition requires a basic restructuring of business, labor, and government. A reorganization of this magnitude is bound to be resisted, because it threatens vested economic interests and challenges established values. The transition has been easier for Japan and for some continental Europeans, both because they never fully embraced high-volume, standardized production and because they have historically linked their economic development with social change.

As America has forfeited world industrial leadership to Japan, American business leaders have become obsessed with Japanese management. The business press daily praises Japanese practices such as the informal worker groups known as "quality circles," said to encourage commitment, soften workplace conflict, and improve product quality. American management consultants advise business executives to convert to less abrasive forms of management, such as "Theory Z," hailed as the key to Japan's success.

The infatuation with Japan's management technique obscures the point that flexible-system processes cannot simply be grafted onto business organizations that are designed for the production of standardized goods. Flexible-system production is rooted in discovering and solving new problems; high-volume, standardized production basically involves routinizing the solutions to old problems. Flexible-system production requires an organization designed for change and adaptability; high-volume, standardized production requires an organization geared to stability.

American business leaders are responding to the superficial novelty of Japanese management without acknowledging the underlying differences in the organization of production. They hope to upgrade their management techniques while retaining intact the old structure. Yet the answer lies not in new techniques but in a new productive organization, requiring a different, less rigidly delineated relationship between management and labor.

The basic premises of high-volume, standardized production—the once-potent formula of scientific management—are simply inapplicable to flexible-system production. The distinct principles of flexible-system production are understood—perhaps intuitively—by many small, upstart companies in America producing new micro-electric products and computer software or creating advertisements and films. They are also understood by a few highly successful larger companies—IBM and Hewlett-Packard, for instance. The same principles dominate many Japanese manufacturing and trading companies, and European producers of such items as precision castings, computerized machine tools, and customized telecommunications equipment.

The tasks involved in flexible-system production are necessarily complex, since any work that can be rendered simple and routine is more efficiently done by low-wage labor overseas. Thus no set of "standard operating procedures" locks in routines or compartmentalizes job responsibilities.

Skill-intensive processes cannot be programmed according to a fixed set of rules covering all possible contingencies. The work requires high-level skills precisely because the problems and opportunities cannot be anticipated. Producers of specialized semiconductor chips or multipurpose robots, for example, must be able to respond quickly to emerging and potential markets. Delicate machines break down in complex ways. Technologies change in directions that cannot be foreseen. The more frequently products and processes are altered or adapted, the harder it is to translate them into reliable routines. Again, if problems and opportunities could be anticipated and covered by preset rules and instructions, production could be moved abroad.

Finally, workers' performance cannot be monitored and evaluated through simple accounting systems. In flexible-system production, the quality of work is often more important than the quantity. As machines and low-wage labor overseas take over those tasks that demand only speed and accuracy, workers' skill, judgment, and initiative become the determinants of the flexible-system enterprise's competitive success. Moreover, in devising and manufacturing such complex items as customized herbicides, titanium alloys, or computer-software systems, tasks are often so interrelated that it becomes impossible to measure them separately; since each worker needs the help and cooperation of many others, success can be measured only in reference to the final collective result.

For these reasons, the radical distinction heretofore drawn between those who plan work and those who execute it is inappropriate to flexible-system production. When production is inherently non-routine, problem-solving requires close working relationships among people at all stages in the process. If customers' special needs are to be recognized and met, designers must be familiar with fabrication, production, marketing, and sales. Salespeople must have an intimate understanding of the enterprise's capability to design and deliver new or customized products. Flexible systems can adapt quickly only if information is widely

shared within them. There is no hierarchy to problem-solving: solutions may come from anyone, anywhere. In flexible-system enterprises, nearly everyone in the production process is responsible
for recognizing problems and finding solutions.

In high-volume, standardized production, professional managers, staff specialists, and even low-level production workers typically get much of their training before joining the organization,
and seldom venture far from a fairly narrow specialty. They move
from one organization to another, but they remain within that single specialty.

By contrast, in flexible-system production much of the training of necessity occurs on the job, both because the precise skills
to be learned cannot be anticipated and communicated in advance
and because individuals' skills are typically integrated into a
group whose collective capacity becomes something more than the
simple sum of its members' skills. Over time, as the group members work through various problems, they learn about each other's
abilities. Like a baseball team, they practice together to increase
their collective prowess. Their sense of membership in the enterprise is stronger and more immediate than any abstract identifica-
tion with their profession or occupational group. They move from
one specialty to another, but they remain within a single organization. The Japanese have been more successful than Americans in
devising the newest generation of large-scale integrated circuits,
because production entails complex and interrelated tasks that can
only be perfected by a relatively stable team. Rapid turnover in
U.S. companies has hindered this organizational learning.

The high-volume, standardized enterprise is organized into a
series of hierarchical tiers. Flexible-system production suggests a
relatively "flat" structure: in most firms that stake their success on
specialized or technically based products, there are few middle-
level managers, and only modest differences in the status and income of senior managers and junior employees. The enterprise is
typically organized as a set of relatively stable project teams that
informally compete with one another for resources, recognition,
and projects.

Finally, because flexible-system production is premised on
ever-changing markets and conditions, it is less vulnerable than

high-volume production to shifts in demand. Its machines and workers are not locked into producing long runs of any single standardized good. For this reason, flexible-system enterprises have less need to diversify into several lines of business as insurance against declining demand in any one. Flexible-system producers thrive on instability. Too much stability, and they would gradually lose their market to high-volume, standardized producers in low-wage countries.

In all these respects, the organization of high-volume production is so fundamentally different from that of flexible-system production that the transformation is exceedingly difficult. Because the roles, experiences, training, and expectations of professional managers and workers in high-volume production differ so sharply from those that flexible-system production calls for, neither group is prepared to adapt smoothly to such a transformation. In fact, they are likely to resist it.

That is what has happened. Because America's blue-collar workers often lack the skills and training necessary for flexible-system production, they have clung to the job classifications, work rules, and cost-of-living increases that brought them some security under standardized production. By the same token, because America's professional managers are ill equipped to undertake the necessary shift from high-volume production to flexible systems, they have resorted to various ploys designed to maintain or increase their firms' earnings without new productive investment. "Paper entrepreneurialism" of this kind merely rearranges industrial assets, while wasting the time and abilities of some of America's most talented people.

Paper entrepreneurialism is the bastard child of scientific management. It employs the mechanisms and symbols developed to direct and monitor high-volume production, but it involves an even more radical separation between planning and production. Paper entrepreneurialiam is a version of scientific management grown so extreme that it has lost all connection with the actual workplace. Its strategies involve generating profits through the clever manipulation of rules and numbers that only in theory represent real assets and products.

At its most pernicious, paper entrepreneurialism involves little more than imposing losses on others for the sake of short-term profits for the firm. The others are often members of the taxpaying public, who end up subsidizing firms that creatively reduce their tax liability. The others are sometimes certain of the firms' shareholders who end up indirectly subsidizing other shareholders. Occasionally, the others are unlucky investors, consumers, or the shareholders of other firms. Because paper gains are always at someone else's expense, paper entrepreneurialism can be a ruthless game. It can also be fascinating, and lucrative for those who play it well.

When the management era began to collapse, in the late 1960s, professional managers, seeking to limit the damage, turned to the tools they had at hand. The ideology of management control was so deeply ingrained that the instinctive reaction of professional managers was typically to define, even more precisely than before, the rules and working relationships within their firms, seeking thereby to solidify their control. But because the environment was changing so rapidly—with the entrance of new foreign competitors, new products, new manufacturing processes, and the opening of new global markets—the rules and controls had to be extraordinarily elaborate. They became even more intricate as the pace of change accelerated.

To coordinate the increasingly complex tasks of production, managers introduced complex techniques of "matrix management" through which employees reported to several different managers for different dimensions of their work. (An employee engaged in, say, the marketing of refrigerators in South America would report to three managers—in charge of marketing, refrigerators, and South American sales, respectively.)

When the matrices became too complicated, resulting in endless conflicts and confusion, organizational-development consultants were called in to design and coordinate "project teams." When this team structure had so muddled personal accountability that employees began to engage in buck-passing and bureaucratic gamesmanship, managers added still more controls: budget reviews, computer-based management-information systems, narrative reports on operations, monthly "flash" reports, formal goal-setting systems, and detailed performance-evaluation and incentive-compensation systems.

These ever-more-elaborate systems of managerial control brought with them additional layers of staff to devise the new rules and procedures, to design and monitor systems of performance appraisal, to referee the inevitable confusion over responsibility, and to mediate conflicts. Between 1965 and 1975, the ratio of staff positions to production workers in American manufacturing companies increased from 35 per 100 to 41 per 100. In certain industries, the jump has been even more dramatic. In electrical machinery, the ratio increased from 46 staff jobs for each 100 production jobs to 56 per 100; in non-electrical machinery, from 43 to 59; in chemicals, from 66 to 78. Companies with 2,500 or more employees have had a higher proportion of staff positions relative to production workers (44 per hundred in 1972) than companies with fewer than 500 employees (32 per hundred). The largest companies have the highest ratio of staff to production workers. By 1979, half of the employees of Intel—the microprocessor manufacturer—were engaged in administration. When an engineer wanted a mechanical pencil, processing the order required twelve pieces of paper and ninety-five administrative steps. It took 364 steps to hire a new employee.

This sudden proliferation of staff positions within American firms is particularly striking by comparison with firms in other nations. In the typical Japanese factory, for example, foremen report directly to plant managers. The foreman in the typical American factory must report through three additional layers of management. Until very recently, Ford Motor Company had five more levels of managers between the factory worker and the company chairman than did Toyota.

Bureaucratic layering of this sort is costly, and not only because of the extra salaries and benefits that must be paid. Layers of staff also make the firm more rigid, less able to make quick decisions or adjust rapidly to new opportunities and problems. In the traditional scientifically managed, high-volume enterprise, novel situations are regarded as exceptions, requiring new rules and procedures and the judgments of senior managers. But novel situations are a continuing feature of the new competitive environment in which American companies now find themselves.

The typical sequence now runs something like this: A salesman hears from a customer that the firm's latest bench drill cannot accommodate bits for drilling a recently developed hard plastic. The customer suggests a modified coupling adapter and an additional speed setting. The salesman thinks the customer's suggestion makes sense, but he has no authority to pursue it directly. Following procedures, the salesman passes the idea on to the sales manager, who finds it promising and drafts a memo to the marketing vice president. The marketing vice president also likes the idea, so he raises it in a executive meeting of all the vice presidents. The executive committee agrees to modify the drill. The senior product manager then asks the head of the research department to form a task force to evaluate the product opportunity and design a new coupling and variable-speed mechanism.

The task force consists of representatives from sales, marketing, accounting, and engineering. The engineers are interested in the elegance of the design. The manufacturing department insists on modifications requiring only minor retooling. The salespeople want a drill that will do what customers need it to do. The finance people worry about the costs of producing it. The marketing people want a design that can be advertised and distributed efficiently, and sold at a competitive price. The meetings are difficult, because each task-force member wants a claim credit for future success but avoid blame for any possible failure. After months of meetings, the research manager presents the group's findings to the executive committee. The committee approves the new design. Each department then works out a detailed plan for its role in bringing out the new product, and the modified drill goes into production.

If there are no production problems, the customer receives word that he can order a drill for working hard plastics two years after he first discussed it with a salesman. In the meantime, a Japanese or West German firm with a more flexible, teamlike approach has already designed, produced, and delivered a hard-plastics drill.

As the bureaucratic gap between executives and production workers continues to widen, the enterprise becomes more dependent on "hard," quantifiable data, and less sensitive to qualitative information. Professional managers concentrate on month-to-month profit figures, data on growth in sales, and return on investment. "Softer," less quantifiable information—about product quality, worker morale, and customer satisfaction—may be at least as important to the firm's long-term success. But such information cannot be conveyed efficiently upward through the layers of staff. Even if such qualitative information occasionally works its way to senior executives without becoming too distorted in the process, it is often still ignored. Information like this does not invite quick decisions and crisp directives.

Even quantifiable information becomes distorted as it moves up the corporate hierarchy, because it must be summarized and interpreted. Distortions also occur intentionally. Lower-level managers, dependent on senior managers for rewards and promotions, naturally want to highlight good news and suppress bad news. In reporting their costs, for example, they may seek to outmaneuver the accounting department (which determines how overhead costs are distributed among units) by shifting some overhead to another unit. Since lower-level managers are competing with other managers for scarce investment resources, they are likely to present overly optimistic estimates for the projects they seek to fund. Their forecasts may underestimate costs, overestimate market demand, and leave out certain expenses altogether. The planning systems that process these estimates become arenas for organizational gamesmanship.

Professional managers at the top of American firms have come to preside over a symbolic economy. The systems of management control that they initiated in the late 1960s in efforts to maintain profitability have become more intricate and elaborate as the global market has grown less predictable, requiring additional layers of managers and staff specialists. As the bureaucratic distance between senior managers and production workers has increased, the rules and numbers in which senior managers deal have become more and more disconnected from the everyday processes of production—distorted by excessive reliance on "hard" data, by communication failures, and by gamesmanship.

Paper entrepreneurialism relies on financial and legal virtuosity. Through shrewd maneuvering, accounting and tax rules can be finessed, and the numbers on balance sheets and tax returns manipulated, giving the appearance of greater or lesser earnings. Assets can be rearranged on paper to improve cash flow or to defer payments. And threatened lawsuits or takeovers can be used to extract concessions from other players. Huge profits are generated by these ploys. They are the most imaginative and daring ventures in the American economy. But they do not enlarge the economic pie; they merely reassign the slices.

The conglomerate enterprise is one manifestation of paper entrepreneurialism. Before the late 1960s, American business enterprises generally expanded only into lines of business related to their original products. They moved into markets where their managerial, technical, and marketing skills could be applied anew, giving them a real competitive advantage.

The conglomerate enterprises that mushroomed during the 1970s—multibusiness giants such as Gulf + Western, LTV, Textron, Litton, United Technologies, Northwest Industries, and ITT—are entirely different. They have grown by acquiring existing enterprises, often in wholly unrelated fields. Gulf + Western, for example, owns Paramount Pictures, Consolidated Cigar (one of America's largest cigar-makers), Kayser-Roth (a major apparel-maker), A.P.S. (an auto-parts supplier), one of America's largest zinc mines, Madison Square Garden, Simon & Schuster (publishers), Simmons (mattresses), the Miss Universe and Miss U.S.A. pageants, and a large sugarcane plantation. ITT (the world's eighth-largest corporation) owns Wonder Bread, Sheraton Hotels, Hartford Insurance, Avis Rent-a-Car, Bobbs-Merrill Publishing, and Burpee Lawn and Garden Products.

Conglomerate enterprises rarely, if ever, bring any relevant managerial, technical, or marketing skills to the new enterprises they acquire. Their competence lies in law and finance. Their relationship to their far-flung subsidiaries is that of an investor. Indeed, many conglomerates function almost exactly like mutual funds, except that the staff at conglomerate headquarters presumably has slightly more detailed information about their subsidiaries than mutual-fund advisers have about the companies within their portfolios.

Some conglomerates have come a step closer to mutual funds by becoming minority owners of a variety of other companies.

Gulf + Western actually maintains a $536 million portfolio of stocks in sixteen companies. Financial advisers within conglomerates like these decide which stocks to purchase or sell according to precisely the same criteria that financial advisers to mutual funds employ. Like the mutual fund, the conglomerate organization does not create new wealth or render production more efficient. It merely allocates capital, duplicating—though awkwardly—the functions of financial markets.

The paper advantages of conglomeration extend beyond speculation and risk-spreading, however. Dexterous tax and accounting manipulations can extract paper profits from economically senseless acquisitions. Whenever a firm's stock-market price falls below its book value (the assumed market value of the firm's total assets, if they were sold off bit by bit), another firm can post significant gains on its balance sheet simply by acquiring the undervalued firm and consolidating the two sets of books. Thus, the acquiring firm's earnings increase with minimal effort. As the American economy has declined, the stock of many companies has fallen to less than book value in this way. The stock market is not being irrational; companies like these are probably worth more disassembled than they are as continuing operations. But conglomeration does not redeploy these assets; it merely displays them more attractively on a new, consolidated balance sheet.

If the acquired firm has lost money in recent years, so much the better. The conglomerate that acquires it can use the losses to reduce its tax liability. Even if the assets of the acquired firm are purchased for more than their stated value in the acquired firm's books, the game is still on—the acquiring company has a higher basis for depreciating its new assets for tax purposes. (The 1982 tax law has made this route somewhat more treacherous.) U.S. Steel's purchase of Marathon Oil Company, for example, saved the steelmaker about $500 million in taxes in the first year and will save at least $1 billion more over the productive life of Marathon's Yates oil field, since tax laws let the oil field be valued for tax purposes at a higher cost than the property represented in Marathon's books. Because U.S. Steel can take new depletion deductions against this high-valued property, the Yates reserves are worth far more to it than they were to Marathon, which had already extracted what it could of the oil field's tax-deduction potential. The field's tax benefits were renewable through transfer, even if the oil was not.

Conglomeration has been proceeding at a breakneck pace. By 1972, 33 percent of the employees of America's manufacturing companies were involved in lines of business totally unrelated to the primary businesses of their companies. In 1977, American companies spent $22 billion acquiring one another. In 1979, they spent $43.5 billion. That year, sixteen firms, each worth more than $500 million, were gobbled up, including Belridge Oil($3.65 billion, bought by Shell Oil); C.I.T. Financial ($1.2 billion, by RCA); and Reliance Electric ($1.16 billion, by Exxon). All records were shattered in 1981, when $82 billion was spent on acquisitions. Du Pont paid a staggering $7.5 billion for Conoco; Fluor, $2.7 billion for St. Jo. Minerals; and Gulf Oil, $325 million for Kemmerer Coal. The pace continued last year with U.S. Steel's purchase of Marathon Oil for $5.9 billion.

Despite widely advertised concern over a capital shortage and calls for corporate tax breaks to spur new investment, firms bent on acquisition have seldom been deterred by price. Corporations have been paying premiums of 50 and even 100 percent over the market value for the stock of the companies they seek to acquire. Even during the "go-go years" of the late 1960s, when "funny money" fueled a short-lived merger explosion, premiums rarely exceeded 25 percent.

All this has been accompanied by some of the heaviest bank borrowings in history. Du Pont borrowed $3.9 billion to buy Conoco, at an interest rate close to 20 percent. Texaco negotiated a loan of $5.5 billion form an international consortium of banks led by Chase Manhattan. Fluor Corporation borrowed $1 billion to buy St. Joe Minerals—a debt equal to Fluor's entire revenues for the first quarter of 1981.

As late as the early 1960s, "unfriendly" takeovers were virtually unheard of. Since then, they have become a standard strategy of paper entrepreneurialism. Fear of a takeover bid haunts America's corporate boardrooms. In a 1981 survey of chief financial officers in America's 480 largest industrial firms, 49 percent thought that their companies were vulnerable to a takeover; even of the remaining group, 38 percent said that they had developed formal plans aimed at thwarting takeover bids. The fear is well founded. Of the 249 firms that have faced unfriendly takeover attempts within the past three years, only fifty-two have successfully withstood the assault and remained independent.

The fear of takeover has generated an array of paper-entrepreneurial strategies. Many targets of takeover bids, fleeing acquisition by a company unfriendly to their present managers, are running into the arms of another, more congenial firm. When WUI, an international telecommunications firm, learned that Continental Telephone Corporation was on its trail, it sought to be acquired instead by Xerox. Some target companies seek immunity by pre-emptively buying companies in the would-be acquirer's own industries, so that antitrust laws block the acquisition attempt. Daylin, Inc., defending itself against W.R. Grace's recent tender offer, sought to purchase Narco Scientific, Inc.—a maker of equipment in a product line so similar to Grace's that Grace would be barred from taking over Daylin. One of the more bizarre—and expensive—defense strategies is for a target company simply to reduce its cash reserves and thus become less attractive to potential predators. This may explain J. Ray McDermott & Co.'s $758 million acquisition of Babcock & Wilcox, and Kennecott Copper Corporation's $567 million purchase of Carborundum.

Increasingly, target companies are paying would-be acquirers high premiums to buy back blocks of stock that the acquirers have amassed. As a lawyer experienced in such tactics recently explained to *The Wall Street Journal,* "Look, I now have 7 percent or 8 percent of your stock. I'm not going after your company. But if you don't buy back the block from me at a premium, I know five or six guys who are interested and could take you over." This is the corporate equivalent of a demand for ransom. And paper entrepreneurs are generating large earnings from such threats.

Even if the target company refuses to pay the ransom, its stock typically shoots up when Wall Street learns that a takeover may be afoot. Thus the paper entrepreneur can generate earnings simply by selling the block of stock in the open market. Bendix recently made $75 million after taxes by buying and then selling back

20 percent of the outstanding stock of Asarco. Gulf + Western announced in September of 1980 that it had made open-market purchases of large blocks of stock in two companies: a 7.4 percent interest in Oxford Industries, Inc., and a 10.4 percent interest in Robertshaw Controls Company. Two months later, both Oxford and Robertshaw bought back their shares, for a total of $2.1 million more than Gulf + Western had paid for them.

The largest gains from conglomeration lie in their potential for opening access to ready cash at low or no cost, while simultaneously avoiding or deferring income taxes. Financial conglomerates offer particularly rewarding possibilities along these lines.

Consider, for example, Baldwin-United—a company that until 1968 was known for the Baldwin piano, which it had been making since 1891. Piano sales were growing slowly, and the pressure from foreign competition was increasing. So Baldwin purchased a bank, twelve insurance companies, a savings-and-loan company, some mortgage-banking companies, America's largest mortgage-insurance company, and America's two largest trading-stamp companies. Many of these companies have been cheap sources of cash. The insurance companies have provided low-cost funds in the form of premiums; the savings-and-loan company has brought in deposits at low, passbook rates; the mortgage-banking and servicing companies have transferred billions of dollars in mortgage and real-estate tax payments from borrowers to lenders, while holding the funds for up to several weeks in the process; and the trading-stamp companies sell stamps to merchants, who give them to customers, who are unlikely to redeem them for months or years, if ever. Baldwin has further enlarged its earnings by avoiding or deferring taxes on these cash flows. Baldwin's mortgage-banking acquisition had unrealized losses in its loan portfolio, which Baldwin then used against its overall earnings; Baldwin also deducts the commissions it pays to its brokers in the year paid, which occasionally generates large tax losses. With these ample deductions, Baldwin has been able to redeem the bonds that it mortgage-insurance company bought, with tax impunity. As a result of all these financial and tax ploys, Baldwin's return on equity has increased from 13 percent to 31 percent since 1968, and its earnings per share have grown at a 20 percent annual rate.

Conglomerates offer no particular efficiency in allocating capital to its best use. Investors who wanted to buy into a particular bundle of industries could simply have bought stocks separately. American investors gain nothing from having the bundle prepackaged in the form of a diversified conglomerate. Indeed, conglomerates undermine the efficiency of America's capital market by eliminating investors' option to buy into Bobbs-Merrill alone, for example, without taking stock in all the rest of ITT's hodgepodge of businesses.

Nor, as we have seen, do conglomerates serve any useful industrial purpose. Unlike earlier multidivisional firms, which featured some complementarity among operations, modern conglomerates are typically little concerned with the actual economic functions of the various subsidiaries, beyond the interest a landlord might take in a sharecropper's labors.

Nor do they benefit employees. When one of a conglomerate's businesses begins to falter, only capital assets are salvaged and redeployed. Workers typically are left to fend for themselves.

Thus modern conglomerates are economically sterile, Their only effects are to facilitate paper entrepreneurialism and to spare managers the need to stake their career on anything so risky as a single firm trying to make products. The growth of conglomerates illustrates managers' discretionary power to serve their own goals, and reveals how far economic change since the end of the management era has separated managers' incentives from socially productive results.

Paper entrepreneurialism does not rely solely on acquisitions, of course. Every month or so, another innovative paper ploy is unveiled. For example, many companies are now engaging in an expensive and financially empty exchange of new stock for old bonds. It works like this: A company that sold long-term bonds when interest rates were lower—and, thus, so was the yield, or "coupon," the bond had to offer—still carries the debt on its books at the original face value, even though the outstanding bonds are in fact, being traded on the market at a discount because they yield less per dollar of face value than new financial assets. (That is, the books may show debt of $10 million, even though the market value of the bonds has fallen to $7 million.) This debt bothers the firm's managers, who want the balance sheet to seem as unencumbered by indebtedness as possible.

So investment brokers have gone into the business of buying up old bonds at their (low) market value and offering to return them to the issuing firm in exchange for new shares of common stock. By buying back its old bonds, the company can claim to have "retired" a deceptively large chunk of debt, based on the financially irrelevant face value of the bonds, and so managers are willing to pay the broker handsomely for engineering the swap.

The company makes a precisely offsetting trade—a certain market value of stock for an equal market value of bonds. the cost: millions in brokers' fees and premiums. The only result: some gullible investors may be led to believe that the company has suddenly become less burdened by debt, and therefore more valuable. And the ruse is tax-free, treated as a non-taxable corporate reorganization so long as the broker handles the mechanics. Since August of 1981, more than a hundred such exchanges have swept at least $2 billion in debt from corporate balance sheets. Even U.S. Steel managed to use this ploy to report a profit for the depressed second quarter of 1982, despite its sizable losses in the steel business. Like other gimmicks, this one will go out of fashion in a year or two, when investors and the Internal Revenue Service catch on, and another innovation will replace it.

Paper entrepreneurs also display their virtuosity in "creative" accounting. In 1978, for example, when slumping car sales began to push Chrysler Corporation deeper into the red, forcing the auto maker to halt production at many plants and cut its dividends by 60 percent, the company still managed to project a fourth-quarter profit. Thanks to a little-noticed actuarial adjustment, Chrysler had merely changed the assumed ra te of return on its employee-pension portfolio to 7 percent from 6 percent, reducing pension costs and adding about $50 million to its profits. This alteration was likely to escape the eyes of analysts and auditors, who are seldom trained in pension matters. Chrysler did nothing illegal. Indeed, it disclosed in a footnote to its annual report that it had made the actuarial change, although it did not state any figures.

Other methods of "earnings management" abound: showing certain transactions as collateral borrowings rather than as sales;

overstating or understating inventories; failing to account fully for the effect of inflation on the value of inventories or profits; overstating the value of good will gained from a merger or acquisition; and understating the price paid for an acquisition. For example, GE paid about $2 billion worth of stock to acquire Utah International in 1976, but "pooling-of-interest" accounting rules let GE show a price of only $548 million on its balance sheet. Utah International's $196 million profit in 1977 looked much better on $548 million than it would have on $2 billion.

None of these ploys is illegal. Nor do they violate generally accepted accounting principles, which give firms wide latitude in reporting their earnings. Given the complexity of modern business practices and the uniqueness of each firm, more rigid accounting rules might actually lead to greater distortions. And that is the point. The set of symbols developed to represent real assets has lost the link with any actual productive activity. Finance has progressively evolved into a sector all its own, only loosely connected to industry. And this disconnectedness turns business executives into paper entrepreneurs—forced to outsmart other participants, or be themselves outsmarted.

All of this paper entrepreneurialism takes place against a background of mounting lawsuits. Professional managers in companies targeted for takeover are suing their predators. Shareholders are suing managers. Acquiring companies are suing the officers of the companies they have acquired. Purchasers of futures contracts are suing sellers who cannot meet the payments. The number of business lawsuit stemming from breach of contract, antitrust, or alleged "wasting" of corporate assets has increased fourfold since 1965.

One must be clear about the problem of paper entrepreneurialism in America. Paper entrepreneurialism does not directly use up economic resources. Every economy needs some paper entrepreneurs to help allocate capital efficiently among product entrepreneurs.

The problem is that paper entrepreneurialism has replaced product entrepreneurialism as the most dynamic and innovative occupation in the American economy. Paper entrepreneurs produce nothing of tangible use. For an economy to maintain its health, entrepreneurial rewards should flow primarily to products, not paper. As Lord Keynes recognized nearly fifty years ago, "When the capital development of a country becomes a by-product of the activities of a casino, the job is likely to be ill-done."

Ours is becoming an economy in which resources circulate endlessly among giant corporations, investment bankers, and their lawyers, but little new is produced. Financial resources are kept liquid in order to meet the next margin call, to enter the next position, or to exploit the next takeover opportunity. They are not applied in earnest to any single undertaking, for fear that they will soon be needed for something else. There is scant investment in new products or processes, because such endeavors tie up resources for too long.

In 1979, RCA Corporation complained publicly that it lacked the $220 million that would be needed to develop a video-cassette recorder, although recorders are the fastest-growing appliance of the decade. RCA thereby ceded the video-cassette market to the Japanese. But RCA had no qualms about spending $1.2 billion to buy a lackluster finance company that same year. In 1979, U.S. Steel decided to scrap its plan for building a new steel plant. Instead, it began building a cash reserve to acquire some other, more promising company, such as Marathon Oil.

While business leaders are otherwise engaged, America's industrial base remains wedded to high-volume, standardized production. Flexible-system production does not fit well into large conglomerate enterprises. The enterprises are too diffuse and fragmented to generate team spirit, too unwieldy and bureaucratic to accommodate novel approaches to new problems. Real-product entrepreneurs bridle at the red tape. Employees are discouraged from choosing unorthodox solutions. It is often difficult, from the mire of conglomerate headquarters, to identify unique customer needs. Big companies also tend to wait for markets to develop; they are not equipped successfully to pursue the markets that do not yet exist. Exxon's plunge into the "office of the future" has been an unmitigated disaster. The company is losing money at a rate that would bankrupt almost anyone else—in 1980 alone, its office-equipment division lost $150 million on sales of $270 million. Industrial giants such as Monsanto, Ford, and Sylvania, which tried several years ago to develop their own commercial semiconductor operations, failed miserably and withdrew from this rapidly changing market. Other large companies—RCA, TRW, Westinghouse—have not done much better.

But perhaps the greatest cost is in human talent. Today's corporate executives spend an increasing portion of their days fending off takeovers, finding companies to acquire, conferring with their financial and accounting specialists, and responding to depositions in lawsuits, instead of attending to their products. Indeed, approximately 40 percent of the chief executive officers of America's largest firms have backgrounds in law or finance and rose to their present positions from company legal or financial staffs. This is in sharp contrast to the past. In 1950, only 13 percent of America's key chief executive officers had legal or financial backgrounds. Most came up through the ranks from marketing, engineering, or sales.

Increasingly over the past fifteen years, the most sought-after jobs among business-school graduates have been in finance and consulting, where the specialty is rearranging assets and shuffling corporate boxes—and from where bright young MBAs have their best shot at becoming corporate executives. Only 3 percent of Harvard Business School's 1981 graduates took jobs in production and 18.6 percent in sales and marketing, while 21.6 percent went into finance. Young people seeking quick affluence without much risk have turned to the practice of law, where America's highest-paying entry-level jobs are found. In a recent survey, 24 percent of Harvard freshmen said they were planning a career in law; only 7 percent were going into science. In 1982, New York city's largest law firms were paying their young recruits, fresh out of law school, $48,000 a year. In 1980, the median income for partners in New York's law firms was $242,685, up 50 percent from 1975. Law firms can afford to pay these exorbitant salaries because legal fees keep rolling in.

Between 1949 and 1960, only about one American in 600 was a lawyer. Between 1971 and 1981, the number of practicing attorneys increased by 64 percent. America now has more than 590,000 lawyers—one for every 400 citizens. Over the same decade, however, there was only a 15 percent rise in the number of engineers, and a 25 percent rise in the number of laborers. Only about one of every 10,000 citizens in Japan is trained in law, while one out of twenty-five Japanese citizens is trained in engineering or science. More than 65 percent of all seats on the boards of Japanese manufacturing companies are occupied by people who are trained as engineers; roughly the same percentage of seats on American boards are taken by people trained in law, finance, or accountancy. Thus, in Japan, many problems that arise in business are viewed as problems of engineering or science, for which technical solutions can be found. In present-day America, the same problems are apt to be viewed as problems of law or finance, to be dodged through clever manipulation of rules or numbers.

Increasingly, professional education in America stresses the manipulation of symbols to the exclusion of other sorts of skills—how to collaborate with others, to work in teams, to speak foreign languages, to solve concrete problems—that are more relevant to the newly competitive world economy. And more and more, the career ambitions of America's best students have turned to professions that allow them to continue attending to symbols, from quiet offices equipped with a telephone, a Telex, and a good secretary. The world of real people, engaged in the untidy and difficult struggle with real production problems, becomes ever more alien to America's best and brightest.

Paper entrepreneurialism is both cause and consequence of America's faltering economy. Paper profits are the only ones easily available to professional managers who sit isolated atop organizations designed for a form of production that is no longer appropriate to America's place in the world economy. At the same time, the relentless drive for paper profits has diverted attention and resources away from the difficult job of transforming the productive base. It has retarded the transition that must occur, and made change more difficult in the future. Paper entrepreneurialism thus has a self-perpetuating quality that, if left unchecked, will drive the nation into further decline.

II. FREE MARKET OR GOVERNMENT INTERVENTION?

EDITOR'S INTRODUCTION

Like physicians, economists usually agree on what ails the patient, but quarrel bitterly over what is required to restore him to health. These disagreements over how to halt the decline of American industry, formerly confined to academic journals, have become a prominent feature of the daily press, and candidates for political office now routinely seek advice from the economists whose views best suit their own convictions. On the one hand, the Republican administration espouses the doctrine of free-market capitalism and came to office promising to stimulate the "supply side" of the economy with measures recommended by the economist Arthur Laffer. However, another group of analysts has risen to prominence that offers a very different approach to the restoration of economic health: a national industrial policy.

Advocates of such an industrial policy hope that concerted government action can encourage productivity and hence lead to rising levels of employment and standards of living. Government planning and support, they believe, could make American products more competitive in world markets, and at the same time shield workers from the unpredictable crises that have put millions of people out of work and left whole communities idle.

As the case of the Chrysler Corporation has shown, it may be possible for dying industries to recover when government support through a difficult period enables them to reorganize and become more productive. But the argument for selective aid to certain companies has an inevitable corollary: who would decide which companies to support, and what would the criteria be? Can we know which technologies, which industries, and which markets will be lucrative in 1990? Can the government guess more accurately than the stock market?

As the following articles from *Business Week* and *The Nation* show, implementation of such a policy would be difficult, even if its advocates could agree on what form it should take. The reporters for *Business Week* point out, however, that there has not been a "free market" for a very long time; federal support for growing industries such as railroads and agriculture was commonplace during the 19th century, and in our own time this practice has continued in the provision of price supports for dairy and arable products, and loan guarantees for Lockheed and Chrysler. The question, the writers ask, is not whether we should have an industrial policy, but what form should it take?

An article in *The Nation* dampens enthusiasm for utopian planning by pointing out that a degree of confusion is essential to democracy. Would not an industrial policy come dangerously (and unconstitutionally) close to state capitalism? Would not all the policies so far mooted simply tend to concentrate even more money in the hands of the great corporations?

Writing in *Harper's* magazine, Robert M. Kaus takes an acerbic view of the debate and those conducting it. He points out that reality is too complex to control with policy: sometimes the market should be allowed to push the weakest to the wall; sometimes, as in the case of Chrysler, it should not. Since no one can agree on these issues, why not let the present array of opposing forces sort things out?

INDUSTRIAL POLICY: IS IT THE ANSWER?[1]

Capital is wayward and timid in lending itself to new undertakings, and the State ought to excite the confidence of capitalists, who are ever cautious and sagacious, by aiding them to overcome the obstacles that lie in the way of all experiments. Alexander Hamilton, 1791

Hamilton may not have been the first American leader to make the case for a national industrial policy in the U. S., but he undoubtedly said it best. Hamilton argued that the new American republic needed strong government measures such as protectionist

[1]Reprint of an article from *Business Week*. p54–7+ Jl 4, '83. Copyright 1983 by McGraw-Hill, Inc. Reprinted by permission.

tariffs, bounties, and premiums to nurture its infant industries. Besides, other nations used these competitive weapons, so the U. S. had no choice but to retaliate. Thomas Jefferson denounced Hamilton as a statist, but the great democrat himself fashioned one of the nation's most ambitious economic and regional development policies: the Louisiana Purchase.

Some 200 years later, Americans are still arguing over whether to have a national industrial policy. Once again, the nation is beset by a spreading sense that economic survival is at stake in the face of subsidized foreign competition that resembles the mercantilism of Hamilton's era. The U. S. has been falling behind Japan for more than a decade, and pressures are intensifying from Europe and newly industrialized countries. But the U. S. has ample reasons to blame itself for its current plight.

Failures by labor and management to check their adversary relationship, contradictory government regulations and policies, and the decline of infrastructure and the educational system are just a sample. A decade of recessions, bouts of roaring inflation, near-depression levels of unemployment, the deteriorating competitiveness of basic industries, sliding productivity, the painful adjustment to dependence on high-priced foreign oil, and a stagnating standard of living have shaken America's confidence in its ability to prosper and remain the world's leading industrial power.

Thus, the U. S. is searching frantically for ways to revive its economic vitality. And that search increasingly is zeroing in on industrial policy, or IP as economists call it. In broad terms, an IP can be anything from a plan to aid semiconductors, for example, with subsidies, tariffs, or tax breaks to a centralized planning appraoch that attempts to choose future growth areas—the so-called sunrise industries—as part of an overall economic growth strategy.

Every Democratic contender for the Presidential nomination has embraced some form of industrial policy, and it promises to be one of the 1984 campaign's hottest issues. Congressional committees led by Democrats are studying it, and other Democrats have already proposed IP legislation.

Partly as what one White House aid calls "a preemptive strike" against the Democrats and partly in response to urgent pleas by groups of business and academic leaders, President Reagan is creating a Presidential Commission on Industrial Competitiveness. Robert Anderson, chairman of Rockwell International Corp. and co-chairman of a study by the prestigious Business-Higher Education Forum that helped prod the White House into action, eschews the idea of a "national super-planning organization." But when asked whether his group wants an industrial policy, he replies: "Oh, no question about that." However, the White House still shuns the term IP because it suggests increased government intervention, and Reagan remains firmly committed to getting government "off the back" of business.

The new commission will aim to "generate a national dialogue on how to make the U. S. more competitive," according to White House assistant Edwin L. Harper. He says the emphasis will be on seeing "what the private sector can do for itself." But the group will also ask what federal policies, especially in research and development, education, and training, are "required to retain our edge in knowledge and technology."

Says Lester C. Thurow of the Massachusetts Institute of Technology: "Suddenly, everyone is willing to talk seriously about a national industrial policy, and the reason is a four-letter word called fear. We all fear we may be going down for the count as an industrial power if we don't counter Japanese and European growth strategies built around industrial policies." Robert B. Reich of Harvard University's Kennedy School of Government agrees with Thurow that it is getting late to argue over the propriety of industrial policy in terms of having more or less government. "Foreigners may argue," says Reich, "over which IP option is best but never over the appropriateness of IP itself. For them, its the third leg on the policy stool, as critical as monetary and fiscal policies for economic growth and stabilization."

But since few politicians are really sure about what IP is or what a national IP should be, a lot of time will be spent defining it. In a sense, the U. S. has always had an IP without calling it such. In the 19th century, federal support helped build the nation's railroads, canals, and university system as well as protect growing industries with high tariffs. In the 20th century, a paternalistic government created or bankrolled a large part of the nation's highways, synthetic rubber, computers, and integrated-circuit industries as well as a host of other projects, products, and industries. The world's greatest agricultural sector is almost as much a product of government aid and research as it is of American farmers' sweat and pluck. However, despite the almost countless ad hoc ventures by government into the private sector, Americans are still not sure it is the right thing to do because it violates the country's laissez-faire philosophy.

Most experts clearly recognize that a national industrial policy could become a political bureaucracy for picking winners and losers and playing high-finance triage with America's industries at the behest of various interest groups. "The onus will be on the proponents of IP to define it and show how it can be made to work," says Robert F. Wescott of Wharton Econometric Forecasting Associates Inc. On the basis of his own research on past U. S. approaches to industrial policy for a book he wrote with Nobel laureate Lawrence R. Klein and F. Gerard Adams of the University of Pennsylvania, Wescott concludes that the U. S. abounds in such policies now but that many of them were undertaken "for political, legal, social, military, moral, and environmental reasons that have knowingly hurt industrial development." He cites the aborted effort of U. S. antitrust enforcers to break up International Business Machines Corp. for noneconomic reasons years after the government helped make the company the world's leading computer maker.

Thus the natural first step toward creating a national industrial policy would indeed, be to get government off business' back. That in itself would be a passive form of IP. In terms of an active policy, the choices get much trickier. The types of national industrial policy now being discussed vary widely in goals and the extent of government involvement:

In general terms, Reich explains his approach to IP by contrasting it with supply-side economics, which uses tax incentives to try to raise the economy's overall level of savings and investment. Reich's IP is also supply-oriented but is "more concerned with capital allocation than with aggregate capital formation. Instead of working on the overall level, it focuses on the most productive pattern of investment."

More specifically, the accelerationist would try to pinpoint industries that promise to become strong international competitors—especially those with high-value products. They would help position these industries to move quickly into world markets. This aid would go beyond the research stage to process development, which is where the Japanese and others really outgun U.S. industry. The aim is not to replace business decision-making with government planning but to accelerate changes already signaled by the marketplace.

This group would offer adjustment assistance to declining industries in return for commitments that they would slim down, modernize, and help their workers relocate and train for new skills and jobs. The adjusters believe workers, businesses, and communities hardest hit by economic changes should be given aid to defuse potential resistance and avert pressure for ad hoc bailouts.

Some advocates would target a select group of industries or sectors to turn them into new engines for economic growth. These areas include high technology, especially information processing and semiconductors; energy, with emphasis on coal and synthetic fuels; agriculture; and service industries, such as finance and health care and equipment. A key part of almost every list is a program to refurbish the nation's crumbling infrastructure of ports, roads, bridges, sewers, and water systems. What distinguishes the targeters is that their program is aimed at promoting overall economic growth rather than purely trade-related industries.

A fourth school of IP advocates would link it more closely to macro policies. "You must start with growth-oriented macro policies, but they aren't enough because of the nation's structural problems," says Klein. "You won't get there if you don't make sure you've got the resources to do it."

To Gar Alperovitz of the National Center for Economic Alternatives, that means "we must go beyond indentifying leading growth sectors and identify other sectors as well that could become bottlenecks and engines of inflation once you start to grow." In this linkage approach to an industrial policy, Alperovitz says: "It's a mistake to write off an industry like steel. By throttling down its capacity too much, we could quickly run into shortages in a high-growth situation and excessive dependency on foreign steel." Alperovitz's strategy comes the closest to comprehensive planning.

These IP proponents believe that a federally backed industrial development bank should provide what they call "patient capital," money that can ride on a high risk venture for 5 to 10 years or more. Says American University's Nancy Barrett: "We're like an LDC that doesn't have an adequate banking system for development loans."

Another reason for creating a federal facility to do the job, says Felix G. Rohatyn, chairman of New York City's Municipal Assistance Corp., is that a federal bank "could make sure that the aid would be conditional on management and labor concessions needed to make the business viable." The Glass-Steagall Act bans commercial banks from owning stock in such ventures. But a new Reconstruction Finance Corp. or a National Industrial Development Bank—as the Democrats now call it—would function like an old-time investment bank and have the clout to force companies to make tough decisions, as was done on an ad hoc basis in the Chrysler Corp. and New York City bailouts. In addition, the banker IP would require that the private investors put up at least 50% of equity to make sure the idea was worth the backing of the market.

How much of all this is achievable, assuming a public consensus can be reached to do any of it? The move is on in Congress to find out. Representative John J. LaFalce (D-N.Y.) has launched his House Banking subcommittee on economic stabilization—the panel that originated the Council on Wage & Price Stability and the New York bailout—on six months of hearings to develop an industrial policy bill by early 1984. Says LaFalce: "What is needed is a coordinative mechanism, a holistic approach for an American transition into a postindustrial world where our emerging industries have to compete with foreign governments."

In addition, Representative Richard L. Ottinger (D-N.Y.) leads a "national economic recovery project," backed by some 150 House Democrats, to develop a "high-production strategy." A Senate Democratic Policy Committee task force is working up a similar package for Senator Edward M. Kennedy (D-Mass.).

And a phalanx of House Democratic neoliberals—Stanley N. Lundine of New York, David E. Bonior of Michigan, Richard A Gephardt of Missouri, and Timothy E. Wirth of Colorado—has written a master plan called the National Industrial Strategy Act. This bill would create an Economic Cooperation Council, with government, business, labor, and other public participants, to collect and analyze data and recommend steps to improve U.S. industrial competitiveness. It would also create a National industrial Development Bank with authority to lend $12 billion over four years and grant an additional $24 billion in loan guarantees.

Other less formal proposals afloat in Congress incude moves to ease antitrust rules to allow joint R&D ventures, to extend existing R&D tax credits, to grant private researchers patents for discoveries made in federal laboratories, and to offer import relief in exchange for adjustment concessions by management and labor. The import-relief idea comes from Pennsylvania Republican Senator John Heinz. Indeed, more and more Republicans are joining the Democrats in proposing IP-style strategies.

Most of the industrial policy schemes will not be passed or implemented soon, certainly not during the Reagan Administration. But the Kemp-Roth tax bill had the same vague look of wishful— and to some, dangerous—thinking when it was first introduced in 1978. The growing fervor for industrial policy reflects a widening public fear that the economic formulas of the past are no longer working—or are not enough by themselves to restore U.S. international competitiveness. It is time to decide whether the U.S. really needs or wants an explicit national industrial policy. Here are the arguments on both sides.

No: Let the Market Work

An industrial policy—in any manner, shape, or form—will be nothing less than an economic disaster for the U.S. It will stifle economic growth. It will slow down the shift of resources to productive industries by trying to shore up declining industries. And it will waste money on "targeted growth" industries that may have no commercial future. An industrial policy will create layer upon layer of bureaucrats who tinker with planning, bailouts, and loan guarantees.

Most industrial policy proposals are so vague that they are meaningless. They are "pure catchwords and slogans," says Michael L. Wachter, economist at the University of Pennsylvania. There is only one consistent theme: The government should have a bigger role in setting the course of U.S. industry.

History shows that the bigger the role for the government, the more messed up business becomes. Says Nobel laureate George J. Stigler: "One thing we know about government is that it is not a good entrepreneur. Look at the splendid triumphs of government: It supervised the railroads into bankruptcy, destroyed interurban transportation with regulation and regulated thousands of banks out of existence in the 1930s." To Alan Greenspan, a Reagan advisor and president of Townsend-Greenspan & Co., industrial policy is primarily a way of parceling out more government money. "When you strip away the philosophical paraphernalia," he says, "industrial policy is a mechanism by which the politically powerful get their hands in the till."

Even liberal-leaning Charles L. Schultze, chairman of the Council of Economic Advisers during the Carter Administration, opposes any industrial policy that gives government the right to allocate capital. He concedes that the U.S. has economic problems, but "an inability to make the necessary transition from old industries to newer, growing ones is not one of them."

Proponents of industrial policy argue that the government must intervene to help declining industries because so many other countries are subsidizing theirs. "Nonsense," responds Herbert Stein, an economist with the American Enterprise Institute and chairman of the Nixon Administration's CEA. Subsidizing industry only makes the taxpayers shoulder a greater burden, he says. "Such subsidies don't increase the country's ability to compete."

Moreover, there is little empirical evidence that foreign subsidies are the main force behind the decline of U.S. industries. High labor costs in the steel and auto industries make steel and autos uncompetitive. In addition, the steel companies' decision not to upgrade steelmaking technology and the auto makers' failure to move into the small car market fast enough with a high-quality product are now coming home to roost.

Most proposals floating around Washington would not just ease the adjustment of old industries but would also target the new. This goal is based on the view that Japan created its postwar economic miracle by identifying "sunrise" industries and nurturing them through protection and subsidies. Now, the argument goes, the U.S. should do the same.

But this view of Japan's sucess is overly simplistic. "MITI was much less influential than people think," says Schultze. For example, the Ministry of International Trade & Industry wanted the Japanese auto industry to consolidate into two companies. They refused to go along, and the Japanese industry, with nine major players, became the most efficient in the world.

Clearly, MITI had an important role in guiding Japan's industrial development after the war. At the same time, even Naohiro Amayo, former vice-minister at MITI and now a special adviser, concedes that Japan had its failures: too much protection for agriculture and banking. And now MITI finds itself trying to shrink industries, such as aluminum and petrochemicals, that it earlier encouraged to grow.

MITI's actions in the late 1940s and 1950s are hardly a suitable model for U.S. policy in the 1980s, anyway. Back then, it was easy for the Japanese to see which technologies to develop. With its industrial base nearly destroyed, Japan was playing a game of catch-up. It was logical to focus efforts on improving the quality and lowering the manufacturing costs of products that already existed.

Today, Japan's catch-up game is over. One sign is that businesses in Japan are beginning to resist joint research under the auspices of government, says Jimmy W. Wheeler, an analyst with the Hudson Institute. As the life cycles of new products get shorter because of technical change, "fast footwork and privacy are more important than they used to be."

Now, both Japan and the U.S. are grappling with the same high-risk challenge: figuring out what the marketplace will favor in the future. No one knows—certainly not government experts. Asking anyone to point to those industries is like asking someone "to buy only stocks which go up," says Greenspan. "It presupposes a degree of knowledge that does not exist."

Outside Japan, the evidence that government can target sunrise industries is even weaker. Atomic power in the U.S. and the Concorde in France and Britain are examples of costly, futile government investments in research and development. "The European experience has just been terrible," says the University of Pennsylvania's Wachter. No one knows which technologies—however glamorous they may be—will form the commercially successful industries of the future until they are tried out and buffeted by the marketplace.

Even if planners could foresee the commercial successes of the future, they are handicapped by poor knowledge about the present. Pierre A. Rinfret, a New York economic consultant, supports an industrial policy but thinks it could be a "disaster" if it is based on current government statistics. He notes that the Commerce Dept's Industrial classifications were set up in the 1940s and reflect the composition of industry in the 1930s. "Government statisticians are out of date mentally on the technological change in the country," he says.

Of course, the U.S. government has always been involved with industry, building canals, railroads, and highways. And its multibillion-dollar defense and space programs pour money into certain kinds of companies. So, the argument goes, why not simply extend government intervention to other sectors?

But by and large, government involvement has been in public works and defense, areas that even Adam Smith considered appropriate for government. Subsidies for railroads and highways, did indeed, influence the course of industrial development. But the government did not "target" trains or autos. These investments were made in response to public pressure after entrepreneurs had tried out the new products and technologies in the marketplace.

The government's efforts to protect industries do not make a good case for industrial policy, either. For example, the U.S. began regulating trucking in the 1930s partly to shelter the railroads from cutthroat competition. But economists generally believe that price protection weakened the railroads rather than strengthened them. The government has also aided U.S. agriculture. But it was the mass exodus from farms starting in the 1920s that ultimately made U.S. agriculture the most efficient in the world. That exodus also provided the labor force to fuel postwar industrial growth.

To oppose industrial policy is to argue that economic change should be allowed to happen efficiently. And the most efficient manager of change has proven to be the marketplace. This offers little comfort to workers who are out of jobs as a result of major changes in industries such as autos and steel. But trying to out-guess the market to save those jobs will be self-defeating and, in the long run, destructive to the economy as a whole.

Yes: Industry Needs the Help.

The U.S. faces a critical choice. It can move toward a coordinated national industrial policy to restore its international competitiveness or it can let market forces—and such industrial rivals as Japan and Germany—work their will and reduce the nation to a second-rate economic power.

An open, explicit commitment to a national industrial policy would help put the country back on a sustainable high growth track. It need not be a matter of picking winners and losers or telling business what to do, says Representative Richard A. Gephardt (D-Mo.), but of "building a national consensus on what changes are needed to get through this transitional period and make our industries more competitive."

Lester C. Thurow at Massachusetts Institute of Technology sees no great difficulties in picking winners, since identifying high-tech industries as growth sectors does not require genius. "If you really think that Americans are so incompetent that they cannot pick sunrise industries, then you can simply use the Japanese list," says Thurow. Of course, government mistakes will be inevitable in targeting industries for growth. But the private sector has been known to have its Edsels, too.

Japan's list is certainly no secret. With an array of strategies backed by cash subsidies, tax incentives, export aid, import barriers, cheap loans, and even government manipulation of exchange rates, the Japanese and other foreign competitors have been driving U.S. smokestack industries into the ground, and now they are taking aim at the infant industries of high technology.

Japan's Ministry of International Trade & Industry, to take just one example, decided to spend vast sums in trying to beat the

U.S. to a fifth-generation computer. The Japanese, Germans, French, and others—all with the aid of industrial policies—are also giving U.S. producers a hard run for their money in rapidly developing technologies as robotics, very large-scale integrated circuits, bioengineering, fiber optics, lasers, ceramics, and powder metallurgy.

A European consortium is threatening to rocket past the National Aeronautics & Space Administration in commercial applications of the space program. Meantime, the U.S. drive to commercialize space flight is hampered by a debate over allowing private participants proprietary rights on discoveries they may make in the government's space lab.

U.S. industrial policy is carried out largely without rhyme or reason—at least, without reasonable attention to competitiveness. Almost anything done for defense qualifies for government help, so the U.S. is countering MITI's computer race with a similarly costly project at the Defense Advanced Research Projects Agency. But other research and development ventures go begging.

According to Harvard's Robert B. Reich, the U.S. government now spends five times more on R&D for commercial fishing than for steel. It also provides almost $750 million a year in tax breaks for the timber industry but a small fraction of that for semiconductors. Housing subsidies, just through various tax breaks for homeowners, will come to $12 billion this year. This may be good for the recovery, but it is one of many examples of how Washington channels capital toward industries that are sheltered from international trade and away from those with a chance to gain or recapture a competitive edge in the world market, such as specialty steel. Not that the U.S. neglects trade. According to economist Robert Wescott, dozens of government policies affect U.S. exports, from the small change spent on trade promotion to the $4 billion in new loans and $8 billion in loan guarantees the Export-Import Bank is issuing this year.

In short, the U.S. has been in the industrial policy game at least since 1643, when Massachusetts granted a new smelting company exclusive ironproducing privileges for 21 years to encourage the industry. Many people think the U.S. should drop its guise of economic innocence and start to fashion its policies in a coordinated, efficient way.

Years of runaway inflation, a major cause of the loss of U.S. competitiveness, should have shown the nation the limits of Keynesian demand management. If they have not, the high interest rates and huge budget deficits now bedeviling policymakers clearly demonstrate the limits of trying to manage an economy solely with traditional monetary and fiscal policies.

Other remedies, such as wage and price controls, are even less in keeping with the U.S. character than industrial policy and have proved to be failures. Voluntary givebacks and other concessions from unions may help in the short run to ease structural change. But does the U.S. really mean to improve prosperity by asking workers to accept a permanently lower standard of living?

The huge tax cuts of supply-side economics may take many years to raise the nation's capital stock. Even if they succeed in the long run, they do nothing to direct that capital toward potential growth and export leaders. The early scorecard for the Reagan Administration's tax cuts shows such questionable effects as encouraging the nation's leading steelmaker to buy an oil company for $6 billion, a New York brokerage house to create a lucrative syndication in used billboards, and other businesses to start a giant market in selling tax credits without necessarily creating much new physical capital.

Some combination of Keynesian, monetarist, and supply-side policies will continue to dominate U.S. macroeconomic management. But these are blunderbuss approaches. The policymakers can no longer ignore the relationship of the microeconomic components to an overarching growth strategy, and industrial policy is one way to fill the gap.

The greatest cost of doing without a national policy is the continual danger of falling behind on the economic power curve. In 1975, when MITI saw the U.S. tightening up on imports of basic steel and developing countries such as Korea about to beat Japan at the low-wage game, it spurred its steelmakers into specialty market—well before its basic steel industry had peaked. Today, the need to anticipate market changes is even more urgent.

The U.S. has been more than lucky with the success of its Lockheed, Chrysler, New York City, and Consolidated Rail bailouts. But that kind of ad hoc action can wind up being even more expensive than an explicit policy. If business, government, labor, consumers, and others had a vehicle for anticipating change—as signaled by the marketplace—politically motivated bailouts could be averted, and fortunes could be saved. Perhaps more important, the human costs—in broken lives, welfare, unemployment compensation, and the breakup of communities—might be reduced if industries were nudged toward change before they became extinct.

Still, the question remains: Why should the welfare of U.S. industries be the concern of government? When it comes to R&D, even conservative economists have little trouble justifying government help. It is generally agreed that the innovations resulting from R&D provide social returns—in improved quality of life, jobs, and expansion of knowledge—that far exceed the private investor's return on his outlay.

R&D tends to be underfunded by the private sector, but it pays the public to make up the difference and thus capture that social spillover. The same argument can be applied to public investment in infrastructure and education, and it has obvious relevance to other elements of the industrial policy approach. Government cannot and should not try to do everything, but it can do much more to help the private sector regain its competitive position in the world economy.

INDUSTRIAL POLICY—NOW THE BAD NEWS[2]

Despite indications that the economy is staging a short-term recovery, it continues to stagger under the weight of long-term stagflation. Democrats are racing to devise plausible alternatives to Reaganomics, and to package them with attractive slogans that will captivate the voters in 1984 as the Republicans' supply-side proclamations did in 1980.

[2]Reprint of a magazine article by Samuel Bowles, David M. Gordon and Thomas E. Weisskopf, authors of *Beyond the Waste Land: A Democratic Alternative to Economic Decline*(1983). *The Nation* 236:687+Je 4 '83. Copyright © 1983 The Nation Associates.

Among those Democratic alternatives, "industrial policy" is rapidly emerging as the frontrunner with both candidates and liberal pundits. The proposals advanced under that rubric sound appealing and sensible—especially in comparison with the heartlessness and voodoo economics of the Republicans. But within the fold of industrial policy there are some wolves in sheep's clothing—proposals that pose a threat to democratic politics or whose internal contradictions emerge under close scrutiny. Progressives should think twice before leaping into the arms of corporatists and neoliberals, no matter how egalitarian their rhetoric. We shall take a critical look at the economic assumptions of industrial policy and then propose a democratic alternative. The contrasts between the two should clarify the political issues in the current economic debate.

Proponents of industrial policy occupy the center of the political spectrum, and they are just as frightened of the social and political consequences of Reaganomics as leftists and progressives. For example, Felix Rohatyn, a Wall Street investment banker and a leading corporatist spokesman, warned recently in *The New York Review of Books,* "America cannot survive half rich, half poor; half suburb, half slum. If the country wakes up, it will not do so by way of laissez faire."

Industrial policy is the principal mainstream alternative to monetarism and supply-side economics. Its adherents range from Wall Streeters like Rohatyn and Peter Peterson, former Commerce Secretary and chief organizer of the Bipartisan Budget Appeal (a campaign to shift government spending priorities), to liberal academics like Lester Thurow of M.I.T. and Robert Reich of Harvard. Because they reject both traditional liberal programs and Reaganomics, we shall call them "centrists."

The main differences between them and conservatives are twofold. First, the centrists do not share the conservatives' distrust of government. They call for a more coherent government policy to boost profits and the rate of capital formation. They recognize the necessity—even the inevitability and desirability—of substantial government involvement in the economy.

Second, the centrists condemn the free-market model of the economy. Their model is not one of perfect competition among millions of individual households and small enterprises, but one of bargaining and consensus among the few giant corporations, large unions and government agencies that dominate the economy. Their prophet is not Adam Smith but Joseph Schumpeter, the twentieth-century Austro-American economist who championed advanced capitalism and liberal democracy as a dual system of economic and political competition among elites. Centrists rhetoric speaks not of individual gain but of the common good; it was Jean Jacques Rousseau, not Jeremy Bentham, whose picture appeared with the 1980 declaration of a reindustrialization program by the editors of *Business Week*.

The basic economic logic of the centrist position may be easily summarized, despite variations in terminology and political orientation among its sympathizers. Although unregulated competition among businesses, workers and consumers gives rise to waste and needless social conflict the centrists say, capitalism, while less decentralized and competitive than in Adam Smith's day, is still capitalism and profits are what make it go. Therefore, extensive and carefully planned government involvement in the economy is necessary to rationalize production and distribution and to maintain high levels of profitability and an efficient market-based system.

The centrists give top priority to increasing the rate of investment through substantial transfers of income to the largest corporations. That means curtailing America's consumption in the short run in order to permit high corporate profits. "The U. S. is being asked to consume less and invest more," wrote *Business Week*. "This means sacrifice." The centrists say the necessary sacrifices will be made voluntarily, rather than obtained by compulsion. They pin their hopes on their ability to appeal to the common good. They call for a new "social contract" between management and labor and for a new sense of discipline among the citizenry at large. Their vogue word is "tripartism," the use of centralized planning boards with representatives of management, labor and government, who would compromise their conflicting interests in behalf of the public welfare.

That is the sheep's clothing; it is hard to argue with a program that recognizes the need to consider the common good. But the wolves begin to emerge when the centrists talk about how the common good is to be pursued.

Many centrists, on Wall Street and in the academy assume that the economy has stagnated in large part because of a capital storage, a squeeze on investable resources. That is why they insist on transferring resources from consumption to investment— through wage concessions, taxes on consumption (sales taxes and the like) and reductions in Social Security spending. But their premise is false. The roots of stagnation lie not in a capital short- age but in what could be called the costs of corporate power—the costs of sustaining corporate control over production and invest- ment. The centrists would ask Americans to sacrifice their earn- ings and to consume less in order to enlarge the pool of investable resources, which is already ample, and to enhance the power of a corporate structure whose wayward decisions caused our prob- lems in the first place.

The centrists would also insist that profitability serve as the ultimate guide to government intervention in the economy. Thus, they propose that the government channel capital into "sunrise" industries and identify new high-tech industries that will be prof- itable in the future; the "sunset" industries should be allowed to die natural deaths. But the "free" marketplace in which they vest their faith has proved to be a poor allocator of goods and services. It has generated enormous waste in the economy—$1.2 trillion worth in 1980 alone, by our calculations, in underutilized capacity and misutilized resources. (This means the production and con- sumption of goods and services in that year could have been almost 50 percent higher than they actually were.) Are profitability and the rules of the marketplace the only criteria by which the govern- ment should decide how to allocate public funds?

The centrists also propose strategies to restore America's dom- inance of the world economy. Whether out of decency or political acumen, they avoid openly imperialist rhetoric, calling instead for subsidies to companies that are logical candidates for export growth. But they remain largely mute on the need to reduce mili- tary spending (although some, like Thurow, have criticized the wastefulness of the Reagan arms buildup). Finally, they speak out strongly for free trade. Some questions inevitably arise. Is it possi- ble for the United States to regain the economic power it enjoyed immediately after World War II? Does it make sense to tie economic recovery to the export prospects of high-tech companies? Doesn't free trade actually mean that U. S. workers are free to compete with the wages and working conditions of millions of oppressed workers in the Third World?

These questions aside, our principal reservation about centrist strategies results from the dangers they pose to democratic institutions. They would transfer resources to the wealthiest and the largest corporations. By insisting on the primacy of profit, they would increase corporate power and reduce corporate accountability. And they would strengthen the role of corporate interests in formulating international economic policy, while failing to confront the potential peril of increased defense spending in conjunction with a more aggressive search for markets abroad.

If these policies are adopted, the losers in our society will far outnumber the winners. Centrist strategies would require that the people's elected representatives be excluded from economic decision making in order to insulate soak-the-poor redistributive policies from popular protest. We have already seen an example of the curtailment of the democratic accountability of government bodies—New York City's Emergency Financial Control Board, which took management of the city's budget away from local officials and placed it in the hands of a committee consisting of bankers, business representatives and state officials. The board's architect, Felix Rohatyn, believes that the lessons learned during New York City's 1975 fiscal crisis have a broader application. "The direction and philosophy of a large unit of government was fundamentally and permanently changed as a result of the involvement, some would say intrusion, of the private sector in government," he said recently. "In my judgement, this is a principle that is applicable to a vast array of national problems for reasons not too dissimilar to the New York City experience . . . The United States today in many ways is similar to New York City in 1975." Such an exclusionary policy could undermine the democratic process in the United States.

Is this the banner to which the Democratic Party will rally us in 1984?

We propose a democratic program for restructuring the economy. We think it has two fundamental advantages over conservative and centrist strategies: It would promote economic recovery more effectively than supply-side, monetarist or centrist programs, and it would emphasize economic democracy. Those advantages are to us overwhelming.

Our proposals do not stem from a romantic fondness for political democracy. Mainstream economists argue that there is a trade-off between political democracy and economic efficiency. We agree that economic efficiency is important. But we disagree with the view that more democracy necessarily means more inefficiency and waste.

Ours is not the traditional Keynesian critique that waste is inherent in laissez-faire economies. Keynesians focus on demand-side waste. They teach that unnecessarily low levels of output and employment occur when the market operates entirely on its own and when, as a result, demand for goods and services is much lower than it might be without such market failures. That analysis played a central and salutary role in postwar economic policy. We do not aim to bury Keynesianism, since its basic critique remains resonant, but we do not intend to praise it either.

The problem with the inherited Keynesian wisdom is not that aggregate demand shortfalls never happen or never matter. They often happen. And they do matter. But demand-side expansion is never enough for economic growth. A viable Keynesian program must take into account the supply side as well—the systems responsible for the production and distribution of goods and services. Supply-side policies may seek to promote private production and profits within the market setting, as did John Kennedy's probusiness tax cuts in 1963 and many other government policies in the postwar years. They may include oppressive controls on labor to contain the explosive potential of full employment (which dramatically enhances workers' bargaining power), as were imposed in Hitler's Germany. Or they may seek changes in private-sector approaches to production and distribution, advocating either selective or wholesale democratic planning. But some kind of supply-side analysis must be part of any strategy that relies on the expansion of aggregate demand.

What distinguishes our programs from those of centrists and traditional Keynesians is our analysis of what we call the "slack economy." The rules under which the contemporary American political economy operates—the rules of capitalism—result in enormous waste, as we have said. Under those rules, profits are the final arbiter of the worth of a person or a product. If one accepts the rules as binding, one must accept the inevitability of supply-side waste. But why must these rules govern? If we can change them in sensible ways, we can start regenerating our slack economy.

The new rules we propose are based on three principles, which differ sharply from the principles of the centrist approach:

Centrist strategies insist on profit-led growth. We stress the necessity and advantages of *wage-led growth*. By rewarding the vast majority instead of suppressing it, wage-led growth policies would stimulate employment and investment. Growth would result from the demand-side effects of full employment and the supply-side effects of greater worker motivation and innovative pressure, as workers respond to the incentive of rising wages and firms respond to wage pressure by technical innovation.

Centrist strategies let the market guide the allocation of economic resources. We call for *needs-based allocation*. An economy most directly and democratically serves the people when there is substantial planning to identify and meet their needs in terms of consumption and personal development. A democratic planning system can better fulfill the basic needs of society than can the flickering and wayward signals of the marketplace.

Centrists want to restore America's economic hegemony over the rest of the world. Our proposals advocate *cooperation for economic security*—in both the domestic and the international spheres. We stress the importance of cooperation not merely for moral reasons but because of the waste and insecurity that efforts at economic domination have historically produced.

Those principles may sound vague and even utopian. But they are embodied in a detailed twenty-four-point program—an Economic Bill of Rights (see box for the headings of the program). The proposals can be applied within the existing constitutional and political framework of the United States. The Economic Bill

An Economic Bill of Rights

I. Right to Economic Security and Equity
   1. A Decent Job
   2. Solidarity Wages, Comparable Pay and Equal Employment Opportunity
   3. Public Child Care and Community Service Centers
   4. A Shorter Standard Workweek and Flexible Work Hours
   5. Flexible Price Controls

II. Right to a Democratic Workplace
   6. Public Commitment to Democratic Trade Unions
   7. Workers' Right to Know and to Decide
   8. Democratic Production Incentives
   9. Promoting Community Enterprises

III. Right to Chart Our Economic Future
   10. Planning to Meet Human Needs
   11. Democratizing Investment
   12. Democratic Control of Money
   13. Promoting Community Life
   14. Environmental Democracy
   15. Democratizing Foreign Trade

IV. Right to a Better Way of Life
   16. Reduced Military Spending
   17. Conservation and Safe Energy
   18. Good Food
   19. A National Health Policy
   20. Lifetime Learning and Cultural Opportunities
   21. Payment for Home Child Care in Single-Parent Households
   22. Community Corrections and Reduced Crime Control Spending
   23. Community Needs Information and Reduced Advertising Expenditures
   24. Equitable Taxation and Public Allocation of Resources

of Rights is for the 1980's, not the twenty-first century. Although our Bill of Rights could pay for itself by promoting economic recovery, its principal virtues are political, not technical. It offers a viable long-term alternative to trickle-down economics, and it provides the basis for popular mobilization and an alternative direction for economic restructuring.

The Democrats will be much in the news over the next eighteen months with their centrist alternatives to Reaganomics. A truly democratic alternative cannot easily compete for public attention. But the questions to ask about both centrist and democratic approaches are simple and self evident. Do they make sense? Would they promote economic recovery without compounding the waste that currently afflicts our economy? Would they promote democracy rather than constrict it? By any of these standards, would they provide a dramatic alternative to the economic wasteland?

CAN CREEPING SOCIALISM CURE CREAKING CAPITALISM?[3]

Felix Rohatyn, the New York banker, wants an "industrial policy" to invest in declining industries. Lester Thurow, the MIT economist, wants an "industrial policy" to invest in rising industries. Barry Bluestone, an economist further to the Left, wants a "progressive industrial policy" aimed at "creating more hospitable, more interesting, less authoritarian, and safer work environments." Bruce Scott, a Harvard Business School professor, wants an "industrial policy" to promote efficiency. Frank Weil, a former Commerce Department official, wants his industrial policy to be made an "Industrial Fed," similar to the Federal Reserve Board; Robert Lekachman wants something called a "National Investment Authority." Gary Hart wants an "industrial policy." Walter Mondale wants an "industrial policy." It's one of the

[3]Reprint of an article by Robert M. Kaus. *Harper's* 266: 17–22 F '83. Copyright © 1983 by Harper's Magazine. Reprinted by permission.

Democrats' vaunted "new ideas"—though even John Connally wants an "industrial policy." All God's chill'un want "industrial policy."

What people who talk about "industrial policy" mean, if they mean anything at all (and some don't), is a new level of intervention by the government in the economy—basically, attempts by government to guide the fate of particular industries. These people say it's not enough for the government to worry about the size of the budget deficit or the money supply, and about general incentives for saving and investment. Instead, the government must be prepared to roll up its sleeves and get its hands dirty promoting or discouraging particular industries, or even particular firms. Most industrial policies involve some scheme for government investment in America's faltering "basic industries" (steel, rubber, machine tools) in exchange for a government role in "restructuring" those industries. Most also involve an attempt to boost the high-technology "sunrise" industries (semiconductors and the like) that are said to populate our future.

The collection of would-be industrial czars, academic hustlers, and self-promoters who are currently riding the "industrial policy" concept is enough to give anyone pause: in addition to Rohatyn, who basically wants the taxpayers to give him a blank check for $5 billion, aspiring industrial policymakers include Charls Walker, the wealthy tax lobbyist whose previous ideas have brought us twelve-figure federal deficits, and Gar Alperovitz, an est devotee and leftish economist-about-Washington who has his own press agent and a rap as smooth as an encyclopedia salesman's. Other "industrial policy" promoters tend to babble with disconcerting confidence about "sectorial policy," "managed adjustment policy," "market promotion policy," "policy tradeoffs," and "policy responses." So much policy, so little time.

Still, some of these idea salesmen may be selling ideas worth buying. And they can always point across the water at our industrial rivals as examples of satisfied customers. "Industrial policy" may or may not be responsible for the Japanese miracle, but there is not much doubt that the Japanese have it and think it helps.

The goal of "industrial policy" is economic prosperity, and the great question about it is how government bureaucrats can be expected to outguess private business executives, who have stockholders' money and their own jobs on the line, about where prosperity lies. Every investment dollar directed by an "industrial policy" into steel on the one hand, or semiconductors on the other hand, is a dollar less for investment in anything else (including semiconductors on the one hand, or steel on the other). Why aren't these decisions best made by the free market? Advocates of "industrial policy" have several answers, often contradictory.

Let's start with the problem of declining basic industries. Steel is the prime example here, and our steel industry is in deep trouble. American steel mills are operating at about 35 percent of capacity, a consequence of the prolonged recession. But the recession (which is hurting other countries' steel industries too) is not our steel industry's major problem. Aging facilities and high wages are. Last November, the steelworkers' union turned down a package of wage concessions, in part because the steel companies would not promise to reinvest the savings in the industry. (The last time U.S. Steel got a big pool of capital together, it bought an oil company.) About all the workers and the managers can agree on is that the industry should be protected against its more efficient competitors, which it now is by a complicated "fair trade" mechanism that is used to force the Japanese and Europeans to agree to import quotas (euphemized as "suspension agreements").

The free market's prescription for steel is straightforward: if American steel mills cannot produce the stuff cheaply enough to compete with the Koreans or the Brazilians, they should shut down. Their owners should reinvest in industries that are profitable, which will be those where America has a "comparative advantage" over other nations. Unemployed workers should look for jobs in those industries—taking wage cuts if necessary, moving to the Sunbelt if they have to, just as workers left Southern farms and moved to Northern cities generations ago.

The market cure falls into the "brutal but effective" category, as far as encouraging a shift into more profitable industries is concerned. Industrial policy advocates of virtually every stripe reject it, and propose instead that the government intervene in declining industries like steel, typically through a revival of the Depression-era Reconstruction Finance Corporation. It is an indication of the slipperiness of "industrial policy," however, that the two leading advocates of a revived RFC, Thurow and Rohatyn, would use it for what seem to be diametrically opposed purposes. Rohatyn, who thinks the idea of writing off loser industries is "nonsense," would have his RFC "turn the losers into winners . . . and use whatever U.S. government resources are necessary to do the job." Thurow says that "sunset" industries like steel, due to quirks in our capital markets, "often have access to plentiful funds for new investment," but that "often these investments should not occur." *His* RFC would make sure they didn't, by directing a Japanese-style "orderly retreat" from the steel industry that would free up funds for investment in "sunrise" industries. Rohatyn calls the migration to the Sunbelt "one of the gravest events in our history." Thurow wants the government to pay people's moving expenses.

What could either of these approaches do that a well-functioning market couldn't do just as well? "What an RFC does that a market doesn't do," says Rohatyn's associate Eugene Keilin, "is make deals." Rohatyn's talk of business-labor-government co-operation often evokes images of a sort of Bohemian Grove chum-miness among these various elites—but what he really wants to do is knock heads. In exchange for lending a few billion to a steel company, for example, a Rohatyn RFC would demand concessions from unions (such as wage cuts or changes in work rules), from companies (including the removal of top executives or prom-ises to reinvest in a new steel mill rather than another oil compa-ny), from banks (in the form of matching capital or stretch-outs of existing loans), and from suppliers (more favorable terms, con-version of debts into equity, etc.). A more familiar model than the RFC might be the International Monetary Fund, which goes around demanding that debt-ridden nations change their ways as a condition for further loans. It is the possibility of new invest-ment, in this scenario, that brings the various parties to the table and overcomes the general adversarial hide-boundness that pro-duced debacles like the recent steel talks. This, as Rohatyn has by now reminded everyone in America, is how he saved New York City from bankruptcy as chairman of the Municipal Assistance Corporation.

Sounds good. But if losers can be turned into winners in this
fashion, why doesn't some smart entrepreneur get together a pot
of capital and do just that? This is, for example, precisely what
Rupert Murdoch does, on a smaller scale, with failing newspa-
pers. If Rohatyn is so confident about his ability to turn ailing
businesses around, as a prominent investment banker he is in a
particularly good position to put large sums of money where his
mouth is.

There are several possible answers to this question. The pot
of money required to revive the steel industry (as opposed to the
pot required to revive the *Boston Herald American*) may simply
be too big for anyone but the government to get together, and the
risk too great for anyone but the government to spread. As even
Murdoch has discovered, unions organized across whole industries are reluctant to negotiate concessions with individual firms.
And not too far from the front of Rohatyn's mind must be the notion that an RFC could do more than just write checks. It might
also dangle in front of firms and unions the sort of temptations that
only the government can offer: temporary trade protection, environmental waivers, tax incentives. Finally, even a free market
needs some procedure for dealing with failing companies. The
RFC can be seen as a better alternative to our current procedure—bankruptcy, essentially an industrial policy run by judges
and lawyers.

Rohatyn thinks his RFC can actually make a profit on the taxpayers' money—which, if it happened, would be some sort of
proof that government can achieve what private investors can't.
But Rohatyn doesn't seem to care whether the RFC is vindicated
in the market-place, since he doesn't accept the wisdom of the
marketplace. He is a preservationist who wants to save basic industries even if the market would say to pull the plug. Industrial
change, he argues, has a negative impact on society that cannot
be fully reflected on the balance sheets of the economic players
who bring it about. As suppliers close down and communities
shrivel up, workers are forced to move, investments in schools and
roads become obsolete or cannot be supported by a declining tax
base. Even national security might be jeopardized by reliance on
foreign steel to build American weapons. This argument is a stan-

dard item in the left-wing protectionist repertoire (ironically, since such people are usually *for* change and *against* defense spending). The trouble is that it can justify preserving practically every industry, however outmoded, that employs people. It's hard to see where it stops.

Thurow, for one, wouldn't take it very far. He is what you might call an "accelerationist" who wants to speed up the market's changes, the better to beat Germany and Japan to the high-tech frontier. As such, he has a harder time than Rohatyn justifying RFC-style meddling in the market. How could an RFC hope to pull the plug on losing industries, or pick future winners, better than the market?

Thurow offers a variety of economic arguments, most of them unsatisfying. He points out that, thanks to a law called the Glass-Steagall Act, which bans commercial banks from owning stock, America lacks true investment banks with the sort of large equity position in major corporations that might give them the incentive (and power) to force tough decisions on large firms before they approach the brink of disaster. Similarly, Thurow argues that current corporate tax laws give firms an incentive to retain their earnings, giving older, established firms an unjustified advantage when it comes to raising capital. Finally, Thurow hypothesizes that if there are four weak firms in a declining industry (as there are now in the farm equipment industry), the wrong ones, or all four, might die unattended, whereas a government-backed "orderly retreat" might be able to preserve the two healthiest competitors.

What Thurow's arguments illuminate is that we *have* an industrial policy now, through a huge variety of regulatory, tax, and antitrust policies that work together to influence the future of various industries in ways no one has stopped to calculate. If the problem is that the market isn't being allowed to do its job efficiently, however, a more sensible solution might be to repeal the Glass-Steagall Act, reform the corporate income tax, and rewrite the antitrust laws so that weak industries can reorganize on their own, rather than to add yet another layer of "policy" on top.

And who is to know better than investors which of the four tractor makers is worth saving? What if one of the firms slated for extinction refuses to cooperate? Japan's industrial policy-makers, fearing a surfeit of automobile companies, tried to get Honda to "retreat" out of auto manufacturing. Honda resisted, and now makes what are arguably the best cars in the world. The strength of American capitalism has been its approach of "let a hundred flowers bloom, and see which one lives."

Thurow's most convincing argument is political, not economic—that if the government doesn't step in and organize the "orderly retreat" of a losing industry, the market—having delayed the inevitable—will ultimately produce a rout, and the industry (and its workers) will end up forcing the government to bail it out through protectionism or Lockheed-type loans. Then the public ends up footing the bill without getting a leaner, more competitive industry in return. "Given that you're going to have government interference," Thurow says, "better to do it by the front door and do it right than do it by the back door and do it badly." Or, as another economist put it, "as long as you're going to get taken to the cleaners, you might as well get your clothes cleaned."

Free-marketeers see this sort of argument as a Mutt 'n' Jeff routine played out by liberal economists and their Frostbelt allies. First the dying industries demand protectionism, allowing the "industrial policymakers" to rush in with their "second-best" proposals, which suddenly look mighty attractive. But Thurow does have recent political history on his side. Even the Reagan administration, with its commitment to the free market, found it politically necessary to protect the troubled auto and steel industries. As a result, consumers are paying higher prices while the unions and executives who benefit from the quotas have promised nothing in exchange. Even an incompetent industrial policymaker would have a hard time striking a poorer bargain.

A whole different strand in the web of "industrial policy" is concerned not with "loser" industries but with "winners": semiconductors, fiber optics, exotic composite materials, biogenetics, etc. Many people urge the government to subsidize these industries of the future, the better to get the jump on our competition. That is what Japan, Inc., with its powerful Ministry of International Trade (MITI) has done; that is what the French are doing by "force-feeding" their telecommunications, computer, and airplane industries (while, like the Japanese, they protect them from foreign competition in their home market).

Why should successful industries be subsidized? Just like dying industries, growing ones are said to generate social benefits that aren't reflected in their owners' cost-benefit analysis. An investment at the cutting edge of technology, in particular, might produce benefits that won't be captured by the firm making the investment. Abstract, theoretical research has long been subsidized for this reason. James Watson was in no position to reap all the profits from commercial applications of the discovery of DNA. If we left it to the profit motive, there would be insufficient investment in society's Watsons—so we don't. The champions of high tech—notably the "Atari Democrats"—argue that a lot of less abstract technological research shares this characteristic with "basic research." If we leave it to the market, there may be too little money invested in developing "applied" technologies. The question of risk reappears here also—with Thurow and others arguing that some large cutting-edge projects are too risky to be financed even by today's relatively healthy venture capital markets. "If you have a $100 million idea, you're okay," Thurow asserts, "but if you have a $3 billion idea you're in a lot of trouble."

Aside from such big-ticket items, however, and some pleas for capital from the small high-tech companies in California's Silicon Valley, it's hard to find anybody in the industrial policy camp who wants to subsidize the ordinary business expenses of "sunrise" industries. "Picking winners" in this sense (as if the government could beat the stock market by guessing which companies will succeed and which will fail) is rightly ridiculed—but it isn't on the "policy agenda," as we like to call it. Even Thurow, the apostle of "acceleration," goes out of his way to admit that it is "clearly impossible" to pick which industries are about to experience "sunrise."

What is on the agenda seems to be something far more modest: an expanded definition of the sort of "R&D" that the government will fund, along with more money for technical training and various schemes for making the Pentagon (which funds about 30 percent of all American R&D) more sensitive to the commercial potential of its projects.

Applied research can be expensive, of course, and risky. The Japanese government directed millions over four years into developing large "random access memory," or RAM, computer chips. The Japanese won a major victory by capturing most of the market for RAM chips of the 64K size, prompting much handwringing in the American business press, as well as praise for the foresight of MITI. But there is now a possibility that the future belongs not to RAM-type chips but to a different breed of chip called the EEPROM, which has the advantage of not losing its memory when its power source is turned off. If so, Japan, Inc., may be in trouble, and the American firms that gambled on EEPROMS will be in a good position to clean up: a victory for the "let a hundred flowers bloom" approach.

To ensure that some risks are taken, but not stupid ones, most proponents of expanded government R&D argue that private businesses should be willing to put up 50 percent of the costs. This sensible rule, they point out with some satisfaction, would at least weed out turkeys like the Supersonic Transport, which no airplane builder was willing to spend much of its own money on, but which the French and British governments have spent billions on, to their regret.

There is another kind of investment that is increasingly crucial to our economic success in the world, and that is education and scientific training, otherwise known as investment in human capital. Emerging industries are built less on a base of natural resources (look at Japan) or on buildings and heavy machinery, and more on the skills and knowledge in people's heads. Almost everyone agrees that the United States has been underinvesting in human capital lately and, what is more, almost everyone agrees that this particular investment is primarily a government responsibility. The *Wall Street Journal* may not like to think of education as an "industrial policy," but in a way that's what it is.

Should America buy an industrial policy? Before deciding, we must sort out three genuine controversies among the salesmen. The first is the debate between the preservationists and the accelerationists. The choice between "picking winners" and "helping losers" may be a false one—in part because nobody really wants to pick winners very far off into the future, in part because you have to do a bit of winner-picking even to help losers. (Some specialties of steelmaking, for example, look more promising than others.) But the choice between speeding up or slowing down the market is not false. You can't do both. If we are going to put more capital into older industries in order to preserve jobs and communities, there will be less money to be put into "sunrise" industries in hope of a big payoff. (And there's no rational reason to suppose it makes sense to subsidize both ends at the expense of the middle.)

The accelerationist goal—of easing the pain of industrial change only enough to make it bearable—seems the better choice. The preservationists' appeals for "regional equity," and elaborate plans to ensure it, can block the necessary path of economic progress. Many of the "social costs" of economic decline in the Northwest, after all, are balanced by the "social benefits" of economic growth elsewhere. America is a nation; the Northeast isn't. Some nasty side effects of industrial change—like the decline of local tax bases—could be cured by more reliance on a national tax base to fund public services. America is a nation; the Southwest isn't. A reversal of the "new federalism" would enable hard-hit communities to maintain their schools, roads, and sewers while they went about the business of acquiring new industries.

The second genuine controversy is over the size and power of the apparatus that would be necessary to administer an "industrial policy." Here the issue is creeping socialism. On one side are what might be called the Fixers (including both Rohatyn and Thurow), who argue that the government can do what is necessary ("restructuring" particular industries, boosting new technologies) without running the entire economy. Arrayed against them are those, like Alperovitz and the champions of "democratic planning," who eagerly anticipate the involvement of the government in questions ranging from the nature of the transportation system (cars vs. trains), to the location of industries, on down to plans dictating (as Alperovitz described it to me) the "use of steel at historic levels." Once you "cross the line" into industrial policy, Alperovitz argues, planning is inevitable—"you cannot be half pregnant on this." Free-marketeers, of course, would tend to agree; but they don't want to be pregnant at all.

Certainly the Fixers could not simply patch up individual firms one at a time. Suppose International Harvester were on the brink of bankruptcy, to pick a hypothetical example. Should the RFC lend it half a billion dollars? Will that be enough to save it? Would it make more sense, if the government wants an "orderly retreat" from the farm equipment industry, to let IH go under and to help strengthen a firm that's healthier, like John Deere? There is no way the government could know how to act intelligently without a clear idea of where the whole industry is heading—in other words, a plan.

Other slippery slopes dot the industrial policy terrain. Robert Reich, in his forthcoming book *The Next American Frontier*, proposes to mitigate the costs of "labor adjustment" by contractually obligating corporations to take care of their workers, in exchange for government loans. If the firms diversified, or closed plants, they would have to retrain their workers to take on new jobs, keep them in their old jobs, find them employment, or pay them unemployment benefits. Reich denies that his proposal is anything like "national economic planning." But since virtually every corporation is "adjusting" to some extent—closing some plants here, laying off other workers there—his scheme would have to mean the pervasive involvement of government in business, if only to negotiate the terms of corporate paternalism. Thurow, for his part, has on occasion indicated he'd like the government to assist not just in helping winners and losers, but also in helping firms in the middle that have simply "been hit by a sequence of bad luck and perhaps bad judgment." But if the government is going to restructure firms that are young, old, and in between, what's left?

Many industrial policy types look longingly at MITI, staffed by the best minds of the University of Tokyo, with a desk to keep track of each industry much like the State Department keeps track of individual countries. Washington's bureaucratic imperatives being what they are, however, the prospect of an American MITI should not be entirely pleasing. Thurow now says that he would keep his "hands off" the auto industry (even though it has been "hit by a sequence of bad luck"). Would bureaucrats who have spent their lives monitoring the auto industry be able to exercise similar restraint?

Still, the Planners seem a bit too eager to find a blazing arrow pointing from "industrial policy" to "national economic planning." A couple of government investment banks—one to restructure the "losers," another to fund some high tech R&D—would not turn us into the Soviet Union, or even France. The original RFC, though it employed 3,000 people even before its World War II expansion, did not in the end throttle capitalist initiative. More ambitious proposals for a centralized super-agency to "coordinate" the often self-contradictory forays of government into the market, on the other hand, raise a reasonable fear of Washington, Inc. The coordination problem could better be solved by expanding the control of the White House over the various agencies—often legally independent—which now feud and litigate both with private industries and with each other.

Silliest of all are proposals to create a fancy government agency and then deny it the power to do anything. This is the course recommended by the House Democratic Caucus, which has called for something they dub an "Economic Co-operation Council," as well as *The New York Times*, which has warmly endorsed a similar idea it calls "MITI-minus." The Democrats' council would be composed, needless to say, of "representative, distinguished, respected, and influential" people who would "map long-term strategy," "monitor carefully the changing nature of America's domestic economy," and "evaluate global economic trends." We have enough committees run by the special assistants of great men, and enough bureaucracies, public and private, to propose high-minded solutions. There's no point diverting more creative minds to Washington unless they are actually going to put some of them into practice.

The third and perhaps most important choice to be made has to do with democracy. Democracy poses a big dilemma for would-be industrial policymakers, for although they all, by definition, reject the market, many don't like the polity much better. The more democratic the system, they tend to feel, the more it will produce favoritism, pork barrel, protectionism, propping up inefficient industries whose workers vote to preserve their jobs, while denying funds for efficient new industries whose workers don't vote because they don't exist yet.

Some embrace these consequences of popular rule and, like Alperovitz, draw up complex and somewhat cynical plans for sacrificing economic efficiency in order to appease the voters—calling it "regional equity" or "community stability." Others hew to the ideal of efficiency, and conclude they cannot afford to be democratic. Almost no one, apparently, believes that politicians will ever be capable of taking actions that appeal to the long-term interests of Americans in a strong economy, as opposed to the short-term interests of particular regions or industries.

Rohatyn is the most openly contemptuous of the political system, and his proposed RFC represents the most striking violation of democratic principles. "Today, we could not build our road system, the TVA, or the Manhattan project," he writes in the *New York Review of Books*. "Between the Congress, the courts, the numerous interest groups, these projects would all die on the vine." His solution is that someone like himself be delegated the power to run things without interference. Hence his insistence that an RFC must be "independent" of politics, like the Federal Reserve Board.

But Rohatyn, were he to get his wish, would have even more power than Fed chairman Paul Volcker. Rohatyn estimates the necessary endowment of the RFC at $5 billion, with authority to issue another $25 billion in loan guarantees. With this money he would hope to mobilize another $60 billion in matching private funds—giving him a hand in a total of $90 billion in new investment, a sum equal to about one fifth of all the credit in the nation in 1980. Rohatyn could—and the whole idea of his RFC is that he *would*—use his billions to punish managers, workers, mayors, and governors who he felt were out of line with his ideas of "regional equity" and "social justice." Americans tend to laugh when Latin American generals stage a military coup with the stated goal of restoring "order" to the economy. But what Rohatyn is suggesting is not far from the same thing.

Is the American political system so hopelessly fragmented that in order to pursue a sensible "industrial policy" it must set up such a benevolent dictatorship? If so, then the system would surely make certain that any industrial czar fell victim to the same pressures, either by limiting his powers from the outset or by second-guessing his decisions, much as the decisions of the far less important Federal Trade Commission are now second-guessed in Congress.

If our democracy is really incapable of improving on the decisions made by the market, that is a good reason for sticking with the market—or for repairing our democracy, so that policies that actually help the economy can be administered by leaders accountable to the people. Before we ask the government to cure our sick industries, maybe we should first cure our sick government.

III. DECLINE OR RENEWAL?

EDITOR'S INTRODUCTION

Confronted by statistics that show the decline of the gross national product, and witnessing daily the predominance of Japanese goods in the domestic market, few Americans would now subscribe to the confident attitudes of the 1960s, when possibilities for growth seemed endless. But the bleakness of the macroeconomic picture, which represents the U.S. economy as a whole, is relieved by contradictory signs of microeconomic health among smaller businesses whose efficiency and inventiveness has enabled them to prosper.

William Van Dusen Wishard celebrates the energy of the American entrepreneur, and promises a more hopeful future than the one depicted by macroeconomic forecasting. The two following articles, reprinted from the *New York Times* and *U.S. News & World Report,* both concern "smokestack industries," but in disagreeing about the prospects for such industries, they reveal the resilience and inherent strengths of American manufacturing companies. Next, Bradley Schiller, writing in *Society,* shows that productivity figures should be treated sceptically because current methods of measuring production fail to take into account the less tangible products of service industries.

Seeley G. Lodwick, formerly under Secretary of Agriculture, analyzes the prospects for another large American industry whose productivity, far from declining, has increased to the point at which the world market, hampered by trade restrictions and embargos, can no longer absorb it. Speaking in praise of the vast capacity of American agribusiness, he makes a plea for a system of free trade in which the government will no longer have to pay the American farmer not to produce.

Seth Kantor's article from *Nation's Business* shows how Japanese competition may, in the long run, prove the salvation of the U.S. auto industry, which has responded to falling sales by adopting new machinery and management techniques in the hope of beating the competition at its own game. The success of Chrysler, which has risen from near-bankruptcy to profitability in the brief space of three years, shows what can be done by determined management, and casts doubt on the proposition that the government should never intervene in the free market.

The final article in this section deals with the Bendix Corporation, whose attempt to take over the Martin Marietta Corporation drew public attention to the art of creating profits on paper without selling a single product.

PRODUCTIVITY AND AMERICAN WORLD COMPETITIVENESS[1]

My invitation today is to offer some remarks on productivity and America's world economic competitiveness. By way of approaching this, I would like to consider the greater context which frames American economic leadership and the productivity equation.

So, may I begin by offering you a rather sobering thought? America and the world have entered a zone of disorder and danger seldom, if ever, equalled in human experience. That's pretty heavy for openers, isn't it?

But there's a flip side to that observation. America and the world are also entering a period of economic and technological possibility literally beyond the imaginings of history's most hopeful dreamers. Which scenario shapes the future, will be decided in the next 10-15 years.

It is against that perspective that we daily wrestle with the nitty-gritty of productivity, recession and inflation.

Recession and inflation, of course, are not solely national problems; they are global questions. With the creation of a worldwide system of credit, with instantaneous global electronic finan-

[1]Speech by William Van Dusen Wishard, Consultant, U.S. Chamber of Commerce, delivered at the Meidinger, Inc. annual luncheon, Louisville, Kentucky, December 1, 1983. *Vital Speeches of the Day*, 48:316–20, Mr 1 '82.

cial markets, with multinational corporations flicking millions of dollars from one country to another in a matter of minutes, with billions of petro-dollars sloshing through world financial conduits, no one nation can avoid recession or inflation by itself. Even Switzerland, that bastion of financial stability, has seen its inflation rise from a low of 1.0 percent during the 70's to above 7 percent this year.

Government, business, and individuals obviously must all take maximum, coordinated action to achieve price stability. But the long-term inflation we've experienced over recent years is not only economic in character. It is a reflection of the fact that the world is passing through one of the great watershed periods of history. Nations are moving from one context of life to another, from one manner of organizing and supporting human affairs to a new and more complex one. Inflation is, in part, a symptom of this transition, just as sustained price rises have marked the three previous epochal socio-economic advances of the past millennium.

Let's take a moment to glance at the outline and contours of the watershed period in which we live. I ask you to consider the following: First, the world continues to shift from self-contained national economies to a worldwide interlocking system, where events in any part of that system ripple throughout the system as a whole and affect everyone.

Second, while economic trends are increasingly unifying the world, political trends are moving the opposite direction, fragmenting political entities as never before.

Third, within the next 19 years, the nations of the world will have to generate net real capital at an annual rate a least twice as high as today's; to develop and deliver as much new energy as has been produced in all history; to meet demands for food, raw materials and products that are 100 times greater than today's needs; to employ 30 to 50 percent more people while increasing productivity enough to halt inflation.

Fourth, the rise of third world economic powers creates new markets, new competition, as well as new inflationary pressures as more people want more goods.

Fifth, we are in the process of deciding who will produce what in the world as whole industries are shifting from one nation to another.

Sixth, new modes of "production sharing" are emerging as, for instance, automobile parts for particular models are made in several different nations, transhipped, and then assembled in one country.

Seventh, last year the Japanese displaced America as the world's largest producer of automobiles. This followed Germany's displacing the U.S. as the world's leading exporter of manufactured goods.

Eighth, the Soviet Union is in the midst of the most massive arms buildup in the history of mankind. At the same time, the Soviet economic mechanism is entering a restructuring process equal in scope and significance to the reconstruction period that followed the devastation of World War II. In effect, the myths of Marxism are yielding to the realities of a global economic system and computer logic.

Ninth, the world annually spends some $800 billion on military armaments. This has an inflationary consequence of gigantic proportions.

Partially as a result of the above trends which have been building for three decades, inflation in the OECD countries rose at less than 2 percent in the 50's, 4.5 percent in the 60's, 8.2 percent in the 70's, and is now running at 10 percent.

Let's narrow the focus a bit and look at our own national context. Between 1945 and 1975, only two truly new industries emerged—computers and systemic drugs. Except for those two industries, most of the technologies of the 1950's, 60's, and 70's, were, in the main, based on science and knowledge that has been produced between 1914 and 1930.

The remainder of this century, however, will see industries emerge based on research and knowledge produced in the 1940's, 50's and 60's. Microelectronics and biotechnology are only two of the most visible of these new industries. Experts tell us that these two scientific advances alone will change our lives more fundamentally than did the industrial revolution. Think about that a moment, for that's a prospect that boggles the mind. There is a structural change occurring in the U.S. economy at least as great, and probably greater than the mid-19th century shift from agriculture to railroads, steel and industry.

The overriding issure is: who is going to lead in this era of new technologies? Who will do for the world of the 21st century what America did for the world of the 20th century? Will it be the Japanese? The Germans? The newly industrialized countries of Korea, Brazil, Mexico, Taiwan and Singapore? Or will it be the United States of America?

I believe not only that it could and should be America, but that unless it is America, the magnitude of world danger and disorder will grow beyond manageable proportions. For America to take such a lead, however, requires a national understanding of and commitment to the quest for greater productivity. Without productivity gains, inflation may be impossible to control, the rate of new job creation declines, social conditions deteriorate, America's ability to compete in world markets is weakened, and we have less real wealth to support our democratic experiment.

We've all read the productivity figures. Between 1967 and 1977, U.S. productivity grew 27 percent. West Germany productivity grew 70 percent; France increased 72 percent; Japanese productivity rose at a phenomenal rate of 107 percent. In 1979 and 1980, U.S. productivity declined. If the U.S. trends of recent years are not reversed, and if foreign trends continue at the present rate, by mid-decade, the U.S. could rank fifth in productivity among industrial nations.

The question of why this decline raises many uncertainties. There is, however, much we do know. The drop in the rate of growth in the capital/labor ratio, for instance, plummeted from an average 2.7 percent per year in 1970-74, to .7 percent in 1975-79.

Over-regulation by government is credited with a 25 percent loss of our productivity growth in recent years. Inflation reduces productivity. Price has a significant signaling function in economic life, and with persistent inflation, the efficiency of this signaling function is impaired. Markets become less efficient, and that entails some drag on productivity.

Take an example—the cost of money. Between 1934-48, the prime rate changed twice. During the 1950's, the prime changed 16 times. Same for the 60's. During the 70's, however, it changed 130 times!! In 1980, 39 times. So far this year it's changed 21 times, which suggests probably 200 changes during the 80's.

Now how can businesses plan when their principle cost changes like that. And what does inability to plan adequately do to productivity!

Shifts in the structure of the work force affect productivity. The labor department tells us that 86 percent of all the new jobs created during the 1970's were in the service sector. As economists estimate that productivity in the service sector is roughly 40 percent below the national average, most of the new jobs of the past decade would seem to have decreased productivity growth.

Managerial experience plays some part in the decline of productivity growth. In recent years, many companies have selected CEOs from the ranks of finance and marketing rather than from operations. Some of these managers are inclined to focus more on p/e ratios, cash management, and quarterly returns than on production performance and long-term productivity levels.

Certainly the decreased spending on R & D in recent years has had a direct effect on declining productivity growth.

Finally, and perhaps most significant of anything we've mentioned thus far, the discontent of workers with their jobs and job environment —which is to a large extent a management issue— has negatively affected productivity.

What can be done? What can put America on a new course? Just as we've seen there is no one single cause for decline of productivity growth, so no single act is going to radically change productivity direction. It must be a combination of factors.

Increasing use of new technologies, for example, will produce major productivity gains. Industrial robots, for instance, will climb in sales from $90 million last year, to $500 million in 1985, and $2 billion by 1990.

Decreasing costs of computer power—cost which has been dropping by 50 percent every 30 months—will enable virtually all business and professional concerns to greatly increase productivity. Increased use of CAD/CAM systems—computer-aided design, computer-aided mnanufacturing—will be an enormous boost to productivity. Westinghouse Electric Corporation's use of CAD/CAM has cut manufacturing lead time by 25 percent and increased productivity as much as 400 percent.

New flexible manufacturing systems (FMS)—which group several numerically controlled production machines and a transport system under computer control—will have substantial impact on productivity. Using FMS, machine-tool utilization has increased as much as 45 percent in some cases. These are some of the factors already at work which will contribute to higher productivity growth rates.

But let me suggest other areas where I believe major national initiatives might be taken if we are to increase productivity growth to the degree that is needed.

First, we must rebuild the financial base of the American economy. Let's look at the facts.

The cumulative U.S. capital investment requirements for the 1980's totals about $5 trillion. This exceeds the sum total of all capital investment undertaken between 1900-1980, and it will average $350 billion more per year than was spent in the last two decades.

The average annual U.S. inflation rate during the 70's was 7 percent. A conservative estimate for the 80's puts the average inflation rate at 9 or 10 percent. The 3 percent increase of the 80's over the 70's will add $650 billion to the capital requirements of the corporate sector.

But where will the money come from?

The rate of savings in the United States is the lowest of any developed country. The personal savings rate in Japan is 19 percent; in France 16 percent; in West Germany, 14 percent; in Britian, 14 percent; and in Canada, 11 percent. In the United States, it's less than 5 percent.

The Japanese, with an economy half the size of ours, last year invested more money in capital equipment than did U.S. business.

Debt as a percentage of total capital has increased from less than 30 percent to over 40 percent in the last decade. Between 1961-64, interest payments on debt of nonfinancial corporations averaged 8.6 percent of pretax profits. By 1980, interest payments had risen to 31.2 percent of pretax profits. Over that same period, retained earnings dropped from 30 to 11.2 percent.

At the same time, individual investors have been net sellers of stock for 10 years; in 1969, equities represented 39 percent of the financial assets of the average family. At the end of the 70's, the equity portion was only 23 percent. At the start of the 70's, there were 31 million individual stockholders. Today there are 24 million.

Just at the point when we need more capital than ever in our history, companies are facing lower earnings, less equity financing, eroding profits, towering interest costs, and lower bond ratings.

Some observers argue that the investment picture isn't so bleak. Indeed, recent figures indicate that the average rate of overall business investment—as a percent of GNP—was actually greater for the 1970's than for the 1960's. The rate of growth, however, of new investment—that is, increasing rather than replacing the stock of capital—dropped almost 1.5 percentage points. The portion of U.S. capital stock that is five years old or less has been declining steadily since 1969. Most importantly perhaps, the share of our total investment going to build technological capital has declined alarmingly.

President Reagan is attempting to reverse this trend by offering rewards for savings and investing. Reductions in marginal rates, more generous retirement plan deductions, capital gains reductions, "max tax" on unearned income—all should supply incentives to save and invest.

The business tax cut amounts to $153 billion over the next five years. While this enhances the internal financing capacity of corporations, the tax savings are only achieved when firms spend for plant, equipment and R & D.

There is another aspect to rebuilding our financial base, however, which merits mentioning. Tax incentives, as crucial as they are, cannot by themselves build the financial base of our nation. The savings base of any country is, in part, a reflection of its underlying value system. As such, no nation can build an adequate financial base while annually wasting $25 billion on lost productivity, $30 billion lost or wasted by government, $2 billion lost in revenues as a result of unreported income on dividends, $50 billion lost in revenue as a result of the "underground economy", $40 billion lost in "white collar crime", $90 billion spent on cocaine and marijuana, and how many billions on fighting crime. Such annual wastage alone exceeds America's yearly capital investment expenditures throughout the last decade.

There is no shortage of money in America for essential needs! A new financial base can only be built, however, if we can foster a national climate that encourages people to spend with some sense of social responsibility, and with a view to what is essential for building the future.

We are facing an undeclared national emergency. As such, we need to make hard choices about the use of capital which lacks any apparent redemptive social value, and is unrelated to building the future economic strength of the nation.

A second initiative to increase productivity is for the government, mainly federal, to adjust its role to one of only providing those services necessary to a healthy society and economy. The administration is trying to rachet back the rate of growth of the federal budget from 15 to 5 percent. This is not easy. 75 percent of the budget is virtually uncontrollable under current law. Almost half the budget is indexed.

The administration's program attempts to slow the rate of growth of human services programs by $128 billion between 1981-84. While such a budget slowing process sounds severe, entitlement programs will still increase by $50 billion this fiscal year—the largest increase ever

Without going into as much detail as this subject deserves, it is clear such massive reductions in budget growth will succeed only if the private sector assumes a greater role in addressing the myriad of America's social problems and tackles them on a scale beyond anything so far envisioned.

Take structural unemployment. There are more structurally unemployed Americans than there are citizens of countries like Panama or Nicaragua.

Willian Norris, chairman of Control Data has proposed a program whereby business would employ one million disadvantaged youth within a three-year period, and 500,000 a year thereafter. Now that represents the scale of initiative the private sector must undertake across the board if resolving social needs is not to go right back into the hands of government.

A third action to increase productivity would be a national educational policy aimed at developing enough scientists and engineers for the future. The critical problem in high technology industries is the shortage of people required to sustain the high growth potential inherent in the industry. Between 1968-78, the number of scientists and engineers working in industry increased 62 percent in Japan and 59 percent in West Germany. In the U.S. there was a drop of 13 percent. The American Electronics Association estimates that 13,000 candidates will be available this year for the 29,000 openings for electrical engineers and computer software engineers. By 1985, it predicts, the supply of engineers will be 15,000 but the demand will hit 51,000.

The number of engineering Ph.Ds awarded by U.S. schools dropped 20 percent over the past seven years. Of these degrees awarded, nearly one half were to foreign students. In 1980, 10-15 percent of the nation's engineering faculty positions were unfilled. We are in an extremely serious situation.

Why is this happening?? Partially because industry is siphoning off new graduates who prefer a high salary rather than an advanced degree.

It goes right down to our secondary schools. Russia has ten times more high school seniors studying calculus than we have, while the Japanese and German students study a third again as much math and science as do American students.

Many students are being taught math and science by unqualified teachers. In Maryland last year, 50,000 secondary students were being taught math by more than 400 teachers who were not certified to teach math. In North Carolina, 45 percent of all teachers teaching math are not certified in the subject.

Again, part of the problem is the teachers who receive $15,000 for teaching math, can get $25,000 working for a computer firm. Beyond that, working for a computer company is far less of a hassle than trying to teach our nation's children under the conditions of the average high school.

In order to have a qualified work force to sustain productivity growth and a new era of high technology, America urgently needs an educational policy that defines what a minimum education is in today's world, and gives teachers a salary that is competitive with what they can receive elsewhere.

Without such a policy, we simply will not have enough scientists and engineers to support a high technology society.

Finally, we must take seriously the productivity studies suggesting that perhaps the commanding factor of increased productivity is whether new management practices can be diffused rapidly enough throughout the executive suites of America.

This diffusion is underway. Indeed, American corporations, prodded by Japanese competition, are undergoing the most far-reaching management revolution in decades. The key question is whether it will spread deep enough, wide enough, and fast enough.

Can we, for example, cut out the excess? We're in for rough times, and only the lean and competent companies will survive. The average American auto company has 12 layers of management while its Japanese competitor averages only 7. U.S. automobile assembly plants employ one full-time inspector for every 20 production workers. Toyota and Nissan, by comparison, have a ratio of one inspector for every 30 production workers.

Can we reduce the need for work-in-process inventory? This might help reveal any waste of time or materials, any use of defective parts. It would push us closer to a concept of "zero defects."

We need to become customer-oriented rather than product-oriented, technology-oriented, or strategy-oriented. Again, the automobile industry provides a good example. The industry was so focused on maximum profits, that even after their own surveys showed 95 percent of the public preferring quality and economy to new styling, they completely missed the greatest customer preference shift in the post-war period.

If we become customer-oriented, then we shall have a new respect for quality. For too long most of American business has followed Alfred Sloan's dictum that to gain market share, it is not necessary to have greater-than-competitive quality. The result is that Americans have been turning their backs on U.S.-manufactured products. The reason is simple. As one Japanese manager noted, "We realize that your willingness to stop at 95 percent quality coupled with our refusal to go as low as 95 percent, is what makes us able competitors."

Despite the shortening cycles of economic fluctuation, we must somehow shift from a short-term to a long-term perpective. We all know of investment strategies that have aimed at quick returns rather than developing future resources and markets; or earnings that have been distributed as profits or stock dividends when they should have gone into plant modernization; or management energies that have been absorbed with keeping stock prices high to defend against acquisition. Such practices force a short-term perspective when we should be committing ourselves to optimizing market position and technological competitiveness for the long run. We've got to be ready to make investments that may not pay off for 10-12 years or longer.

Experience is showing us there is no way to compete in the world of the 80's and 90's without a global perspective. A national market has yielded to competitive boundaries that are worldwide in scope. This means exporting must become an integral part of corporate strategic planning. Even though U.S. international trade as a proportion of GNP increased a spectacular 140 percent during the 70's, our share of world exports in manufactured goods slipped 5 percent.

There are some 20,000 American firms which could be exporting, but are not. 20 percent of the exports that do leave our shores are sent by companies owned by the Canadians, British, Dutch, Germans, and Japanese. Do you know who the fourth largest exporting company is in America—right behind Boeing, GM and GE? It's Mitsui & Co. If you put Mitsui and Mitsubishi together, they handle nearly 10 percent of all U.S. exports. In today's global market, countries that do not export gradually become less competitive.

Perhaps the most vital need is for business and labor to look at their relationship in a new context. The adversarial struggles of yesterday may have made sense within the framework of yesterday's realities. But today's realities are different. Today it is not labor against management. It is American labor and management versus the world.

For management, this means a new awareness of and respect for the underutilized capacities of the American worker. Labor must be treated not as a "cost," but as a resource. Workers must be given more responsibility not only for their work environment, but for quality, scheduling, line stoppages, job structure, and increased involvement in planning and supervision of operations.

For the worker this means a new sense of responsibility for the total production process and the final product. This involves major changes such as keeping wage demands related to productivity gains, or changing rigid union work rules. Overall, it means trust, cooperation, and a common aim must replace the traditional adversary relationship.

There are many more issues affecting productivity we could discuss—energy, the spread of "best practices" in a given industry, the growing shortage of skilled labor, and the rising cost to business of the nation's deteriorating physical infrastructure. For, in truth, productivity represents the totality of our life. It is the sum total of our physical assets and how we utilize them, our attitudes of mind, and our relationships to each other. It is far more than just an economic equation.

In closing, I suggest that nothing we have discussed today will regain American world economic leadership unless we as a people find a new promise for the American experiment. That experiment is an on-going process. It was born in the ferment of belief that swept the western world in the 18th century. Men came forward who expressed enduring truth in such a fashion as to take an entire age forward to a new level of human dignity and achievement.

Our times are every bit as revolutionary as was 1776. Perhaps more so. As such, our priority need is for a new interpretation of the transcendent purpose of the human journey. We need to provide our youth, indeed, our whole nation, with a vision beyond satiated boredom, with a hope beyond apocalypse. Yes, we need to answer the productivity lag, recession, inflation, and the thousand-and-one problems that bedevil us.

But underneath these surface economic problems lie deeper needs and questions. Who will be the Jeffersons and Madisons of a new epoch? What is the character and meaning of the society we want to shape with our all-powerful technology? In light of our increasingly splintering cultural base, what is our relationship and responsibility to each other as citizens? What common convictions form the foundation of national attitude and direction? Is our present structure of self-government—particularly the division of powers between the executive and legislative—adequate for an age where instant communication links global financial flows and economic events?

What is our aim in a world torn by the strains of transition a world where people barely beyond ancient agricultural conditions hold vast power over the entire global economic system? Is America responsible only to our own rational genius, or should we be the instruments of some larger purpose? These are some of the underlying questions we must consider. In truth, these questions form the central core of the productivity issue. For most of our economic problems are only symptoms of underlying social, moral and cultural patterns.

In our time, we have explored the outer edges of our solar system; we have penetrated the core of life and matter. But it still remains to us to probe the deepest possibility of human spirit; to lift humankind above the bondage of prejudice or sectional interest; to provide a belief in the future that is both realistic and grand enough to encompass all races and nations on earth.

We see the collapse of old structures and beliefs all around us, and we reach back in nostalgia for a past greatness. The challenge of the times, however, is not to reach back, but to go forward and build the edifice of a new period of history.

The English historian Thomas Carlyle once remarked that "Destruction of old forms is not destruction of everlasting substances." It is for us to take those everlasting substances— human ingenuity, imagination, hope, perseverence, sacrifice, faith, generosity, courage, belief—and to shape a new age that is as different from industrial America as industrial America was different from the agricultural America of our forefathers.

Given the terminal quality of the dangers facing the contemporary world, the task ahead is very possibly the greatest challenge to have confronted any generation since the beginning of time. So with all the vision and commitment at our command, let us reach for the promise of that new age which beckons us forward.

GÖTTERDÄMMERUNG OF THE GIANT
CORPORATIONS?[2]

One of the best-kept secrets, though the underlying evidence is everywhere around us, is that obsolescence has overtaken our fundamental economic structure in which the giant corporation plays the dominant role. Many huge companies, which served America so well through most of this century, have succumbed to competitive pressures that have transformed successful companies into dinosaurs, economic units unsuited for today's hotly competitive world. In other words, we are in the midst of an economic evolution—or call it a revolution if you will—that if further ignored can undermine our democracy or, at the very least, result in government takeover of the giants, just as we are now witnessing in France.

Indeed, the recent spate of giant takeovers has been primarily fueled by the bleak futures that giants foresee for present operations. Insecure with their decaying businesses and entranced by the "grass-is-greener" syndrome, the giants react by lashing out at takeover targets in attempts to diversify. Unfortunately, the giants are inept in implementing their acquisitions, and so the merger mania of recent decades has not only destroyed or weakened a generation of the nation's promising growth companies but also has sometimes boomeranged to further undermine the giants' capacity to innovate.

When the history of our times is written, the unrestrained mergers of recent decades will replace the debacle of the stock market of the 1920's as the cataclysm most destructive to the nation's financial and economic foundations. *In view of the stagnancy of our giants, our future lies with innovative small businesses.*

Now there is one bright ray of hope for the nation's economic future. It is our capacity to spawn creative entrepreneurs ready to challenge new horizons. An example of their impact is *Inc.*

[2]Speech by Arthur Burck, President, Arthur Burck and Company, delivered to the Computer and Communications Industry Association, Palm Beach, Florida, December 8, 1981. *Vital Speeches of the Day,* 49:73–9, N 15 '82.

Magazine's December 1981 list of 100 fast-growing private small companies. In 1976, the Private 100 employed a total work force of slightly more than 2,300 people. Five years later, that work force had grown by more than 30,000 jobs, at a compound annual growth rate of 93 percent. As job generators, the fastest-growing smaller companies are far ahead of their giant corporate counterparts. In the same five-year base period, for example, the nation's 500 largest corporations hiked their employment by 7 percent, a compound growth rate of only 1.8 percent.

However, one doesn't have to go outside of this room for an example of what creative American entrepreneurs can accomplish in the way of jobs and prosperity for their fellow Americans. The David against Goliath image certainly comes to mind when one compares the 25 percent compounded annual growth of the 65 entrepreneurial companies, many under ten years old, represented by the Computer and Communications Industry Association, with the overall stagnancy of the Fortune 500. What makes your record so inspiring is that you are not competing against our wornout has-beens; your areas are dominated by such respected giants as IBM, Honeywell, Control Data, AT&T, to name a few.

Entrepreneurial companies manage to thrive even though they are in the "third world" in terms of comparative wealth and government neglect. Most of the "goodies" of government aid go to the Goliaths—not even free slingshots for the Davids—through taxpayer bail-outs of floundering giants such as Chrysler or Lockheed, or the 1981 tax loophole that lets corporations, mostly weak giants, "sell" tax credits. Put in simple language, we taxpayers are giving back-door subsidies to stagnant giants that some experts estimate can reach $50 billion, at a time when wide-scale budget cuts hurt the poor—and when countless small businesses fail because of capital shortages.

Indeed, despite the prosperity in a few segments of the innovative small business sector—such as your group—overall, the small entrepreneur became an endangered species in the decade of the 70s. Starved of capital because of capital gains tax up to 49 percent until 1979, handicapped by high interest rates or even inability to borrow, deprived of incentives, submerged in bureaucratic red tape and surrounded by the burgeoning bigness of the corporate giants, the small business sector has become a victim of the continuing upheavals, inflation and the recessions since 1970. Yet it has been the innovator—the smaller business—that has provided most of the jobs, the technology, and the continuing growth that fueled the post-war prosperity which has tapered off in the past decade.

The greatness of American industry has been based in large part on the creativity of entrepreneurs who start small but whose companies eventually become leaders. From Lilliputian beginnings, there have emerged in recent decades not only technology giants such as Xerox, Polaroid, Control Data, and Texas Instruments, but also innovative growth companies in mundane industries: McDonald's in hamburgers, Revlon in cosmetics, Block in accounting, Beatrice in foods, Eckerd in drug stores, Occidental in oil, and Hyatt in hotels are but a few examples.

Indeed, when the history of our times is written, the period 1950-1970 will go down as our Economic Golden Age, when through technological and other advances we did for living standards and material well-being what the fifteenth century Italian Renaissance did for the arts. To be sure, the large companies made their fair share of contributions to the national weal, but it was the entrepreneur who often provided the spark and the genius that propelled our economy.

Despite all the obstacles of recent years, the future can be bright for innovative small and medium-sized businesses if government gives a fair share of the help that the giants are getting. Why? Giantism by its very nature opens up manifold opportunities for the quick and the alert. The static bureaucracy leaves many openings for nimble entrepreneurs to launch new business. So long as small businesses do not dance with the elephants, they can find many delectable morsels. And what often starts as gadfly activity can eventually open up entire new industries. The stage is therefore set for proliferation of new ventures—if entrepreneurs are given a reasonable chance to launch and expand innovative businesses.

How can we best help small business achieve its desperate need for more capital? Encouraged by the largesse the government endows on weak and ailing giants, many spokesmen for small business are "me too" supplicants for government subsidies and handouts. However, national policy should channel more capital—through incentives, not handouts—to deserving small and medium-sized business. What oil is to the Arabs, capital is to America: our most valuable economic asset, which must be husbanded and fully utilized.

In my judgment, one little tax deferral advantage could bring a flood of capital to deserving small business—and at no cost to taxpayers. Huge pools of sterile capital lie dormant in stocks and properties where there are large unrealized gains. If owners could sell and reinvest the proceeds in small businesses and defer capital-gains taxes until a subsequent sale of the follow-on investment, abundant capital would become available. In other words, give prospective small-business investors the same sort of deferral advantage enjoyed by homeowners or investors who sell to the giants through a tax-free exchange of stock.

Why can nimble small competitors often run rings around the giants? R. H. Baumgardner, President of Apogee Enterprises Inc., a thriving growth company, put it lucidly:

The enormous capital investment made by some of our larger companies encourages them to stay married to the past rather than obsolete their investment by embracing new technologies. My personal experience has been that we have no awe of enormous companies as competitors. We find that being innovative and nimble we can successfully compete with the giants. Unfortunately, I think the whole world is beginning to learn that lesson. This trend puts our large corporations in jeopardy of being nibbled to death.

Reflect a moment on this simple analysis by a perceptive entrepreneur. Isn't this the key to why most giant companies are in a state of decline, their future clouded?

The answer is everywhere around us, amid the wreckage of so many of our basic industries; autos, steel, tires and consumer electronics are but a few of the industries where our once-respected giants have been relegated to second-rate status by nimble foreign competitors. Our decaying giants too often lose the capacity to create new products.

An insightful summary of our current industrial scene is in a recent interview of George Gilder, author of *Wealth and Poverty*:

SS: If, as you say, the largest corporations at the peak of their productivity tend to turn into inflexible bureaucracies, how can they be saved, or should they just be allowed to go up and come down in the normal course of events?

GG: Some large corporations do rather well. IBM continues to compete successfully, particularly in the world economy. Exxon has succeeded in launching a number of new products in recent years. I think that some of these corporations can continue to play a valuable role, but the odds seem to be against them. There does seem to be a life-cycle in the corporate experience. As corporations get terribly good at producing and selling a particular product, they become increasingly rigid and sterile in producing new products. Ultimately, most economic growth derives from producing new products rather than enhancing productivity or reproducing old ones.

Indeed, one wonders whether, under current conditions of heated worldwide competition and fast-changing technology, the up-down cycle doesn't run much faster than anyone imagines. For example, take Control Data, the exemplar of entrepreneurism that reached the top within a generation of its inception in 1957. Chairman William Norris lamented, in 1978 Senate testimony:

"The haves end up not to be the risk takers or the innovators that the have-nots are. I have seen it happen at Control Data as we grew. . . . The day came when growth had changed Control Data's environment to that of a big company. That was when acquisitions began to fall short of objectives and some of our most creative acquired people began to leave. In spite of all kinds of creative approaches, we were simply unable to maintain an environment satisfactory to many of the more innovative people."

It is simple as this: when companies get too big, through merger or otherwise, they often lose the capacity to create new products. The failure to innovate then opens the door to destructive competition. We then pay the penalty for having permitted many of our basic industries to become concentrated, usually as the result of mergers, many in the musty past. In concentrated industries, there is often no domestic competitor in a position to bring about innovative change. The vacuum is then filled by foreign competitors. And so the nation also is the loser, just as in autos and steel.

Nostalgia Concerning Big Business.

Just how could this happen to our respected giants? We all grew up in the belief that big companies were as much a part of America as apple pie. One deeply imbedded instinct we share with the Russians is that big is good, and so it is not surprising that there has been currency for the notion that "what is good for General Motors is good for the nation." No wonder it seems almost heretical to criticize big companies. Except for populists and extremists, bigness in business has been a sort of sacred cow. An English observer notes:

"Linked with political and economic power, but far less quantifiable, is the social power of big business. In the U.S., particularly, this is considerable. America comes close to being a 'business society,' in which the glamourized lives and occupations of executives represent a wide-spread social ideal." (Fikri, *Readings on Mergers and Takeovers*, p. 391).

There has been good reason for such beliefs. One can't overlook that large firms have been creators of wealth and jobs, a reason why America until recently enjoyed a standard of living never before achieved in history. An eminent Harvard professor, John D. Glover, recently (1980) authored a monumental work titled "The Revolutionary Corporations: Engines of Plenty, Engines of Growth, Engines of Change." As a history of some of the past accomplishments of the giants, Glover's work cannot be faulted. But it fails to deal with the vital issues raised by this paper.

Why Did the Giants in Recent Decades Lose Their Capacity to Innovate and Change?

Through much of our early industrial history when the nation was booming and expanding, our giants prospered in concentrated industries because of relative insulation from major foreign competition. In most of our basic industries that had become "shared monopolies" through early mergers, their concentrated little "clubs" were never really invaded by impudent foreigners; they were able to innovate and change at their own pace. Thereafter our insulation—our privileged position—was extended for another half century by the happenstance of two world wars, and their recovery aftermaths, that left us relatively alone with undestroyed plants, advanced products and established markets. So it was not until the late 50s, when the industrial nations began to recover, that giants first felt the impact of aggressive foreign competition. In retrospect, it is not surprising that the giants were unable to make alert response since, never having experienced such aggressive competition from within their concentrated industries, they were burdened by lethargic habit patterns formed for another time and era...

In brief, the fault lies mostly with management bureaucracies, especially of companies in concentrated industries, that had lost the competitive touch, usually through no fault of their own. They were victims of the easy one-way street that was enjoyed by American business after World War II. In hindsight, it is easy but unfair to label these people as "myopic, unimaginative, over-privileged, inflexible," and content with the status quo, but their transgression if any was merely to follow the way of life that was the norm at the time.

In view of the wreckage we now see everywhere on our industrial scene, we now have ample proof that the huge industrial bureaucracies have outgrown their day of usefulness in a hotly competitive world where innovation is the name of the game.

The clear lesson is that under today's changed circumstances the nation is served only when there is the largest possible number of viable, independent companies engaged in vigorous competition. For too long, with an outmoded Maginot-line mentality, we have worshipped giantism and the idolatory of "economies of scale." We now know that there can be no meaningful economies of scale when products face obsolescence; and in a uncertain world, the only certainty is that every product will eventually become obsolete.

The Bigger They Are, the Harder They Fall.

The reason is simple. When investments in the status quo are huge, it is human nature for managers to resist jettisoning the investment no matter how clearly they see inevitable obsolescence. For example, it is unthinkable that the managers of General Mo-

tors and Ford didn't see what was coming—after all, they ran efficient small car operations in overseas locations and therefore were
as well informed as anyone. But with big cars still so profitable,
timely dumping of the multibillion investment just wasn't in the
cards. Similarly, the fact that U.S. Steel had $11 billion in assets
and Bethlehem Steel $5 billion didn't prevent agile foreigners
from obsoleting their technology and plants—indeed, it was their
very size in concentrated industry that made them vulnerable.

Takeovers Often Boomerang to Harm the Acquirers.

The gigantic mergers that are altering the face of our economy
not only are symptoms of the underlying malaise but also hasten
the process of stagnation. The conduct of huge companies speaks
louder than words; many giants know that their future is so bleak,
they struggle to shore up their position by the almost promiscuous
acquiring of whatever targets of opportunity happen to appear on
the scene. For example, moribund U.S. Steel, which lost out to
foreigners in its own industry, has been seeking to cure its ills by
diversifying into the oil business through Marathon, ignoring that
oil is finite and therefore a business with its own future problems.
Once mighty DuPont fell into the same trap with Conoco, and in
the process has probably forfeited its independence to Seagrams,
the enemy that Conoco struggled so hard to escape.

And so it goes these days; in recent years hundreds of big companies have been taken over in activity that has been described as
"orgies of corporate cannibalism" implemented by "Pearl Harbor
tactics." Indeed *Business Week* (11/23/81) vividly described the
dramatis personae of these uninspiring scenes: ". . .the war games
of mergers and acquisitions are a mock battleground for *capos,
consiglieres,* and soldiers eager to make their mark." With their
multimillion fees, Wall Street firms are the only winners in this
nasty game that is undermining the nation's economy.

Moreover, many of these mergers are really digging a deeper
grave for the giants. First of all, the bigger they become, the more
vulnerable they are to decay. It should not be forgotten that companies such as General Motors and U.S. Steel were built on mergers.

Then even if they acquire a viable giant, they are on the horns of a dilemma. If the takeover is hostile, the key people leave while those who stay vegetate rather than make waves. The acquired business is then destined to erode because the vibrancy of most businesses lies in the people who made it successful. On the other hand, if the merger is "friendly," the acquired bureaucracy is left untouched and the extra layers of bureaucracy hasten stagnancy and decay. After all, inflexible bureaucracies are the Achilles heels of the giants. Why? We castigate bureaucracy in big government but overlook that big bureaucracy has an even more adverse impact on business. Government follows tradition, with minimal change; in business change is the name of the game. Yet the very nature of bureaucracy is resistance to change. It is easier to do what is familiar than to break new ground.

Why are Stocks of the Giants So Low In an Otherwise Inflationary World?

In an inflationary world where everything seems overpriced, only the stocks of the giants are dirt cheap, probably a third of 1960s prices in today's dollars. Why? The easy answer is the stock market is "undervalued." But you entrepreneurs in the computer and communication field know this is not so: when your companies are vibrant and growing you command high prices and P/E ratios. Not so with the giants. This is pretty good proof that investors, who are not as inastute as many think, view the decaying giants for what they are—dinosaurs incapable of meeting competitive challenges of the future. It is ironical that the investors who hold these stocks in such low regard are primarily the trust departments of big banks. Yet it is the loan departments of these same banks that make the huge loans that float these takeovers, on the basis of the security of huge asset values. But are the assets of dinosaurs worth more than is reflected in their stock values? Do we have a situation where one hand of the big banks doesn't understand what the other is doing?

The giants have deeply damaged our economy through the destruction or weakening of most companies they acquired. Tens of thousands of viable and thriving businesses were acquired by giants in recent decades, and most were eventually ruined or weak-ened. To understand how this happened, we must first understand why the giants are such destructive acquirers. Most huge compa-nies are run by bureaucracies not unlike those of big government. Like oil and water, it is difficult to mix staid bureaucracies and creative entrepreneurial companies that are often fragile. It is al-most as hard to blend two big bureaucracies when the merger in-volves two giants. Moreover, bureaucracies are quite unsuited for the delicate task of buying a business, an art that usually requires entrepreneurial skill, judgment and intuition.

The widespread ripples from the damage reach just about ev-ery community. The business loses its momentum. Key people have left. Employee morale and efficiency have eroded. When workers become part of a sprawling, faceless bureaucracy, the identity with "their" company is lost. Productivity suffers. Cre-ativity fades. In time, the damaged company is quietly "phased out" or sold off if it is salvageable. And so recent merger waves have been followed by a less-publicized divestiture wave in which the giants have dumped thousands of their ugly ducklings that were star performers when they were bought.

Others exposed to the debilitating damage inflicted on ac-quired companies make even harsher judgments. For example, here are the words of one of the nation's top business leaders who has seen first-hand what has happened to many of his Control Data acquisitions. Willian Norris, Chairman and CEO, is per-haps unique in American business in many respects: in 1957 he founded Control Data on the proverbial shoestring and already his company is among the leaders in American industry, a classical example of what a dedicated entrepreneur can accomplish in a single generation. On July 28, 1978 when he and I were called as witnesses before the Senate antitrust subcommittee, he testified:

"The innovation-stifling and job-creating resource-destructing scenario is not built on theory or second-hand information. I personally have lived it by being cast in roles on both sides—once with the acquired company and many times as the acquirer. . . . The most serious economic damage results from the destruction of job-creating resources. Technological in-novation is the wellspring of new jobs. . . . Immediately after a takeover an innovation-stifling process sets in. The aggressor blankets the other with bureaucracy, layer upon layer. . . . Proposals for new products languish. . . . There is the gauntlet to run . . . of the majority who belittle new undertakings. On top of all this is the foot-dragging, road-blocking administrative processes . . . in carrying out the project. This innovation-stifling process is compounded by employee trauma because the more creative employees resign first. The result is the dispersal of the entrepreneurial team, the major job-creating resources of the company."

Not only have the companies been blighted, so have their host communities. The founders and executives of thriving companies—people with roots in the town—are eventually replaced by hirees of the acquirer. Local lawyers, bankers and professionals are replaced by others in some distant headquarters. As the acquired company decays, workers are laid off, doing still more damage to the economy of the community.

Workers of course have been the primary victims of these upheavals, and the tragedy is that many of the nation's most productive workers have been affected. When companies are small, American workers often compare favorably with the Japanese in esprit and efficiency—and they are often better because many possess traits of independent creativity and ingenuity that can make significant contributions—the same qualities that in World War II made our GIs more resourceful than the trained automatons of the Axis armies.

Indeed, America's great "hidden asset" is the inherent competence of its work force, one that has never been better educated. Yet too often we blame labor for our ills. To be sure, in the big companies the productivity of overpaid labor lags, often woefully; but it often just mirrors the stagnancy of the setting. To see what happens when labor is properly motivated, critics should look at America's vibrant small and medium-sized independents. If we are ever going to revitalize our stagnating industry, we must return to the basics of restoring motivation from top to bottom in our work force. That can be accomplished only in smaller settings, certainly not in government-sized corporations.

What happens to executives and employees following takeover was graphically described by Control Data's veteran acquirer, William Norris, in his Senate testimony:

"Employee trauma starts at the top of the target company and usually extends to all other workers. . . . Virtually every young executive aspires to be a member of top management . . . the main interface between the enterprise and its stakeholders. . . . A profound difference (exists) between . . . executives in top management . . . and those of division management. This difference is what the aspirations and rewards of top management are all about. A position in top management lost through takeover is often not retrievable. . . . Further down, executives find not only their jobs threatened or changed, but their career paths as well. At other levels job jeopardy is in the forefront of employees' minds."

It is ironic that communities make such effort to attract new industry, but just when a company reaches fruition, it is whisked away by some giant. Recognizing that a company is helpless when a predator offers a premium over depressed market prices that often is far below real values, many states have structured anti-takeover laws in an effort to block or slow down the one-sided nature of these contests. The states are being frustrated because these laws are now crumbling before the constitutionality assaults of the legal teams of big companies. And so under today's lax attitudes there is no more concern given to public welfare in the takeover of a billion-dollar firm than on the sale of the corner hot-dog stand.

When the giants learned the hard way that most of their smaller acquisitions turned sour, they changed directions and channelled their efforts into buying mature companies and other giants, hundreds of which have been acquired in recent years. It is too early to tell whether these gigantic acquisitions will be able to withstand the attrition inherent in the acquisition process, but some of the early results are not promising. Billion-dollar boondoggles include such mammoth purchases as Reliance Electric by Exxon, C.I.T. Financial Services by RCA, Scientific Data Systems by Xerox and Marcor by Mobil Oil. Other recent big fiascos include the acquisition of National Airlines by Pan American World Airways, Seven-Up by Philip Morris and Mostek by United Technologies.

Some companies have been revolving doors for their acquisitions. For example, W. R. Grace has divested over 60 businesses but Whittaker is probably the winner in the discard sweepstakes with 90. However, today both are successful companies that illustrate a point needing emphasis: the giants should not be blamed for the damage they do with their acquisitions. It is up to legislators and not management to change the rules of the game. Operating under current rules, managements have the duty to promote the welfare of stockholders, even if disaster overtakes some acquired companies.

In assessing the impact on the nation's economy of the damage to acquired companies, we must remember that the giants for several decades have been beating the bushes to find the most tempting takeover targets, the cream of the crop of emerging growth companies and leading independents. In other words we have lost a generation of our most promising companies, the industrial future of America.

What makes this damage especially inopportune is the fact that we also lost much of the following generation of incipient growth companies. As above noted, the decade of the 70s was a disaster for the innovative small business sector. The "double whammy" of having undermined two successive generations of our industrial future is an impediment that may long be with us.

No wonder our economy is stagnant, with lagging productivity and lack-luster innovation.

Mergers Have Inflicted Deep Damage in Many Other Ways.

There are other areas of damage that should not be overlooked:

Instead of expanding the nation's productivity through new plants and products, the giants have recently spent hundreds of billions in buying that which already exists, sterile investments to which they can contribute nothing. As one short-range consequence, our capital goods industries suffer. Long-range, how can our economy grow when the giants divert massive capital outside of their areas of supposed expertise?

The huge borrowings that finance the deals soak up funds in short supply for smaller businesses that are imperiled by lack of capital and high interest rates.

Mergers have taken a frightful toll on competition. Antitrust is a sieve; the majority of big acquisitions eventually hurt competition, often in many subtle ways. It often takes decades for the damage to surface. Also, when a giant with "deep pockets" takes over one of the leaders in another industry, it is not easy for the independents in that industry to compete. Not only small competitors are hurt, also consumers which pay over $100 billion a year in higher prices, according to a recent Congressional study. We all dislike overregulation and yet we forget that big government is a response to big business. "When business engulfs the state, it forces the state to engulf business," is the way Adolf Berle put it. Similarly, we dislike that Washington becomes too powerful and yet that usually happens because local governments are unable to cope with the complex problems of ever-enlarging big business. Likewise, huge labor unions have excessive power. Big unions can be traced to growth of big business, with which only big unions could deal on an equal footing. And so, to reduce the power of unions—or the federal bureaucracy, as the Administration proposes—we must first reduce the size of our labyrinthine busines bureaucracies.

Today's rampant inflation is worsened by the happenstance that most basic industries are in a few hands—"shared monopolies"—largely as the result of early mergers. Linked with equally powerful unions in what J. K. Gailbraith calls a "mating dance," these giants lift prices in unison, regardless of productivity. In contrast, in industries that are fragmented with many competitors, the raising of prices is a much more difficult task—one of the reasons that small businesses are victims of inflation.

If a man from Mars were to descend on Wall Street and make a study of the merger mart of recent decades, he would be mystified and shocked that any nation, with no other excuse than laissez-faire, would permit such helter-skelter destruction of its industry, a destruction that may yet be fatal if foreign competition continues to widen its inroads, as many predict it will. Yet we did somewhat the same thing in the 1920s when the policy of "anything goes" dominated the nation's stock and financial markets and its business practices. In retrospect, the crash of 1929 was a blessing in disguise since it forced us to put our financial house in order. Do we have to have another similar cataclysm in order to come to grips with the current problem?

We must never forget that capitalism works only when it is kept vibrant through corrective measures that eliminate the abuses that periodically develop. Proper mergers of course play an important and necessary role. Some are vital to a dynamic capitalism; businesses must be sold for many valid reasons including owner liquidity and/or maximizing viability or growth potentials. Also, it goes without saying that some companies must be huge, such as in capital-intensive industries. The problem comes, however, when Napoleon-like leaders take them into industries where size is no advantage.

It is ironical that the taxpayers have been subsidizing the damage and wreckage caused by giant mergers. Invariably these deals depend on tax-free exchanges of stock and/or the tax deductibility of interest on the huge borrowings needed to float the deal. So half the carrying charges are borne by the U. S. Treasury.

The solution of course is simple: remove the tax incentives that so long have fueled giant mergers. In that way the activity will shift to the small and medium-size companies. That is the sector where mergers are needed to keep our capitalism dynamic, to restore the imbalance caused by the burgeoning bigness of past giant mergers. The industrial future of America lies not with the decaying giants but with the nimbler businesses that can open up new horizons, and merger is often the best way to hasten the growth of these creative entities.

But that will not happen. Legislators traditionally cringe before the "deep pockets" and power (the PACs are becoming a most telling weapon) of the giants who always resist even the most common-sense restraint—for example, it took Congress 20 years to pass a much-needed law requiring acquirers to inform the government of larger acquistions.

Nevertheless, if our economy slides further into recession and unemployment widens, there might come a time when legislators and the Administration heed the admonition of Control Data's Norris:

If public concern for social trauma of takeovers doesn't bring constraints, the increasing economic damage from unemployment certainly should. As unemployment relentlessly persists and slowly rises, the time will come when the public will understand how difficult and critically important it is to preserve existing jobs and to create new jobs. By that time it will be clear that all reasonable effort must be made to avoid the loss of job-creating resources.

Takeover by the Government Is the Likely Ending.

If recent merger trends continue—as is likely—our economy within a few decades will be dominated by a handful of supergiant companies. Even if democracy can then survive, it is unlikely that the mega-corporations will be able to withstand the next logical step: takeover by the government.

Americans bent on preserving our free enterprise system should reflect soberly on the current French program to take over dozens of big banks and companies. Government's appetite for big business is already evidenced by state control of most of the top 20 in France, eight of the top 10 in Italy, basic industries in leading democracies such as Britain, Sweden and Austria, and 17 of the 50 largest industrials in Western Europe—and of course everything in Eastern Europe. Also in Greece the new socialist government proposes takeover of most large companies.

It can't happen here? It is by no means a new idea that excessive concentration by merger is likely to bring about nationalization; way back in 1901, historian Woodrow Wilson, alarmed by the merger wave that then threatened to engulf the nation, wrote:

". . . No doubt [mergers] did give to a few men a control over the economic life of the country which they might abuse to the undoing of millions of men. . . . Extremists proposed a remedy which was but a completion of the process: the virtual control of all industry by the government itself."

In a similar note, President Francois Mitterand recently explained:

"Our society in 1981 . . . [is] characterized by the accumulation and concentration of capital. . . . We believe these companies should not have at their disposal the economic, and therefore political, power that lets them influence decisions in the general interest."

Mitterand's words could make a ready-made platform for a future power-grabbing political leader. A dangerous level of concentration already exists, and it gets worse with every huge merger.

Not only are the nation's industrial and financial assets falling into fewer and fewer hands, the ownership of these companies also continues to shrink in number as financial institutions, especially bank trust departments, become the dominant holders. The concentration is expected to accelerate (1) under the new huge financial conglomerates that recent mergers have created and (2) when interstate banking is authorized. So in time we will face the specter that most of our industrial and financial economy will be owned by a few supergiants and the controlling stock of these Brobdingnagian companies will in turn be owned by a few gigantic financial institutions.

We therefore face the reality that in time awesome political and economic power will be vested in relatively few hands, far beyond that which Mitterand now berates. Indeed, in America there already is a political time-bomb in the economic and political power, little short of life and death, that these private dictatorships now hold over the destinies of more human beings than many nations, a power that is beyond the constitutional checks and balances that limit other power centers. This is fertile fodder for a populist demagogic leader to expound the imagined need to "democratize" these private dictatorships. Also, Americans area already conditioned to the quasi-nationalization implicit in government bail-outs of giants such a Chrysler and Lockheed. In a recent business visit to France, I was astounded by public support for Mitterand's measures, even by many in the business community. America's huge companies enjoy little "grass roots" support, and so nationalization here just might move ahead with the same incredible ease that we are now witnessing in France. And so, like lemmings awaiting the mysterious call, the giants will mark time until the trumpet announces vassalage to the government.

THE TWILIGHT OF SMOKESTACK AMERICA[3]

It is quiet in Buffalo. No shoppers to speak of, no noon-hour rush to lunch, no bursts of traffic accelerating from stoplights, no movement on the Erie Canal, the artery that turned Buffalo from

[3]Reprint of a newspaper article by Peter T. Kilborn. *New York Times.* p27+. My 8, 1983. ©1983 by The New York Times Company. Reprinted by permission.

just another town to a thriving port. Buffalo is a fading steel city, a fading flour-milling city, a fading automobile-rubber-chemicals-building supplies-machinery city.

At its periphery stand dormant industrial smokestacks and the tall, stuck-together columns of the H-O Oats grain elevator, vacant and crumbling. Along a two-mile stretch of Route 5 West into the lakeside city of Lackawanna, loom the soot-black facilities of the Bethlehem Steel Company where more than 20,000 people once worked, but which will only employ 1,300 by the end of the year.

Buffalo today has plenty of roads, homes, sewers, schools and electrical power to accommodate the 580,000 people who lived there in 1950. But there are 360,000 people in Buffalo now, and many don't have work, which is why it's so quiet.

Buffalo could be Detroit or Akron or Youngstown, the cliches of unemployment and shut-down factories in the nation's depressed industrial core. It could also be less obvious cities like St. Louis, Toledo, Seattle, Louisville, Dayton, Hartford, Peoria, even Atlanta and Birmingham—all hit hard by the long, 1981-82 recession and all hopeful that work will resume again, as it always has, with economic recovery.

But what is happening in the Buffalos of America exceeds the usual thrashing of periodic recessions. For two decades now, more awesome, glacier-like forces have been at work in the American economy, rolling across the nation's industrial landscape, burying neighborhoods, factories and the once-secure skills of millions of American workers. "Since the late 1960's, the American economy has been slowly unraveling," writes Robert B. Reich, a Harvard political scientist, in his new book, "The Next American Frontier." Recoveries only camouflage the process. Recessions just grease the skids.

For Professor Reich and others who have recounted the "deindustrialization" of America, the United States economy, which to generations of Americans seemed invincibly secure and ever more prosperous, has undergone an irrevocable change. The emblems of its wealth—the heaving smokestacks of giant industries, the calloused hands of its armies of factory workers—have given way to new emblems of stagnation and decline—the cadavers of urban factories and the lines of the permanently unemployed.

"In those industries that have been the underpinning of our industrial structure—like steel, autos, textiles—we are no longer competitive," said George Gols, vice president for management economics at the business consulting firm of Arthur D. Little, "It's difficult to see where you start to correct these things, if they are correctable."

Analysts blame two insistent, compelling forces for the declining might of industrial America. One is the constant drubbing the American economy has taken in recent years as the Government's stop-go economic policies, perverse tax incentives, heavy-handed regulatory policies—and inflation—have eroded industry's ability to plan and prosper. American economic growth has averaged below 2 percent a year for the past decade, a worse record than that of any major industrial nation except Britain. The villainous, 1973-75 recession gave the American economy a severe jolt and for some of the weakest businesses in hard-pressed heavy industry, the recession that lifted late last year delivered the coup de grace.

The victims of industry's decline are the jobless, record numbers of them. Employment in the iron and steel industry, which peaked in 1957, at 952,000, plummeted to 653,000 last year and, according to analysts at the Interindustry Forecasting Project at the University of Maryland, the numbers are headed lower for the next decade at least. In auto production the story is similar: The industry's employment peaked at 1.02 million in 1978; last year's job level was 716,000. Though auto jobs may grow somewhat by the end of the century, they aren't expected to regain their peak. The chemical industry shows the same grim trend: The peak job level was reached in 1978 and there's scant chance of regaining that level for the rest of this century, analysts say.

But American industry has been humbled by more than the economy's repeated stops and starts and Government policies that leaders of both parties now concede were ill-conceived. The second major force undoing industry is America's new vulnerability to global competition. Once United States industry could feast undisturbed on the vast domestic market, but today it shares that market with foreign competitors, especially the Japanese. The dollar has become the world's leading currency, and as its value gyrates against other currencies, so too do the fortunes of the American economy.

Last year, 5.9 percent of the goods and services sold in the United States were foreign-made. Twenty years earlier, only 2.3 percent of the American market was absorbed by imports. And America's once exalted ability to crank out more and more goods at less and less cost—its productivity—has turned flat while productivity elsewhere keeps improving. For heavy industry, this turn of events has been particularly painful. Exports of steel have barely budged in a decade from an annual level of two billion tons, but in 1981, imports touched 20 million tons. So it goes for automobiles and motorcycles, farm tractors, ships and machinery.

"For the first time, we've got an economy that's ingrained in the world economy," said Lester Thurow, the M.I.T. economist who has written widely on the American economic dilemma. But "somehow we haven't ingrained that into the system in any fundamental way."

Among professors and politicians, the search for a route out of stagnation has become a vital business for the next decade. Younger Democrats on Capitol Hill—like Senators Bill Bradley of New Jersey, Gary Hart of Colorado and Paul A. Tsongas of Massachusetts, and Representative Richard A. Gebhardt of Missouri—are grappling with the issue along with their academic gurus like Professor Thurow and Professor Reich, and with Charles Peters, editor of the Washington Monthly magazine.

These politicians disavow the "Atari Democrat" label, first given them for their concern with promoting high-technology. More often now they are called "neo-liberals," as Mr. Peters defined the thinking in the current Monthly. It's a new blend of liberal and conservative concerns, a third alternative to the classical Republican free market theology of Ronald Reagan and the traditional Democratic concern for the underdog, at any price.

The quest for answers to America's industrial problems has spawned dozens of books, by the two Cambridge professors, by Bennett Harrison of M.I.T. and Barry Bluestone of Boston College, co-authors of *The Deindustrialization of America,* and by John Naisbitt, author of *Megatrends.* The books have coined the buzzwords of a growing debate over the future of the American economy—words like Low Tech and High Tech, Sunset Industries, Sunrise Industries and Smokestack Industries, and Targeting, which is what the Japanese do in selecting industries for special encouragement by the Government.

But so far, the pickings for policy makers are rather thin. Despite all the pages and meetings and thought devoted to developing a policy for re-energizing the American economy, none of the proposals on the table so far has won wide attention or support in President Reagan's Washington. But the neo-liberals are aiming at the 1984 election campaign, and beyond.

"I'll bet that in the 1984 election," said Mr. Thurow, "the leading issue will be whether we should have an industrial policy. The Democrats will say yes, and the Republicans, no."

What such a policy might be can be pieced together from talks with various neo-liberals. They speak of retraining jobless workers, of nurturing new industries and helping old ones to modernize. Some of them seek a repository of "patient money"—public and private funds to invest in companies for the long haul, not for the quick bottom line results that Wall Street has come to demand.

Mr. Peters, in his manifesto, calls for tying wage increases to gains in productivity, not inflation, as a way to hold down labor costs and to improve U.S. competitiveness. Mr. Thurow has proposed that businesses pay chief executives a delayed bonus based on their companies' performance during the 10 years following their retirement. And M.I.T.'s Professor Harrison, would modify the tax code to encourage investment in new factories.

This potpourri of options would be difficult—and costly—enough to engineer. But even this wish list simplifies the problems ahead for any initiative to rebuild and reshape America's industrial base. Some fundamental and divisive questions must be answered along the way to an industrial policy. Should the adjustment task ahead, for example, be left mostly to an imperfect free market or to an imperfect Government. Just as basic is the national security question: How far should the United States go in letting its smokestack industries wither away while the service industries prosper. Can the West survive if the United States forsakes the production of steel and becomes a nation of insurance companies and fast-food restaurants?

The country appears doomed to spend the rest of the 1980's—
and the 1990's, too—thrashing out the answers to these questions.
History shows that fundamental changes take time to work
through the economy. In New England, new industries have
emerged and the population is rising again, but only 50 years after
the flight of the shoe and textile industries gave the region a foundation on which to build the high-technology industries that much
of the rest of the country now covets.

To a reporter who has spent two weeks on the road exploring
the wounds afflicting American industry, the prospects of any
quick return to stable growth and low unemployment appear dim.
The difficulties facing politicians and business leaders in cities like
Louisville and Buffalo are complex, diverse, baffling. They seem
to defy easy policy prescriptions from Washington or from the
campus. Often, the solutions to yesterday's problem bear in them
the seeds of tomorrow's.

Take, for example, automation: It's the only road to survival
in the view of most heavy industrial companies, but it is also a road
to more unemployment. In Louisville, the General Electric Company operates a huge industrial facility that accounts for $2.5 bil-
lion of the company's annual sales. The basic problem for G. E.
there is a maturing market. Most American homes now have appliances. New construction provides the only real room for
growth, and until recently new construction has been moribund.

In January, G. E. switched on a $38 million production sys-
tem for a new line of dishwashers—with the latest in automation.
At posts along the assembly loop, workers sit in posture chairs at-
taching parts and tightening bolts as dishwasher tubs move past
them along an overhead track. The worker stops the tub to perform his task and releases it only when he is satisfied with his
work.

"With the old process, we manually transferred the tub and
the door of the dishwasher 27 times," said Homer Moeller, manager of dishwasher production who went to Japan for two weeks
as part of G.E. course in industrial engineering. Now, he said, "we
handle the tub once and the door three times."

Roger Schipke, the senior vice president who runs the G.E.
plant says it once employed 22,000 workers. Now it employs 13,

500, and over the next two years as the economy improves, he said he might recall a couple of thousand more. However, Mr. Schipke said, "our basic philosophy is to produce more with the same number of people."

Automation is also the credo at Bethlehem Steel's plant in Lackawanna, outside Buffalo. Foreign competition has knocked out its whole steel-making business there, and left it with only two small finishing facilities—a mill that fashions 4,200- to 5,600-pound, 32- to 40-foot-long steel bars into rods hundreds of feet long, and a galvanizing mill that presses the bars into long steel sheets. No more than a couple of hundred men are visible in both mills, and the reason is that racks of closet-high process control computers now do most of the work.

The object there is to meet the foreign competition, and the company is confident that, with its computers, it can finally do so. "Japan, Korea, Brazil?" says Richard Murray, the general foreman. "They don't do anything better. We make a better product."

Automation poses tough questions for policy makers in the view of Wassily Leontief, a Russian-born Nobel laureate who is, at 76, a lion among American economists. Professor Leontief puts the chip, and its progeny, integrated circuits and computers, right behind the wheel among man's great technological achievements and alongside James Watt's 1765 invention of the steam engine, the catalyst of the industrial revolution.

The role of humans as ordinary intelligent creatures will diminish," he said, "As scientists and engineers continue to work, they will develop automatic devices that will replace higher and higher mental capabilities." In time, he said, the workweek, the workday, the work life will shrink enormously. He said competition from computers and robots will put immense downward pressure on wages, requiring that the Government develop new ways to distribute income much as it does now through Social Security.

I am standing on the beach, and I can see the wave," he said, in an accent that is still heavily Russian. "What I say will happen will happen. What will happen will be quite analagous to what happened to horses after we got the tractor. I hope the solution will be different."

THERE'S STILL LIFE IN SMOKESTACK AMERICA[4]

Remember Smokestack America, the gritty industries supposedly gasping their last solvent breaths? While the economists and politicians who had given them up for dead weren't looking, they climbed far from the depths of the recession—sometimes amazingly so.

Fueled by the surge in automobile and housing sales, some of the nation's basic businesses—notably chemicals, textiles and a few nonferrous metals—are rebounding smartly and could soon approach prerecession peaks of production. Profits are improving, too.

Even the recovery's laggards, steel and machine-tool producers, are seeing modest improvements in orders and factory operating rates, though not enough to propel them into the black.

Says Van Jolissaint of the consulting firm of Evans Economics in Washington,D.C.: "For the short term, the recovery is much more robust than most people expected, and most of the basic industries are doing real well in terms of increased production, better cash flow and improved profit picture."

Most old-line manufacturing firms are benefiting as well from extensive belt-tightening measures adopted during the recession. Merely to survive, many of them reduced front-office staffs as well as factory work forces, clamped down on inventories, froze pay and closed inefficient plants.

Despite all the positive signs, smokestack businessess still face serious problems. Eleven basic industries now employ 1.7 million fewer people than at the last economic peak, in July, 1981—including 156,000 fewer in steel, 550,000 in machinery and 103, 000 in autos. Economist Michael Evans predicts that two thirds of the 2.9 million manufacturing jobs eliminated since 1979 will never reappear.

Imports from Asia, Latin America and Europe continue to take business from U.S. firms, a trend aggravated by a strong

[4]Reprint of an article by Manuel Schiffres, Staff Writer. *U.S. News & World Report.* S 12, '83. Reprinted from *U.S. News & World Report.* Copyright, 1983, U.S. News & World Report, Inc.

American dollar that makes overseas goods relatively cheap. What's more, because business investment for plant and equipment remains sluggish, sectors such as steel and machinery continue to lose money.

Still, economists trumpeting the fall of the smokestacks have been surprised by the strength of some basic industries. Nowhere has the reversal been more startling than in the auto industry.

Drops in interest charges, fuel prices and the inflation rate caused sales by U.S. auto makers to jump sharply. Analyst Frank Drob of E.F. Hutton expects Detroit to sell 9.3 million cars and trucks this year and 11.4 million in 1984, compared with 7.9 million in 1982.

As a result of improved production techniques and wage concessions by auto workers, the industry has reduced its break-even point from 11.9 to 8.1 million cars and trucks a year, and profits are zooming. Earnings of the Big Three auto makers could approach 5 billion dollars in 1983.

The auto boom and the pickup in housing construction benefit other basic industries. Selling more cars, for instance, helps tire manufacturers, whose shipments to auto makers were up 14.4 percent in the first six months of the year.

Goodyear Tire & Rubber reports a 20 percent rise in shipments to Detroit. A spokesman says that Goodyear can't meet the demand for tires used on bigger cars, which have become fashionable again. "We're shipping everything we can make," he adds.

Also profiting is the textile industry, which makes materials for car interiors as well as for home furnishings. Domestic textile shipments were up 5.5 percent in the first half of 1983 compared with the year-earlier period, and, as of July, the industry was operating at 88.5 percent of capacity. "Demand is firming almost across the board," says Kay Norwood of Interstate Securities in Charlotte, N.C.

Leading the rebound for Belding Heminway, a New York textile producer, are home-furnishing materials, sales of which were up 20 percent in 1983's first half. Explains President Robert Brown: "It's not just the housing recovery, but also the pent-up demand among consumers who have been penny-pinching for a long time to change the appearance of their living quarters."

Stronger markets for cars and housing help the aluminum business, too. Nearly half its products go into housing, autos and consumer items such as refrigerators. "Because aluminum is predominantly used in consumer markets, it was one of the first metals to benefit from the recovery," says analyst William Siedenburg of the brokerage firm Smith Barney, Harris Upham & Company.

Domestic aluminum shipments were up 11 percent in the first half of this year. By late July, Aluminum Company of America's domestic smelters operated at 91 percent of capacity.

Just as important to producers are higher prices made possible by the pickup in orders. The price of aluminum ingots, which had dropped to as low as 42 cents a pound, is now as high as 81.5 cents. For Alcoa, Siedenburg estimates, each penny-a-pound rise for all aluminum products means 25 million dollars in additional profits.

Stronger demand also boosts prices for chemicals. Olin Corproation, citing the housing recovery, in late August raised the price of chlorine by about 17 percent, to $170 a ton. Hercules, Inc., recently increased the price of polypropylene resin, a plastic used in appliances and automobiles, 3 cents a pound, to about 40 cents. "That reflects a strong recovery in volume," says the company's chief economist, Bill Bewley.

"Everything's got a chemical in it," says analyst Leslie Ravitz of Salomon Brothers, the investment bank. He expects the major producers to post average earnings gains in 1983 of about 25 percent.

Profit growth by the smokestacks will owe much to stringent cost cutting begun during the recession. Says Thomas Barger of Chase Econometrics, a consulting firm: "We may be surprised at the strength of the profits. These companies have cut back on work force, have shut down unproductive plants and are getting more productivity out of their employes."

Chemical manufacturer Rohm & Haas reported a 2 percent sales decrease in the first half of 1983, but a 74 percent rise in earnings. During the recession, it reduced its work force by 15 percent, to 11,500, placed a moratorium on new hiring and slashed inventories by 85 million dollars. Firestone Tire & Rubber last year induced 1,300 salaried workers to take early retirement. "We made a substantial cutback in our overhead to get lean and mean," says Firestone President Lee Brodeur.

Burlington Industries, the No. 1 U.S. textile producer, deferred pay reviews for white-collar employees six to 12 months beyond the normal yearlong wait. Dow Chemical estimates that it slashed expenses 325 million dollars last year. Among other things, Dow cut its work force by 12 percent, and it reduced debt by 1.6 billion dollars to save 26 million in interest costs. Dow says that lower costs, combined with higher sales, made June its most profitable month in two years.

For the machine-tool industry, which could lose 100 million dollars in 1983, "weak demand and foreign competition dictate that cost cutting has to be a way to survive, not just to return to prior levels of peak earnings," says Eli Lustgarten of Paine Webber Mitchell Hutchins, the brokerage house. But producers of machine tools, which are used to cut and shape metal, see at least one sign of hope: So far this year, orders have risen each month from the previous one. Even so, orders remain 75 percnet below peak 1979 levels.

Cutting costs to survive is gospel to steel, the ultimate smokestack industry. Shipments are not expected to exceed 70 million tons this year, compared with 100 million just four years ago.

Discounting remains rampant, too, despite 7 percent price boosts in late August for sheet and strip products. The industry could lose 1 billion dollars this year, on top of a 3.2-billion loss in 1982.

A fundamental problem—too much capacity—is being tackled by closing plants permanently. Bethlehem Steel plans to reduce its capacity by 20 percent, to 17.5 million tons a year, by ending basic steelmaking operations in Los Angeles, Seattle and in Lackawanna, N.Y. Since 1979, National Steel has slashed capacity for 11 million tons a year to 5.8 million. It managed to earn 9.3 million dollars from steel operations in 1983's second quarter.

Beyond eliminating jobs and paring the wages of white-collar employes, the industry negotiated cuts in pay and benefits with its unionized workers that figured to 12.7 percent when put into effect in March.

For the short term, with expenses down and capital spending by businesses expected to perk up, steelmakers could become profitable again soon—maybe as early as the fourth quarter. One analyst, Aldo Mazzaferro of Standard & Poor's, predicts that the industry could earn a record 3 billion dollars in 1985 if the recovery doesn't fizzle.

Over the long haul, however, there are still formidable hurdles. For one thing, it is estimated, the nation's 151 million-ton-a-year steelmaking capacity is 15 percent too much. Also, wages and benefits remain 75 percent higher than those of the average U.S. manufacturing worker. "If you can't do something about those wages, we won't be able to compete internationally," says Charles Bradford of Merrill Lynch, Pierce, Fenner & Smith. Imports now account for 19 percent of steel sales in the U.S.

What does all this portend for the future of Smokestack America? Chemical, rubber and plastics companies could see production surpass all-time peaks within a year, experts say. Textiles should bounce back, too, and auto companies have demonstrated that high productivity can generate big profits even with lower sales levels.

On the other hand, American steelmakers are probably not going to match past production peaks in the foreseeable future, and some may find it a struggle to stay out of bankruptcy.

"Basic industries are not dead," says Robert Gough of Data Resources, "but there are companies within these industries that are going to be weeded out." For the most part, though, the smokestacks are belching again in a manner that suggests they won't fall easily.

INDUSTRY-GROWTH SWEEPSTAKES[5]

The jury is still out on Reaganomics. Indeed, even if the president succeeds in pushing all his tax and budget cuts through the Congress, it will be at least two years before we know with certainty what this daring experiment in supply-side economics has wrought. Whatever the final verdict, however, its impact will not

[5]Reprint of a magazine article by Bradley R. Schiller, Professor of Economics and Public Administration at the American University. *Society.* 19:44–47. Jl/Ag '82. Reprinted by permission.

be spread evenly. The surest lesson we have learned from economic growth is that it is a process that moves in fits and starts. While some industries and regions are prospering, others are declining. Even in the most exuberant "boom" cycles, there are enclaves of industrial activity that stagnate. The reverse is also true: some industrial sectors do well even when all national indices of economic activity turn downward.

A second lesson to be learned from our growth experiences, directly relevant to the core of Reaganomics, concerns the role of productivity in fostering economic growth. The economists in and about the Reagan team see productivity growth as the only sure route to economic prosperity. Freeing productivity growth from the "shackles" of government regulation is one of the primary elements of the Reagan strategy for "industrial modernization." Whether it deserves such a priority is open to question. Viewed from the perspective of industry, productivity advances have not consistently been the engine of growth, nor even its companion. Some of the most rapid advances in productivity have occurred in industries whose output growth has been sluggish, while many rapidly growing industries have exhibited negligible productivity gains.

Measuring Growth

Much of the confusion about the nature, causes, and benefits of economic growth derives from the varying ways people measure it. Most people think of increases in output as its basic indicator. But this is neither an all-encompassing nor altogether satisfactory definition, especially when applied to specific industries or regions. After all, what governor would be willing to ignore employment as a basic measure of growth? Local, state, and regional governments pursue industries that promise jobs, not output per se. From this regional perspective, employment is at least as important as any other measure of industrial growth. Another important index of growth is income. If the benefits of growth are to be distributed and appreciated, they must be evident in bigger paychecks. Here again, the political significance is evident: rising wages make for happy voters and larger pork barrels.

It is tempting to dismiss these definitional concerns by asserting that industrial growth brings all these good things simultaneously. But such a promise does not square with the facts: output, jobs, and wages do not generally increase simultaneously. An industry whose output is growing rapidly may not deliver any better job or wage growth than one whose output is increasing slowly. Output growth is *not* synonymous with either job growth or wage growth. It is even less synonymous with productivity growth. As a consequence, state, local, and regional planners, as well as politicians, face some difficult choices in their pursuit of growth; so do those who seek to evaluate the success of Reagan's "industrial modernization" on the basis of any single growth measure.

The variability of growth patterns is evident from our experiences in the 1960s. From today's perspective, the sixties look like an economic boom. The total output of the U.S. economy grew by 48 percent from 1960 to 1969. We had rarely experienced that kind of sustained growth before, and we have seen nothing like it since. The economy grew by only 37 percent from 1970 to 1979.

Despite the strong overall performance of the U.S. economy, many industries experienced negligible growth in the 1960s. The shoe industry, the leather industry, and an assortment of service industries (e.g., laundry and cleaning, beauty shops, amusements) were all "losers," even while the economy was growing rapidly. On the other hand, there were some spectacular "winners" in the output-growth race, most notably office machines, building services, instruments, rubber, and department stores. The same kinds of disparities were evident across regions. The South grew much faster than other regions, with the West a distant second. By contrast, the northeast and northcentral regions enjoyed very few real success stories, as measured by increases in industry output.

The distinction between winners and losers is already a familiar one in research and policy discussions. What is new here is our discovery of how elusive these designations are. An industry that appears to be a winner in terms of output growth often exhibits subpar employment or wage growth. During the 1960s, for example, the office machines industry (including computers) was the premier growth industry, as measured by increases in the value of output. For the decade, the output increased in value by 222 percent. But its job and wage performances were not equally high; it ranked only 7th in employment growth and a dismal 36th in average wage growth. This industry won in only one race, placed in another, and did not even show in the third. Whether this performance constitutes a victory depends on which race you bet.

The other end of the output rankings contains similar stories. Beauty shops and amusements registered relatively slow output and employment growth in the 1960s—beauty shops ranked 46th in output growth, 29th in employment growth; amusements came in 48th in the former category, 56th in the latter. Nevertheless, workers in those industries experienced above-average wage growth—the beauty shop industry ranking 14th; the amusement industry, 9th. Even workers in the footwear industry (which ranked 50th in output growth and 62nd in employment growth) who were fortunate enough to hold on to their jobs enjoyed above-average wage growth (where the industry ranked 19th). They must certainly have felt like winners, even though their industry as a whole declined.

These glimpses of industry experience are not atypical. For fifty industries studied, output and employment rankings were closely related only half the time. On average, there was no distinct relationship between growth in output and wages, and actually a *negative* relationship between growth in employment and wages.

The absence of clear winners and losers in the industry-growth sweepstakes results not only from various growth indices but also from regional variations in an industry's growth, as measured by a *single* growth index. An industry doing exceptionally well in one region may be performing poorly in another. Hence, what looks like a winner at one track turns out to be a real dog at another. The office machines industry, which in the sixties had the fastest output growth *nationally*, is again a good example. It lived up to its promise in the Northeast, South, and West, ranking number one in each of these regions. But the northcentral region hardly even noticed, for there the industry exhibited neglible growth, ranking a paltry 44th. Thus, while three regions enjoyed the fruits of this industry's growth, a fourth region had to look elsewhere for increases in output, jobs, and wages. Other examples abound. The newspaper industry flourished in the northeast and northcentral regions, but stagnated in the West and South. On the other hand, textile mill products grew markedly in the West while floundering in most other regions.

The variations observed across regions in industry-specific growth rates are not unique to output growth. Employment and wage patterns are similar. The health services industry, for example, was one of the best job creators in the 1960s, both in percentage growth (+79) and absolute numbers (530,000 new jobs). But its employment creation was largely confined to the northeast and northcentral regions; it created relatively few jobs in the South. The office machines industry, on the other hand, was the source of tremendous job creation in the South and West, but performed less well in the Northeast and abysmally in the northcentral region. The South found solace in the communications industry, which ranked 17th in that region but below 50 in all other regions in terms of employment growth.

Industry-specific wage growth also varies across regions, although the variations are less striking. Hotels and lodging, for example, which experienced the fastest wage growth of any industry in the South, achieved below-average wage gains in all other regions. Legal services had a similarly diverse regional pattern, with great wage gains in the northcentral region, but below-average increases in the Northeast and West. The immediate implication of these garbled impressions is surprisingly clear: there are no unambiguous winners or losers in the growth game. Individual industries perform differently on alternative growth indices and in various regions of the country.

Productivity growth, the central concern of Reagan's strategy for industrial modernization, is commonly measured in terms of output per worker. The key issue for productivity growth is therefore how fast output grows relative to employment. The record of U.S. industries in the 1960s provides some interesting debate on the relationship of productivity growth to output, employment, and wage growth

Building services (e.g., janitorial) was one of the fastest-growing industries in the sixties' building boom, as measured by increases in output. Its productivity improvements were negligible, however. The same was true of business services, which included not only building services, but also glamorous "growth" services as data processing, photocopying, and temporary office help. Here, too, output and employment both grew rapidly (business services ranked 6th in the former category, 3rd in the latter), thereby constraining productivity (output per worker) growth, where the industry ranked 47th. At the other extreme, variety stores enjoyed a doubling of productivity, where it ranked 3rd in growth, even though it was one of the slowest growing industries of the decade, ranking 42nd in output growth and 61st in employment growth. In these and several other industries, productivity gains were of little tangible benefit to either employment or output.

In theory, we expect wage growth to accompany productivity growth; indeed, productivity improvements are supposed to be the source of wage gains. But this is often not the case. Productivity growth in an industry was not closely linked to industry wages in the 1960s: rapid wage gains were as frequent in industries with slow productivity advances as in more dynamic ones. Grocery stores are an example. Productivity gains were well below the national average in the 1960s (the industry ranked 43rd in this category), yet average wages in that industry grew much faster than the national average (grocery stores ranked 13th). Thus productivity and employment growth were negatively related, on average. And although output and wages generally moved in the same direction as productivity, the relationship was weak.

It is too early to observe whether these disparate patterns of industrial growth continued in the 1970s. Most of the data required to assess the seventies' growth experience is still being processed through the government's computers. However, a few clues are available, and they generally point to the same conclusions as the earlier data.

The only data yet available for the 1970s relate to employment growth and wage growth. Even these data do not yet cover all industries. Nevertheless, they do confirm some earlier impressions. Once again, there are significant differences in the regional growth experiences of specific industries. Two extreme examples are holding/investment companies and water transportation. In their record for employment growth, holding companies were the second-best performers in both the northcentral and southern regions, but were far behind the pack in the Northeast (ranking 35th) and even more so in the West (ranking 52nd). Water transportation enjoyed the fastest rate of job expansion in the northcentral region, but created few jobs elsewhere (ranking 53rd in the Northeast, 42nd in the South, and 55th in the West). The same kinds of regional disparities are evident in industry-specific wage gains. Primary metals, for example, ranked 5th and 6th respectively in the northeast and northcentral regions, but 35th in the West and 46th in the South. Water transportation ranked 3rd in the South, 11th in the Northeast, 18th in the West—and a dismal 52nd in the northcentral region.

The data also confirm the earlier observation that employment growth is negatively correlated with wage growth. Indeed, the two industries with the best employment record nationally in the 1970s, miscellaneous retail stores and furniture, had the slowest wage growth, ranking 55th and 54th respectively. And as we see more clearly by juxtaposing data on water transportation mentioned separately in the previous paragraph, in the northcentral region that industry ranked 1st in employment growth but 52nd in wage growth, while in the south it ranked 42nd in employment growth but 3rd in wage growth.

Finally, a comparison of industry growth patterns in the 1960s and 1970s reveals numerous changes in relative growth. Business services and repair services, both of which experienced sluggish employment growth in the 1960s, enjoyed some of the fastest job expansion in the 1970s. On the other hand, restaurants and securities brokers, two premier sources of new jobs in the 1960s, provided very little job creation in the 1970s.

Lessons for the Eighties

This collage of growth experiences has important implications for our understanding of economic growth and related policies, one of which concerns productivity. Productivity growth is not well understood and is a much-abused goal. People tend to confuse observed productivity growth with improvements in technology and management techniques. But neither need occur. Productivity is typically measured by the ratio of sales to employment. Hence, an industry with rapidly growing sales and employment is not likely to register notable productivity gains, no matter how fast its technology is improving. Recall the experience of business services in the 1960s. On the other hand, an industry like variety stores can register a tremendous productivity gain with slow sales increases and even slower employment increases. It should be noted that variety store employment actually *decreased* during the 1960s, when the industry scored impressive productivity gains.

The central problem for policy, then, is that productivity gains are as likely to reveal changes in the utilization of existing technology (e.g., variety stores) as to reflect changes in technology itself (e.g., business services). The latter is desired, the former may not be. Raising the flag of productivity gains therefore may not lead the troops in the right direction.

But there is more than arithmetic to be learned here. Another important lesson concerns the basic variability of growth indices. More output, more jobs, higher wages, and greater productivity are indeed worthwhile goals. But they do not necessarily, or even frequently, occur simultaneously in a single industry. As a consequence, we must decide which of our goals are most important, and pursue them for their own sake.

To be specific, we should not overpromote productivity as a reason for reindustrialization. The lesson of the past is that productivity gains per se do not necessarily promote either sales or employment. What ails an ailing industry may be a basic lack of demand. Increasing the productivity of buggy-whip production, for example, will not do much for buggy-whip sales. The current emphasis on supply-side economics (including productivity) is welcome, but easily exaggerated. Demand is still important.

Another constraint on output and employment growth may lie in noncompetitive price and wage structures. As noted above, wage gains of the recent past have not been highly correlated with an industry's output or productivity performance. Indeed, some of the largest wage gains of the 1960s occured in industries (e.g., variety stores) directly affected by minimum-wage increases or union collective bargaining agreements (e.g., electric gas, sanitary services, and communications). The potential of reindustrialization to improve output or employment performance in such industries may be modest.

Another observation from the past is relevant. A leading industry does not produce benefits equally for all areas of the country. The experience of different regions with the office machines industry has been noted. Even greater regional discrepancies occurred when industries (e.g., leather, textiles) effectively moved from one region to another. To the extent that reindustrialization is expected to aid depressed areas as well as industries, this spatial dimension of growth will be important as well. Indeed, one could argue that the spatial dimension of Reaganomics is the primary concern of local, state, and regional politicians. If recent experience is any guide, we can conclude that there will be many regional and industry winners and losers, no matter what the general outcome of Reagan's economic policies.

Finally, the diversity of industry experiences across growth measures, geographical regions, and decades should instill great hesitancy about designing and implementing intricate strategies for economic growth. It is hard enough to envision, much less comprehend, the diversity of economic growth. Under these circumstances, it may be presumptuous to think we can both anticipate and redirect the spatial dimensions of growth. Maybe the best we can hope for is a successful *national* program of growth stimulus, supplemented by marginal interventions when specific regional or industry problems become acute.

ARE FARMERS ON THE WAY OUT?[6]

In planning my remarks for this occasion, I have posed a question that you may think is far-fetched—preposterous even. You may think there is only one answer possible for a speaker with a life-long dedication to agriculture.

[6]Speech by Seeley G. Lodwick, former Under Secretary of Agriculture for International Affairs and Commodity Programs, delivered at the Armand G. Erpf Symposia on American Private Enterprise, Berry College, Berry, Georgia, May 5, 1983. *Vital Speeches of the Day*, 49:517–21, Je 15 '83.

You have just heard me introduced as an Iowan who has been a farmer and a farm manager. You heard that I have spent most of my life in agriculture—either farming or representing farmers in the Iowa state house, in the Federal Government, or as an officer in a national organization of farmers.

So when I ask the question "Are farmers on the way out?" the answer may appear obvious. Would I be likely to take the position that there's no future in farming? That would be a denial of everything I've worked for.

But suppose we reword the question: Is there a future for the individually-owned and operated farm—as opposed to an agriculture operated by corporations, banks, or governments? In a time of high-fixed production costs, increased operating expenses, exploding technology, computerization, and sophisticated management, is there still a place for the individual farmer?

Or, even more to the point, is this a future that will provide adequately—more than adequately—for a new generation on the farm? Will farming be a desirable occupational choice for the generation now enrolled at Berry College and at other colleges and universities all over America. And will there be a future for their children and grandchildren?

You may have read that farmers are going bankrupt right and left—that farm prices are depressed—that farm profits and incomes are so low they recall memories of the Great Depression. You may have read that farmers' overseas markets are drying up, and that the Government is taking title to a flood of farm commodities that farmers can't sell. You could easily get the impression that farmers are on the way out. You could get the idea that agriculture will soon be in the hands of bankers, large corporations, or—worse still—the Federal Government. And that's pretty scary!

It is certainly true that farmers in this country have been going through some tough times. Some of the causes are global and cyclical and likely to change for the better in the normal course of events. Other factors are man-made and therefore subject to change by man, provided we recognize the problems and work hard enough at finding solutions.

Three global events have coincided the past three years to put the brakes on export growth and throw the farm economy into reverse. To begin with, the world has been growing more grains, oilseeds, cotton, and other farm commodities than it can readily use—more than farmers can sell or store or even turn over to the Government without driving market prices down. World wheat, feed grain, and soybean crops have all been the largest of record. Cotton and rice are not quite that abundant, but almost.

You can blame the good weather, improved farming methods around the world, and expanded acreages—sometimes artificially stimulated by governments. But the fact is that carryovers this year—the amounts left over before the new crops come in—will be higher than they've ever been before. The global grain carryover, for example, will be more than 250 million tons, compared with 172 million just three years ago.

Coincident with this cyclical swing toward global overproduction is the unfortunate fact that the world's people are less able to buy. For three years, the economies of most nations, including the United States, have been in a serious recession. This has reduced food consumption, especially of the more expensive items such as meat and poultry. When people have less money to spend, they may eat manioc instead of McNuggets, frijoles instead of filet. This was reflected quickly in a decline in the sale of feedstuffs. World trade in corn fell by almost a fifth in these last two years.

The decline in buying power has fallen especially hard on several customer countries where political oppression or mismanagement has made things even worse. Poland is a nation unable to pay its debts because of political conditions there. Iran was once a market for $700 million in U.S. farm products, and it's almost at zero this year. Other nations have been unable to cope with the rise and fall of petroleum prices—Mexico for example.

The third global problem affecting American agriculture is the changing value of the dollar relative to other currencies. Three years ago, the dollar was relatively cheap in terms of other nation's currencies. Today the U.S. dollar is relatively expensive. In many ways, that's good. If you should travel in Europe this spring, you would find travel there to be much less expensive than was the case, say, three years ago. But for the farmers of this country, this means that their products are made more expensive to foreigners who want to import. The German or Japanese importer has to come up with more Deutschmarks or more yen to buy a dollar's worth of U.S. soybeans. He may find it to his advantage to order from one of our competitors, Brazil, for example, or to revise his feeding ration to include less high quality protein and more roughage or something else less costly.

Over a period of three years, the German mark declined from a value of 58 U.S. cents to below 40 cents toward the end of last year. In November 1980, when soybeans were selling in Chicago at around $8.75, a German importer had to put up 16 Deutschmarks to buy a bushel of soybeans at that price. Today, soybeans are $2.50 cheaper in Chicago, but the price to a German importer is almost the same. He still has to put up 15 D-marks for a bushel of soybeans, which means that the lower U.S. price is not being passed through and U.S. farmers don't get the competitive advantage they should have.

In January 1981 when corn was $3.55 in Chicago, a Japanese exporter could buy a bushel for 710 yen. Today the yen is considerably cheaper against the dollar. So the Japanese buyer has to put up substantially more yen (750) for a bushel of U.S. corn, even though the U.S. price is about 40 cents cheaper.

These three factors—oversupply, recession, and changing currency values—are beyond the control of farmers and traders. Even governments have very limited ability to influence them in the short term. On the other hand, these are elements that tend to swing in cyclical fashion. Economic recession will pass. The world will not always have record crops. Exchange rates will be altered in time.

Meanwhile, some of the other factors that inhibit trade are more nearly within the control of nations and their leaders. I refer to two developments that have distorted trade and made it more and more difficult for American farmers and traders to profit from their own efficiencies. One is the restriction of exports. The other is the restriction of imports.

In the world of trade restrictions, no nation can claim to be without fault, not even our own. All trading nations have restrictions of one sort or another. For example, the United States Congress has mandated import restrictions on beef, dairy products, textiles, and many other items. But in all fairness, I must say that this country is still the most open large market in the world.

Unfortunately, however, the United States now has the image of a nation that, if pressed, will use its food exports as an instrument of foreign policy. This grows out of events at the beginning of 1980 when President Carter embargoed farm product exports to the Soviet Union except for an amount of corn and wheat guaranteed by the 1975 agreement. This seriously affected U.S. grain exports along with poultry and other products.

To be fair, I must point out that President Carter was not the first American president to impose an agricultural embargo. In 1973, President Nixon embargoed exports of soybeans and related products for a short time, to all destinations. In 1974 and 1975, President Ford intervened in the export market, not with an embargo, but with interruptions and delays of corn shipments to the Soviet Union. In those instances, the U.S. government interrupted trade because it was worried about having adequate supplies in this country. As it turned out, there was no need to worry. But the damage was done and customer confidence was weakened, not only in the Soviet Union, but in other importing countries as well.

In 1980, the U.S. embargoed for an entirely different reason. The cutoff to the Soviets was altogether political—ordered as a result of foreign policy concerns that were entirely legitimate. There is no argument about that. But the fact is that U.S. farmers were singled out to carry the burden of a foreign policy decision that proved ineffective and costly.

The embargo was a failure so far as foreign policy was concerned. It was extremely costly to the taxpayer. And it had the effect of disrupting agricultural trade and damaging farmer incomes in this country. Those effects are still with us, although President Reagan's efforts in lifting the embargo and encouraging orderly trade are helping a great deal.

Meanwhile, there has been little or no change in the tendency of customer countries to restrict imports. Japan, although it is our largest single country market for farm product exports, has continued to artificially restrict imports and discourage domestic consumption of U.S. agricultural products.

If you were buying a high-quality beef cut in Tokyo today, you would have to pay somewhere between $15 and $20 a pound. Georgia beef producers will tell you that they could export to Japan at those prices and do very well—and Japanese consumers would benefit too. But in fact we cannot share fully in that market because the Japanese maintain rigid import quotas. Meanwhile, the United States continues to accept Japanese products, even when it hurts.

On the other side of the world, the European Community uses an import levy that is adjusted up and down to eliminate any price advantage that imported commodities might otherwise have. For example, U.S. corn is priced at about $3.70 a bushel at the port in Rotterdam, but once that corn is inside the EC it costs the livestock feeder there about $2 more. The EC simply adds a levy of $2.05 to the price of U.S. corn, which erases the U.S. price advantage.

Even more insidious is the EC's practice of using government funds to give its farm exports an unfair advantage in other markets where they compete with us. Having produced more barley and wheat and sugar and beef and poultry than it can use at home, the Community in effect pushes these commodities onto the world market at below the world price.

The American broiler industry, of which Georgia producers represent about 15 percent, spent years building up a market in the Middle East. That market has now been virtually wiped out, so far as U.S. exporters are concerned, by subsidized exports from France and Brazil.

If Georgia broilers can be delivered into Saudi Arabia at a price 12 cents below the cost of French broilers, for example, the Common Market simply subsidizes the French exporters at 12 cents or more, which enables their product to undercut the U.S. price. The U.S. has complained bitterly about the kind of practice—to the EC and to the GATT—but with no effect.

EC and Japanese trade practices are not the predominant cause of the decline in U.S. exports—I would not want to exaggerate. But they are an important cause—one that will have to be remedied if world trade is to grow and expand on a basis of open and fair competition.

The upshot of these various developments in the U.S. agricultural exports are in their second year of decline—from about $44 billion in 1981 to an expected $36.5 billion this year. That's a decline of 17 percent. Even more serious is the decline in U.S. share of the world market, which could be very damaging even after the global situation improves.

The last time the United States suffered a substantial decline in agricultural exports was in the late 1960's when exports tailed off by 12 percent over a 4-year period. That was a more gradual decline and more importantly it came at a time when exports were not nearly so important to farmers as they have now become.

Fifteen years ago, U.S. farmers were devoting only around one-fifth of their cropland to production for export. In the 1980's, almost two-fifths of U.S. cropland is producing for export. U.S. agriculture has been internationalized—its dependence on world trade is real and irreversible. So, when the export market suddenly turns downward, the effect on American agriculture is immediate and sharp. U.S. farm prices in 1982 averaged 10 percent below the preceding year. That, together with a continued rise in production costs, brought net farm income down by almost one-fourth.

But a farmer has to be optimistic. I certainly am, and I sometimes think of the remark of a rancher in the American West that: "We are closer to the next good rain that we've ever been before." Some good things are happening. Inflation is under control; the 1980 inflation rate of 13 1/2 percent has been reduced to below 5 percent. The prime interest rate is now 12 percent compared with 20 percent in 1980. Housing starts are up sharply in the first part of 1983. Industrial output rebounded strongly in March, along with gains in disposable personal incomes and consumer spending.

Unemployment is still too high, and interest rates are still too high. But there is general consensus among economists and policy makers that our country has begun an economic recovery. That's good news. The bad news, according to those economists, is that the farm economy will lag behind other sectors in the general recovery because of the large commodity stocks that still overhang the market. But even the stocks situation is looking toward improvement now, because of the success of PIK—the new payment-in-kind program. Farmers have responded beyond all expectations to this program, which provides payment-in-kind to farmers as an incentive to reduce plantings.

In other words, corn farmers will receive corn out of government hands to make up for corn that is not planted. They can feed this grain or sell it into the market however they wish. The Administration instituted PIK after taking a number of actions to encourage export sales. Innovative export credit programs and other export initiatives have helped—but the over-supply problem was just too massive to be solved by export programs alone. All of us who had a hand in the PIK program recognize it as a short-term effort. There may or may not be another PIK next year, depending on how supplies stack up at the end of this year. But beyond that, we know that the nation has a major decision to make in farm policy.

What role do Americans want their Government to play in the agricultural economy? Do they want more government control and regulation, or do they want the primary government role to be one of opening and expanding markets? Essentially the issue for agriculture is: Are farmers willing to accept increased management of production and marketing by the government? Or, are they prepared to move toward greater reliance on the market with prices essentially to be determined by economic forces here and abroad. I believe the choice has to be and will be the second option. The need and the challenge are to find ways to extricate the government from U.S. agriculture.

This means that any government price minimums established for farm commodities must be at levels that permit products to move into trade. This nation simply will not sustain for long a program that causes farmers to produce for government warehouses. This is too expensive, and it's just not in the cards.

At the same time, it is in the long-term best interest of farmers to produce for the world's people as well as for our own. That's where the growth opportunity is. When you look at agriculture as a global enterprise, you realize that food truly is a growth industry. For three reasons: The globe has more people on it every year. These people want to eat better. The U.S. farmers are best able to serve that want

Thirty years ago, the world had a population of 2.4 billion and geographers were predicting that this figure might approach 4 billion by the end of this century. This year we already have a global population of 4.8 billion—and we have 17 years remaining in the century. We could have 6 billion by 2000. I am not an alarmist on population growth—the rate of increase has actually diminished somewhat. Nevertheless, even with minimum growth rates, world population will continue to expand. And it will need to be fed.

The other certainty, along with taxes, is that the world's people will want to eat better than they have in the past. Those who are hungry and malnourished want to have adequate diets, and the world must find ways to meet that need. Those people with only adequate diets want to have food that is more nutritious, more varied, richer in protein.

Not only do they want more protein in their diets, they need it. As developing countries increase their consumption of poultry, dairy, and livestock products, their people become stronger, healthier, and longer lived—more capable of contributing to the advancement and development of their countries and ours too.

We can no longer afford to squander the energy and talent that are lost in people who cannot fully perform because they are not well fed. The problems of the world are too numerous and too large, and we need the capabilities of all the world's people. This invites innovation on the part of American farmers and traders to find ways of serving those needs. We have the opportunity to expand exports of processing foods and other high value products that increase dollar returns to this country and also create non-farm jobs in processing and food manufacturing.

We also have the challenge to find new methods of trading— barter and countertrade, for example—and the linking of trade with development projects that make imports possible for the poorer countries. All of this adds up to a growth opportunity for those Americans who produce food. Food producers will be the key to progress toward a future world of peace and plenty.

Add to that the fact that the most productive farm unit ever invented is the American privately owned and privately operated farm. Obviously, I don't mean 40 acres and a mule, or even a hundred acres and a 2-plow tractor. An efficient unit could be that small if it were intensively farmed. Or it might be 500 acres in Iowa or several times that in the Great Plains.

An efficient unit might include a half million dollars worth of machinery and involve many thousands of dollars in production inputs every year. And it still might be operated by an individual farmer who has the freedom and opportunity to take his own risks and profit from his own success. That is the common ingredient—the key ingredient. Years ago, an American business leader advised that ". . . a business can reach the highest level of productivity only under the stimulant of a free society and only when the government allows enterprise to receive fitting reward." That's still good advice.

Press reports from Moscow tell us that the new Soviet leadership under Uri Andropov is giving high priority to agriculture. The Soviets have decided on a drastic overhaul to bring better planning and better leadership into their farming system. This may bring some improvement to the U.S.S.R.'s agriculture, which has now produced four straight years of serious grain shortfalls. But that won't be enough—what they need is the freedom to profit! . . .

The Soviet producer is locked into a system that does not provide those freedoms. The system does not provide the stimulant of a free society and the freedom to gain personal reward. That is a problem that a major overhaul of Soviet planning will not correct.

American farmers respond to opportunity because they are the products of a free society—a nation built on the promise of freedom. I know that farmers will always respond to that promise. . . . Every farmer has known adversity or he hasn't been in the business very long. He is willing to take risk, but he needs the opportunity to profit from that risk. He understands that it won't always be easy. As one cattle feeder said, "it's difficult to plan your business when you have to look in the newspaper every morning to see what prices are." Businesses outside of agriculture don't have that kind of volatility.

A farm supply dealer told about a farmer who came by and said, "If I could just get back up to broke I'd quit farming." The thing is, he has to get back up to broke first. Country bankers call that "negative net worth."

I believe that American farmers will emerge all the stronger for the adversity of the past three years. They have an enormous opportunity to be a part of the coming expansion in the world economy. American farming is a growth industry. But it's also a world industry . . . affected by purchasing power in Hokkaido . . . politics in Marseilles . . . as it is by rainfall in Iowa or late spring in Georgia.

I asked the question: Are farmers on the way out? I want to answer that question and close my remarks by saying: Yes, farmers are on their way out . . . and on their way *in* to a new world of growth opportunity.

HOW U.S. AUTOMAKERS ARE FIGHTING BACK[7]

John Telnack leads his visitor through the well-guarded doors of Ford Motor Company's design center in Dearborn, Mich., where work is under way on 1987 cars. As Ford's chief designer for North American automotive operations, Telnack is a key figure in an industry that is investing more than $70 billion in 47 new engine and transmission facilities and 80 assembly plants—and in retooling for the 21st century.

In a courtyard, Telnack shows off a full-scale, fiberglass prototype of a 1984 Mark VII, next model year's top-of-the-line Lincoln at $20,000 plus. It differs radically from traditional Lincolns—just as the entire U.S. auto industry is changing dramatically to meet the challenge from foreign competitors.

Detroit is in an all-out fight. Preliminary findings from a detailed study at the Massachusetts Institute of Technology indicate that only seven to nine auto manufacturers, worldwide, can expect to survive into the next century.

[7]Reprint of an article by Seth Kantor. *Nation's Business*, vol. 71, no.5, 28+. My '83. Reprinted by permission. Copyright © 1983 by the Chamber of Commerce of the United States.

American manufacturers are still reeling from a contradictory recession—interest rates remained high despite widespread unemployment and poor retail sales generally. Only 5.8 million new American-made cars were sold in this country last year, a 21-year low and a grim 40 percent below the record total of 1973, when 9.6 million were sold. The recession intensified what was already a serious problem for the domestic industry—competition from imports, primarily Japanese.

W. Paul Tippett, chairman and chief executive officer of American Motors Corporation, gives this perspective:

"In 1958, the first year the Japanese produced a completely Japanese-designed and Japanese-manufactured car, they produced a total of 333,000 cars and trucks. This year the Japanese are expected to produce a total of 12 million vehicles."

The present situation, in which the United States is building less than 20 percent of the motor vehicles sold throughout the world, is a stunning reversal of the dominance that the American auto industry enjoyed just a generation ago.

In 1950 the United States produced more than 75 percent of the motor vehicles sold in a war-battered world. The U.S. industry's pre-eminence was most secure at home; in 1957, for example, of the 6 million new cars sold in this country, 5.8 million, or 96.6 percent, were American-made.

Last Year, total sales in the United States had risen to 8 million, but the American manufacturers' share had shrunk to 72.2 percent—they were selling the same number of cars as in 1957.

The U.S. auto industry now stands in the shadow of the Japanese industry, which will produce more than one third of the world output of cars this year—roughly twice the U.S. share of the world market.

In 1957—a year when Detroit turned out more cars in 10 days than Japan did in the entire 12 months—Japan exported only 440 cars. Now it exports 4 million a year.

Undaunted by such formidable competition, the U.S. auto industry is launching an all-out campaign that amounts to what Philip Caldwell, chairman of the Ford Motor Company, calls "the biggest industrial revolution in world history." Its principal components are:

A $70 billion investment in new plants and machinery.

Redesign and restyling to improve appearance, performance, economy and efficiency.

Sharply improved productivity through better labor-management relations as well as capital investment.

Significant reduction in federal regulations that add to costs.

Industry critics argue that the Detroit recovery plan is, in large measure, based on techniques that Japan's auto industry has long been using to build its industry to the present level.

But V.J. Adduci, president of the U.S. Motor Vehicle Manufacturers Association, suggests that the Japanese had the good fortune to be "at the right place at the right time with the right vehicle" a decade ago.

Because of high fuel costs and narrow roads, he explains, the Japanese had long been producing smaller, fuel-efficient vehicles and thus were ready for the explosive demand for such cars when the oil embargo of 1973-74 turned American consumers in that direction.

General Motors Chairman Roger B. Smith has declared, "We all know that the Japanese are very efficient producers, and they now have the capacity to build small cars and ship them here at costs far below our own."

To improve its own efficiency, the U.S. industry has been investing in new production facilities that range from robots to assembly plants. "To illustrate the magnitude of that effort," says Ford Chairman Caldwell, "one of Ford's new engine plants has a continuing line of computer-controlled machine tools that stretches one third of a mile in one direction, then back again for another third of a mile and forward again for still another third of a mile."

GM has more than 1,850 robots on hand or on order and expects to be using 14,000 by 1990. In addition to acquiring robots and other modern equipment, Detroit is adopting a Japanese practice known as *kanban*, a system under which parts are delivered to production lines from strategically located suppliers, rather than having them warehoused at high inventory cost until needed.

This approach offers increased opportunities to small firms that are suppliers to the auto industry. Under an arragement with

American Magnetics, of Valparaiso, Ind., for example, GM has reduced its inventory of ferrite magnets from six weeks to six days. The prospect of continued production has enabled American Magnetics to cut its prices to GM by 40 percent.

The product resulting from the massive changes in equipment and procedures, says Ford designer Telnack, will answer the car-buying public's demand for "a departure from that Detroit living-room-on-wheels look. What's emerging now is a driver-oriented, aerodynamic machine." Today, says Adduci, "American manu-facturers can compete with imports . . . head-on in safety, perfor-mance, reliability and fuel economy. . . . Today's American-built cars are 66 percent more fuel-efficient than they were in 1975. That, in itself, is a remarkable turnaround.

On the labor front, the auto industry offers examples of pres-sure on organized labor to be more concerned about the economic survival of employers as critical to the survival of jobs, as well as to the unions' hopes for higher pay and benefits.

GM Chairman Smith says, "You might say that, in the labor area, foreign competition has done for us what we could not do for ourselves."

Organized labor has shown increasing willingness to help American business reduce costs, increase efficiency and become more competitive internationally, Smith adds. "I believe one of the most valuable benefits foreign competition has brought to Ameri-can business is the progress we have made in establishing a viable bond of enlightened self-interest between employes and management."

Government regulation, however, remains one of the indus-try's most pressing problems. The Motor Vehicle Manufacturing Association has targeted 34 specific regulations that will cost the industry $1.4 billion in capital expenditures and add $9 billion to car buyers' costs over the next five years. These rules could be modified or repealed without adverse effects on safety or the envi-ronment, the industry says.

A specific case is Federal Motor Vehicle Safety Standard No. 108, which 43 years ago outlawed use of bulbs in headlamps in favor of sealed-beam lights. The bulbs, it was said, were subject to moisture and corrosion that weakened their power. Ford has developed a bulb-using aero-headlamp that engineers say is as efficient as a sealed-beam light, but cheaper. Use of the lamp could save consumers $1 billion a year, designers say.

William C. Turnbull, a Buick dealer in Huntington, W.Va., and current president of the National Autombile Dealers Association, says the industry does not oppose all federal regulations blindly, but it asks that Washington "keep in mind that cost analysis is vital and that costs must be weighed against effectiveness. In other words, do the benefits outweigh the cost to consumers?"

NADA's ranks are another reflection of what has happened to the American auto industry. Four years ago, NADA had 23,000 members selling new and used cars. Today there are 18,300.

Although the main emphasis of the industry's recovery program is on a competitive product at a competitive cost, some quarters are pressing for varying degrees of protectionism.

One of the most visible of these efforts is the drive in Congress for enactment of legislation designed to decrease imports sharply by specifying the amount of "domestic content" in vehicles sold in this country.

The legislation, which draws major support from organized labor and its allies in Congress, is aimed squarely at Japan. It probably has enough support to pass the House at this point, but not the Senate. Its chief sponsor in the Senate, Donald W. Riegle (D-Mich.), says it would preserve or create a million jobs in the auto industry, including suppliers.

President Reagan has vowed to veto a domestic content bill if one clears Congress, because the idea runs counter to his efforts to expand global trade.

Robert A. Perkins, Chrysler Corporation's vice president for Far East affairs, expects a serious push for a domestic content bill in the spring of 1984, when the Democratic presidential primaries are in full swing. Also, a three-year program of voluntary restraints by Japanese producers on auto exports to the United States will end then. Perkins says Chrysler "would rather have the Japanese voluntary restraints continue, but we are interested in taking a look at domestic content legislation."

Ford and GM are strongly opposed to such legislation, as are leaders in other major industries who fear retaliation in world markets for any protectionist moves by this country. Chrysler Chairman Lee Iacocca, however, is quietly lining up top executives from various industries for a drive to promote American-made goods.

An overview of the U.S. auto industry as the midpoint of 1983 approaches shows grounds for optimism that the "revolution" will succeed. Sales and production are both up substantially this year. Early April sales were up nearly a third over the same period a year ago. The Commerce Department predicts 1983 sales will total 9.2 million cars, a 16 percent jump.

Says the Motor Vehicle Manufacturers Association's Adduci: "The numbers we're seeing these days—though they have the ups and downs so familiar to anyone who has followed our industry over the years—are indeed brighter. Although we're not yet ready to say we're completely out of the woods and the economy is back on track, we sure see some light up ahead."

IACOCCA'S TIGHTROPE ACT[8]

Frank Sinatra. John Houseman. Joe Garagiola. Ricardo Montalban. Chrysler Corp. has hired all of them to tout its cars on television. But the company's premier pitchman is a slightly paunchy, slightly balding 58-year-old who happens to be on the permanent payroll: Chairman Lido Anthony ("Lee") Iacocca. "You can go with Chrysler," he booms into the camera, "or you can go with someone else—and take your chances."

Iacocca, the son of Italian immigrants, is fighting for his corporation's life, and growing numbers of viewers seem to be buying his act. Says Abe Gurewitz, 54, a Brooklyn cab driver: "I saw him on TV and I like the guy. He's turning around a company that was down the drain. He has guts." Nor has Iacocca's commerical charisma escaped notice by Wall Street's saviest auto analyst, Maryann Keller of Paine Webber Mitchell Hutchins. Says she:

[8]Reprint of an article by Alexander L. Taylor III. *Time*. 121:50–4+ Mr 21 '83. Copyright 1983 by Time Inc. All rights reserved. Reprinted by permission.

"I wouldn't doubt that people have bought Chrysler cars just because they wanted Lee Iacocca to make it."

Incredibly, it is beginning to look as if he might. Five years ago, Iacocca was president of Ford Motor Co., and Chrysler's profits were about to career off a cliff. In November 1978, four months after he got the ax at Ford, Iacocca joined Chrysler as president. From that year through 1981, the company lost nearly $3.5 billion, easily the biggest bloodbath by any American company in history. In 1979, the company was so close to bankruptcy that only an act of Congress saved it, and despite the bailout, Chrysler has almost collapsed several times since. It is therefore something of a modern management miracle that last month Iacocca was able to announce that his company had actually made a profit in 1982.

True, it was a small profit, only $170 million on sales of $10 billion, and it came mostly from the sale of the tank division, not from making cars. Yet no one denies that Chrysler's progress has been prodigious. Had not a debilitating five-week strike last fall in highly profitable Canadian plants crippled operations, Chrysler would have eked out a profit in the auto business. More astonishing, the once cash-starved company now has a cash hoard of $900 million. Wall Street has halted its death watch: last year Chrysler's shares more than quintupled in price, from 3 3/8 to 17 3/4. It was the second best 1982 showing of any stock on the New York Stock Exchange, surpassed only by Coleco Industries' rise from 6 7/8 to 36 3/4.

Chrysler's recovery is largely Iacocca's doing, a triumph of brains, bluster and bravado. When the company needed money and the banks dithered, he threatened to go into bankruptcy. When he needed pay cuts and the union protested, he warned that he would shut plants. When Chrysler could not pay its bills, he persuaded suppliers to be patient. It now seems a plausible bet— not yet even money but not 100 to 1 either—that Iacocca's company will survive as No. 3 against its behemoth competitors, General Motors and Ford, and occasionally even threaten them. Of course, the tougher battle is the one that all U.S. carmakers are in together: turning back the competition from Japanese and other foreign automobile companies, who drove off with a record 28% of the market last year.

Iacocca blames this miserable state of affairs in part on past failures by the U.S. industry's leaders, including himself, and with characteristic brashness he predicts that Chrysler, though possibly not its U.S. competitors, will conquer. He proclaims, "I was arrogant, but GM made a science of goddam arrogance. I think the Townsends of this world,* the Henry Ford IIs and some of the GM chairmen wrecked this industry. That arrogance should be gone now. We got our comeuppance. If GM and Ford keep thinking that way, we'll run over them. If they had been on the ball, I don't think we'd have made it. So who wants to wake them up?"

Although Iacocca's company is only one-sixth the size of GM in terms of revenue and less than a third as big as Ford, that kind of talk has made him easily the auto industry's best-known figure. A Gallup poll of heads of small- and medium-size businesses earlier this year found Iaccoca the U.S. business executive they respected most. He got 27 times the number of votes of the runner-up, Frank Cary, who retired last month as chairman of International Business Machines Corp.

A few red-white-and-blue bumper stickers have even sprouted declaring IACOCCA FOR PRESIDENT. Preposterous? Yes, preposterous. Iacocca greatly enjoys the sound of his own voice and often pontificates on political and economic matters, especially as they affect Chrysler. But friends say he does not have the patience for politics, and he concurs. "I'm not interested," he says, and then, as if to explain how stories start: "If you only talk cars, people say you're a provincial son of a bitch. If you're outspoken, then they say you are running for office." Quips Publisher Keith Crane of *Automotive News*: "Hell, Lee doesn't want to be President; he wants to be appointed Pope."

It is easy to dismiss Iacocca as just another supersalesman because he is so good at it. He exudes confidence and conviction: well-tailored clothes, big cigar, self-satisfied smile. But Iacocca has proved he is a remarkable manager as well. He has a knack for getting the most out of people, for making them do more than they think they can. Says St. Louis Plant Manager John Burkart: "All of us at Chrysler believe in the man, I worship the guy."

*Lynn Townsend was Chrysler chairman from 1967 to 1975.

Vince Williams, a Portland, Ore., auto salesman, says he decided to open a Dodge dealership rather than a Pontiac outlet just because of Iacocca.

The boss is by turns charming and demanding. Extremely demanding. His edict to top managers: "I don't need a $100 million mistake. Try to make it a $5 million mistake if you have to make one." Investment Banker Felix Rohatyn, who helped rescue New York City from insolvency in 1975, sums it up: "Lee is a man who can instill leadership in a crisis. He knows his business from front bumpers to back ends. He is the right man at the right time."

Keeping Chrysler alive has been a wrenching process. Iacocca has effectively cut the company almost in half. Of its 52 plants, he has closed 16. Overseas operations and unrelated businesses were auctioned off to raise cash. Five years ago, Chrysler had 157,000 employees: today there are 74,700. In the past years its costs for wages and salaries have been slashed from $2.1 billion to $1.5 billion. Once the world's sixth largest automaker, Chrysler now ranks twelfth.** In Detroit, where the man in charge was briefly known as "Ayatollah" Iacocca, there are dozens of eerily silent rooms with long rows of empty desks at company headquarters.

The smaller, slimmer Chrysler can make a profit selling only 1.2 million vehicles instead of the 2.3 million required in 1980, a big advantage in tough economic times. But this transmogrification is not without high risks. The company can no longer compete across the board with GM and Ford by building car models in every size and price category. It remains burdened by $2 billion in long-term debt. If it should falter ever so slightly, it could again be plunged into a financial abyss. Says GM Chairman Roger Smith: "The jury is still out on Chrysler. It all depends on the product they introduce and whether they can sell it."

Nothing would derail Chrysler's recovery more effectively than a continuation of the disease that has afflicted Detroit for three years: sickly sales. Last year U.S. manufacturers sold only 5.8 million cars, the fewest in 21 years; Chrysler sold 794,000, but

----

**Ranked by cars and trucks produced in 1981, the 15 largest vehicle manufacturers in the world are: GM, 6,240,380: Ford, 3,730,319; Toyota, 3,220,418; Nissan, 3,100,968; Volkswagen-Audi, 2,210,666; Renault, 1,810,365; Peugeot-Citroen-Talbot, 1,593,943; Fiat, 1,209,819; Toyo Kogyo (Mazda), 1,176,608; Mitsubishi, 1,094,793; Honda, 1,008,927; Chrysler, 1,002,464; Lada (U.S.S.R.); 830,000: Daimler-Benz 712,315; Suzuki, 578,876.

its share of the American market inched up, to 10. So far this year the industry is doing only slightly better. Through February, sales were running at an annual rate of 6 million cars. All of the Big Three are offering customers cut-rate financing of 11.9´in an effort to spur sales. Chrysler's decision last month to cut prices by offering rebates of $300 to $1,000 to cash buyers is expected to set off another round of price competition, one that manufacturers say they can ill afford.

U.S. sales of Japanese-made cars were 1.8 million last year, and are not increasing, thanks to Tokyo's recent acceptance of a third year of "voluntary" import restrictions. Although Detroit is at last beginning to approach the Japanese on quality, evidence suggests that an extra twelve months will enable U.S. carmakers to become significantly more competitive on price. After ten years of mostly futile trying, Detroit continues to watch the small-car market slip away to the Japanese, who are now training their sights on the midsize and luxury end of the market as well.

The international competition that challenges the U.S. auto industry today was unknown when Iacocca began his career. His father Nicola immigrated to the U.S. from southern Italy in 1902 and eventually built a small auto-rental business in Allentown, Pa., with 33 cars, mostly Fords. Surrounded by Model A's, Son Lido always wanted to work for Ford. After graduating from Lehigh and getting a master's in engineering at Princeton, he joined the company as an engineer in 1946, then quickly switched to a district sales job. By 1970, he had risen so far that only Henry Ford II, grandson of the founder, outranked him.

Iacocca succeeded by indulging the passionate American love affair with the automobile. He combined a knowledge of an automobile's innards with a shrewd, almost intuitive sense of what car buyers wanted. He stripped the plain-Jane body off Ford's dowdy Falcon and replaced it with a long-hood, short-rear-deck configuration called the Mustang that in 1964 set a record for automobile sales by a first-year model (418,000). Four years later he reached into Ford's spare-parts bin again and launched the limousine-like Continental Mark III on a Thunderbird chassis.

Iacocca personified Detroit braggadocio, the longer, lower, wider mentality that economy- and quality-conscious buyers would eventually find objectionable. He was a used-car dealer writ large. At Ford, where the real power flowed like sap from the family tree, Iacocca managed to tap in through the sheer force of personality. A cadre of Iacocca subordinates grew up who owed their fealty to him, not to the boss whose name was on the cars. One of Iacocca's weapons was a black book he carried, itemizing each manager's quarterly goals, a tradition he transferred to Chrysler. Those who did not live up to their targets rarely forgot it. Says William Fugazy, the New York travel and limousine owner who has known Iacocca for 25 years: "I've seen him just ream guys out for not getting the job done. He'll turn to one of his top people and say, 'I told you what I wanted done. It hasn't been done. Now do it, and I don't want any crap.' He never wants any crap. It's one of his favorite expressions."

Inevitably, President Iacocca and the equally strong-willed Henry Ford II clashed. On July 13, 1978, the chairman called Iacocca into his office and fired him. At the time a story made the rounds that Ford, by way of explanation, offered this: "Let's just say I don't like you." Iacocca insists that is apocryphal, but says he is keeping the real story for an autobiography he is writing. Whatever was said, it was apparently enough to last a lifetime. Neither man has spoken to the other since Iacocca walked out of Ford's office.

Iacocca was evicted from Ford world headquarters in Dearborn and given an obscure office several miles across town to serve out the four months until he could collect his retirement benefits. Already a millionaire, he might have ended his business career then; there are few successful second acts in the automotive industry. But Iacocca loves a challenge. On Oct. 30, 1978, Iacocca was officially through at Ford. On Nov. 2, Chrysler made two announcements: 1) the company had just lost a record $158.5 million in the third quarter, and 2) Iacocca would become Chrysler's president.

Joining Chrysler presented Iacocca with the chance to be his own boss at last and to put his unmistakable stamp on the industry. While the top jobs at GM and Ford had passed on to drab managerial types, Chrysler remained a company where a single, forceful personality could make a difference. It had, in fact, had a sucession of strong-willed leaders, beginning with a brilliant entrepreneur named Walter Chrysler, who founded the company in 1925, 22 years after Ford, 17 after GM.

For a time in the late '40s, Chrysler (whose product line included Plymouth, Dodge and DeSoto) surpassed Ford as the No. 2 U.S. automaker. But then began two decades of losing ground. A costly international expansion program drained resources and diverted executives' attention. Strapped for cash, Chrysler shunned small cars for larger, rather stodgy models that it sold to mostly lower-income buyers. Thus it was ill prepared for the surge in gas prices that began in 1973. Even its reputation for quality began to slide. The company's market share, as high as 26% in 1946, slipped to 12% by 1977.

By 1979, Chrysler Chairman John Riccardo had begun making regular trips to Washington to drum up support for tax credits and relief from regulatory restrictions. He told anyone who would listen that Chrysler's future was threatened unless it could get financial help to transform its aging, oversize fleet into economical front-wheel-drive cars. It took losses of $1 billion, plus all of Iacocca's lobbying during his first year at Chrysler, to ram the message through.

After Congress's approval in December 1979 of loan guarantees covering $1.5 billion of Chrysler's borrowings—money it would need to survive—Iacocca's hardest task began. Congress made the guarantees contingent on Chrysler's winning about $2 billion of concessions on its own: from the United Auto Workers, suppliers, state and local governments and 446 lenders. Those negotiations took six months and were concluded just as the company was days away from declaring formal bankruptcy.

But money alone could not solve Chrysler's problems. When Iacocca arrived, he found management in disarray. Executive responsibilities were ill defined, and there were few of the sophisticated financial tools needed to keep track of operations. The quickest fix Iacocca knew was to hire people who understood the same system he did: other Ford executives. Some were called out of retirement, others were wooed away and enlisted with Iacocca for the challenge of engineering a turnaround. Today the four top officers are Ford alumni: Iacocca; Vice Chairman Gerald Greenwald; Harold Sperlich, president of North American automotive operations; and Executive Vice President of Finance Robert S. Miller. Of the 28 highest-ranking Chrysler executives, only four remain from pre-Iacocca days. Says Survivor Stephan Sharf, 62, executive vice president of manufacturing: "As the newest vice president when Iacocca arrived, I followed a tradition and sat next to the chairman at meetings. Now I'm nearly at the end of the table."

As he swept out the old management, Iacocca also axed some bad business practices. The most insidious was a device known as the sales bank. Unlike other automakers, which build few cars except those ordered by dealers either for customers or showroom stock, Chrysler turned out a lot of cars that simply sat in inventory. Although theoretically this meant that production lines could be kept running efficiently, the sales bank became a tool to hide mistakes. Managers ordered tens of thousands of cars built so that they could boost production figures, as well as their bonuses. Most of the vehicles were eventually sold to dealers at cut-rate prices, often after months of outdoor storage had taken their toll. Iacocca's cure for Chrysler's peculiar addiction to production mandates was to kill the sales bank. The company took some heavy losses to sell off its back log of inventory, but once the last car was gone, Chrysler stopped making cars on speculation.

Iacocca's next task was to convince car buyers that Chrysler was indeed alive, even if it was not exactly well. Again he turned to his old employer and wooed away Kenyon & Eckhardt, the New York City advertising agency that had represented Ford for 34 years. Iacocca's carrot was a $140 million account, the second largest (after Chevrolet) in the auto industry. The agency decided the most sensible way to spend the money was to market the chairman himself.

Kenyon Chief Leo Kelmenson began to find himself on the phone with Iacocca at all hours: designing ads, plotting strategy, evaluating results. He recalls: "Lee used to phone late at night, and then I'd hear from him first thing in the morning. Two days later, the advertising would be on the air. It was fast paced all the time and it went on for months and months."

Iacocca inherited the design of the front-wheel-drive K-cars. Though they were not brought out until the fall of 1980, they had been practically ready to go into production when he arrived two years earlier. (He still could not resist tinkering with the grille and adding louvers to the windows shortly before the designs were locked up.) Chrysler had botched the launch of the luxury New Yorker series in 1978, and the memory haunted Iacocca. Now, with buyers clamoring for fuel-efficient cars and Chrysler short of cash, a trouble-free K-car rollout was critical.

It turned out to be a near miss. Problems with advanced robotic welders and material handlers slowed initial production so that only 10,000 cars, less than a third the number needed, were in showrooms on the official introduction date, Oct. 2, 1980. Chrysler flubbed in other ways as well. Iacocca sent the earliest models out with high-profit options like velour upholstery and electric window lifts that pushed the sticker price from $6,000 up to $9,000. But buyers did not want the extras. Until the production imbalance was corrected, sales did not really take off.

Ever the optimist, Iacocca had predicted before Congress that Chrysler would lose only $482 million in 1980. Instead, the losses ran to $1.7 billion, much higher than 1979's record $1.1 billion deficit. The company was hemorrhaging cash. Just in time, the K-car caught on: in its first year, it won more than 20% of the compact-car market. Despite this, Chrysler's survival continued to be a week-by-week proposition throughout 1981. The losses were lower, if still unspeakably high: "only" $475.6 million. Iacocca and other executives periodically braced themselves for "drop-dead dates," deadlines when, the accountants calculated, accumulated expenses would overwhelm the amount of cash that was trickling in. Iacocca found himself one Friday night in November 1981 with just $1 million left in the bank, a pittance for a company that was spending $5 milllion per working hour. Only by delaying payments to suppliers and strong-arming dealers into buying cars during this period was he able to keep out of bankruptcy. The crisis somehow passed, and Chrysler was still in business. With its break-even point now halved, new management in place and its share of the U.S. auto market back up to almost 10%, from a low of 8.8%, the company was slowly edging away from the financial precipice.

A Japanese colleague, Tomio Kubo, chairman of Mitsubishi Motors Corp., which builds two small-car models for Chrysler, pays Iacocca a compliment. Says he: "In the person of Mr. Iacocca we have developed a sense of security about the corporation and its future." He explains that Iacocca "shows signs of Oriental wisdom." Perhaps Mitsubishi's boss has noticed that in rebuilding Chrysler, Iacocca has turned from American role models and is looking to the Japanese. While he has tried to appropriate the expensive, high-gloss image of European automobiles for his more modest creations, Iacocca has borrowed heavily from the successful management and manufacturing techniques of Japan.

The Japanese have cut inventory costs by building parts plants next to assembly plants and using the same part on several car models. Now Chrysler, instead of shipping big batches of transaxles by rail from its Kokomo, Ind., plant to Belvidere, Ill., for assembly, moves smaller loads by truck, gaining at least 24 hours. Total savings on inventory from such measures: $450 million a year. Chrysler has cut the number of different parts it uses to 40,000, from 70,000. That means, for instance, that van buyers can choose only one kind of tinted glass, not two. Total savings: about $300 million annually.

A far greater challenge involves changing a basic tenet of the U.S. auto industry that was laid down in 1921 by Alfred P. Sloan, creator of the modern GM: produce a separate and distinct automobile for every price category. Since Chrysler can no longer afford the $1 billion it costs to build an entirely new model, it will eventually have to use its basic model, the K-car, as the building block for each of its four car sizes: subcompact, compact, intermediate and full size. Thus buyers have to be re-educated not to mind that their luxurious Chrysler may have started out as a lowly Plymouth.

It is a strategy that some automakers have quietly used for many years, particularly Japanese companies. But Chrysler has taken the approach one risky step further. Americans who pay extra for an intermediate- or full-size car want to be convinced that they are getting additional value, not just a knock-off of an existing model. Bigger and better-heeled automakers can still afford to crank up entirely new designs when they are needed. Admits Ia-

cocca: "We have to say, 'Do you want vanilla or chocolate?" GM
says, 'Do you want vanilla, choclate or strawberry?'" Later this
year, for example, Ford will roll out its replacement for the rear-
wheel-drive Ford Fairmont/Mercury Zephyr, known as the
Tempo/Topaz. The totally new designs will have front-wheel
drive and aerodynamic styling for greater fuel economy, advances
that would have been impossible with Ford's old models.

At Ford, Iacocca dazzled buyers with the élan of a three-card
monte dealer by spinning off the Mustang and Continental Mark
series from existing chassis combinations. Now he is trying to do
the same thing with virtually an entire line of cars. The $5,900
Dodge and Plymouth 1981-model K-cars begat the $8,100 1982
Chrysler LeBaron and Dodge 400, the $12,300 Chrysler LeBaron
convertible and the 1983 Chrysler E Class and Dodge 600, which
sell for $9,000 to $12,000. By stretching the K-car, he produced
the luxury Chrysler New Yorker ($12,800). In the fall of '83 will
come the Dodge Daytona and Chrysler Laser, sleek sports cars
also using K-car components, which are receiving raves in the automotive press. They will sell for $10,000 to $14,000.

To keep the buying public bedazzled, Chrysler is developing
vehicles for special market segments, known in Detroit as "niche"
cars. These are expected to confer some luster on the rest of the
car line as well as to reach relatively small but profitable markets
where other carmakers are not competing. Later this year Chrysler will introduce the ultimate in elongated K-cars, the roomy five-
passenger Chrysler Executive Sedan and the seven-passenger limousine. Iacocca has also ordered up a blatant knock-off of the $40,
000 two-seat Mercedes-Benz 380 SL that Chrysler has code-
named the SL and will sell for about half the price. He is wagering
an enormous amount, $700 million, that he can rekindle buyer in-
terest in vans. Chrysler claims the hybrid minivan will be as revolutionary as the Mustang.

While he has been restructuring the corporation, Iacocca has
never stopped scrutinizing new model designs. A little while ago,
he took one look at a mock-up of a 1986 subcompact, then curtly
told the stylists that the front grille and bumper made them look
like "Dodg'em cars." The lights burned late in the styling studios
for weeks thereafter. Iacocca is unrepentant. Says he: "The guys

who have it tough in this company are the product guy and the marketing guy because I grew up in those areas and think that I know more than they'll ever know." Even with the skillful scavenging of existing models, the cars Chrysler brings to market between 1982 and 1986 will cost $6.6 billion before they roll off the production line. For a company still struggling to stay out of the red, the sum is staggering. But almost anyone in Chrysler's finance department can tick off where the money will come from. Part of the total, some $823 million, was spent last year, and another $2.5 billion or so is in annual budgets through 1986. A large chunk is in hand in Iacocca's $900 million cash kitty. And he is counting on generating the rest from profits and cash flow over the next four years. It is not a scenario that can withstand unpleasant surprises. Says Alan Webber, a former transportation-department aide who is now a senior research associate at Harvard: "One false step and they are off the tightrope."

To sell the new models, Iacocca has greatly strengthened another weak link: Chrysler's dealer base. After losing about 1,000 outlets out of 4,800 during 1979 and 1980, he succeeded in signing up roughly 300 new showrooms last year alone. Equally important, more of the dealers are making a profit: 80% in 1982, in contrast to only 52% in 1980.

Over the long run, and in that big battle for the international market, Chrysler will need help from other automakers to survive. Iacocca talks of plans for a new corporate entity he calls Global Motors. Rather than a megacorporation formed from actual mergers between car companies in different parts of the world, he envisions a setup in which Chrysler would undertake joint ventures with foreign manufacturers to get economies of scale or low-cost labor or design or technological expertise. The combines he talks about do not sound so different from the one GM and Toyota announced last month, a collaboration in California on the manufacture of a subcompact car. However, Iacocca rails against that one because GM and Toyota are so enormous and powerful already.

Back in the 1970s, Chrysler was moving in that new direction. It acquired 15% of Mitsubishi in 1971 and 15% of France's Peugeot in 1978. The ideal combination, says Iacocca, would be a top

Japanese producer at the low end, a high-tech European company for the luxury segment and an American company for the middle of the market. As Iacocca sees it, "That would be Mitsubishi, Peugeot and Chrysler or maybe Nissan, Volkswagen and Chrysler."

If Iacocca worries much about Chrysler's survival these days, he shows little sign of it in public. He delights in twitting skeptics who doubt Chrysler's recovery. And in giving Government officials, including President Reagan, advice about how to manage the economy. Reagan appears to like it; hoping to get some ideas for his speech, he invited Iacocca to a small dinner at the White House nine days before the State of the Union message. Not long after that, Iacocca spent a few hours hobnobbing with the President at Chrysler's St. Louis assembly plant.

For several years, Iacocca has been lobbying for a 25¢-per-gal. increase in the federal gasoline tax. Most proponents of the idea see it as a way to discourage consumption, but Iacocca knows it would help Chrysler sell its new cars, which have been designed to go farther on less gas than their U. S. competitors. Chrysler's fleet averages 27.5 m.p.g., vs. 24.3 for Ford and 24.1 for GM. If falling oil prices spur a demand for old-fashioned big cars, Chrysler will hurt the worst. Says Iacocca: "What's happening with gasoline is wacko. It's crazy. We needed to slap at least a quarter on the pump so that people didn't get into dirty habits and start buying those rear-wheel-drive New Yorkers like they were going out of style."

For all the outspoken rhetoric, Iacocca is basically a shy, even awkward man. Says J. Paul Bergmoser, a friend from Ford days who served as Chrysler's president for 20 months: "Believe it or not, he doesn't like to walk into a room alone. At parties, he is not for giving all the women a kiss, the way some people do." While Iacocca is often seen in public with the likes of Sinatra, Singer Vic Damone and Yankees Owner George Steinbrenner, he seems most comfortable in the company of his own family.

Iacocca has forsaken the much publicized $1-a-year salary that he drew temporarily while steering the loan guarantee through Congress; last year he earned $365,676. His Chrysler stock is worth only $16,625, but he has stock options that would net him $4.9 million pretax if he exercised them. His enjoyment of the trappings of the corporate life has prompted his enemies at Ford to dub him "the Queen of Sheba." In 1981, the Government Loan Guarantee Board ordered Chrysler to give up its corporate jets, including Iacocca's favored Gulfsteam II, to save money. Iacocca stalled until he was caught red-handed: Treasury Secretary Donald Regan saw a newspaper picture of him sitting in the New York Yankees dugout in Florida during spring training and figured that he had not gone there in a Plymouth sub-compact. Chrysler now leases a jet, but Iacocca is irked that he must obtain the permission of the Loan Guarantee Board every time he wants to travel in it.

So far, neither the Treasury nor the taxpayers have lost or lent a cent in connection with the loan guarantee. Indeed, the Government actually nets about $11 million a year from payments Chrysler is required to make. (The money borrowed under the guarantee was raised in the public markets.) All the loans come due in 1990; Chrysler may be strong enough to repay some of them this year.

But Chrysler's long-term survival remains shaky. After giving up $965 million in wage increases and paid holidays, its 65,000 U.A.W. workers make $2 an hour less than industry counterparts, and they hope to make up the difference when their contract expires in January 1984. They could have a powerful ally then in Douglas Fraser, who retires as president of the U.A.W. in May but will stay on the Chrysler board, where he has been since 1980. Chrysler owes the union pension fund $477 million, and has an overhang of $2 billion in unfunded pension liabilities.

For a long time, people did not believe Iacocca when he declared that Chrysler was just the leading edge of the problems of the U. S. auto industry. Now they do. Despite the gains that U. S. automakers have made, their higher labor and manufacturing costs still give Japan a $1,000-per-vehicle advantage. When currency and tax differences are figured in, the Japanese advantage is closer to $2,000. Even if import restrictions are kept next year, as they are likely to be, U. S. automakers still face an uphill battle.

Iacocca insists he has no plans to quit, observing that he has seen too many contemporaries retire and then "die in six months." At the same time, he admits that he is tired. Having suffered rheumatic fever as a youth, he worries about his health and tends to tire easily. During the turmoil of congressional hearings in 1979, he nearly passed out in a Capitol Hill restaurant, though he makes light of the incident now. Says Mary Iacocca: "Lee's been through hell. He didn't realize how bad it was at Chrysler, or he would never have gone."

Taking a look back at his 37 years in the automobile business, Iacocca reflected not long ago: "I don't know what the hell I rushed for. It's a long race. I was trying to sprint all the time. Maybe if I had to do it again I'd slow down a little." The thought is so outlandish that not even Lee Iacocca can sell it.

BENDIX CAN ONLY PROFIT FROM ITS MARIETTA BID[9]

Bendix Corp Chairman William M. Agee appears to have positioned his Southfield (Mich.) company and its stockholders to profit in its takeover battle with Martin Marietta Corp., almost without regard to the outcome. And prolonging the fight may even sweeten the pot.

Agee, an executive who see himself as a wily financier, has attempted to structure his acquisition attempt to guarantee a return for Bendix stockholders whether the bid succeeds or is dropped and whether Marietta lines up a "white knight" or manages to make good on its attempt to acquire Bendix as a defensive move. Concedes a former colleague who is skeptical of the chairman's tactics: "This is a no-loss situation for Bill Agee."

Bendix announced a tender offer on Aug. 25 to buy 15.8 million shares, or 44.5%, of Marietta, a diversified aerospace compa-

[9]Reprint of an article by the staff of *Business Week*. p. 37+. S 13, '82. Reprinted from the September 13, 1982 issue of *Business Week* by permission. Copyright © 1982 by McGraw-Hill, Inc. All rights reserved.

ny based in Bethesda, Md., at $43 a share. That prompted a counterbid the following week by Marietta to buy 11.9 million shares, or 50.3%, of Bendix at $75. Agee declined to up the ante, but he urged Marietta to meet with Bendix management to "negotiate any and all terms" in the original Bendix offer. Most analysts say Marietta now has little chance of emerging from the fray unscathed. "Marietta is gone," says one Wall Street arbitrageur. "Enough attention has shone on it to show that it is a very attractive company, and very vulnerable."

If Agee's bid is successful, Bendix will acquire a $3.3 billion company with heavy ties to the defense industry. Marietta's aerospace operations, which produced most of the company's first-half earnings of $56 million, would mesh well with Bendix's own Aerospace-Electronics Group. And if Agee sticks to his often professed plan to move Bendix toward higher-technology businesses (BW—Apr. 24, 1981), he would also sell off Marietta's ailing chemical, cement, aluminum, and aggregates businesses as soon as he could do so profitably. Marietta has argued that Bendix's bid is too low because it has invested more than $1.7 billion in nonaerospace operations over the past five years.

But Bendix stands to make at least $30 million even if Marietta finds another buyer. The profit would come from the 1.6 million shares of Marietta that Bendix bought at about $24 a share before announcing its tender offer in August. And Bendix could earn almost as much even if it and Marietta should agree to drop both of their bids, since heavy trading by Wall Street arbitrageurs pushed Marietta stock by Sept. 1 to nearly $40 a share, two-thirds higher than a month earlier.

Bendix shareholders would do well even if Marietta's defensive bid to acquire Bendix proves successful. Initial skirmishing sent Bendix stock up from about $48 in early August to $56 by the end of the month—but still well below Marietta's $75 offer. Some Wall Street analysts interpreted the movements in both stocks as indicating that arbitrageurs were playing both sides but were lending more credence to the Bendix offer than to Marietta's.

Marietta, meanwhile, attempted to bolster its defense against Bendix with a $100 million suit filed in Maryland federal district court. The complaint charges Bendix with "selectively leaking" its bid plans, thus pushing Marietta stock prices up and shifting big blocks of its stock into the hands of speculators whose only interest is in selling out to the highest bidder.

IV. INDUSTRY AND THE SOCIETY OF THE FUTURE

EDITOR'S INTRODUCTION

Somber assessments of the present state of American industry have become commonplace, but what about the future for U.S. manufactured goods? Those who believe that the struggle for dominance in the world market for automobiles and small appliances has already been irretrievably lost to the Japanese often predict that American innovations in the field of "high technology" will rescue the economy and usher in another era of prosperity. Americans take justifiable pride in their technological achievements but unfortunately it has been these very innovations that have undermined U.S. industrial pre-eminence by making it possible for countries with predominantly agricultural economies to take low-paid workers from fields to factories where they now assemble electrical components. The United States, which once produced almost all televisions and radios, now produces almost none.

Although the U.S. leads the world in computer technology there are signs that the Japanese are poised to enter the market for semi-conductors, suggesting that history could repeat itself. How hopeful, then, is the future of high-tech industry? Robert Jastrow, writing in *Science Digest,* takes a strongly optimistic view, not only of this sector of manufacturing, but also of the state of the economy in general. Challenging several popular assumptions he asserts that American labor is not prohibitively expensive, that the U.S. does spend enough on research and development, and that government regulation has not crippled business. Our current troubles, he concludes, are merely "a natural interlude between two great waves of economic growth," and that the U.S. has a "secret weapon" to use in industrial competition—its entrepreneurs. The following article from *Newsweek* takes a less sanguine view, pointing out that high-tech industries alone cannot solve the problems of high unemployment.

Declining productivity and revenues have put many Americans out of work and forced others who have retained their jobs to adopt new attitudes and work habits. According to a *Business Week* report on labor and management, economic hardship has had a beneficial effect in companies that have adopted more flexible work procedures and involved workers in decisions that were formerly imposed by management. Martin Morf's article from *The Futurist* asks what work will be like in an economy controlled by a technological elite. He concludes that "the future may bring more work than most people think," largely because an army of service workers will be needed to do the tasks that the elite are too busy, or too sophisticated, to perform.

The last two articles in this section concern the role of industry in encouraging social change. President Reagan, while cutting federal subsidies to community projects, has exhorted private enterprise to take up the government's role. To promote such efforts two congressmen have sponsored "free enterprise zones." Harvey Shapiro's article from *New York* magazine assesses the chances of the success of such a zone in the South Bronx, that perennial symbol of urban blight. Writing from the standpoint of the business community, William Frederick, in an article from *California Management Review*, points out that Reagan's efforts to "get government off the backs" of business suggest that corporations will slacken their efforts to assist the public with philanthropy. Although the number of corporations actively involved in public policy is still very small, Frederick hopes that more and more business people are realizing that a commitment to improving the quality of life is not necessarily inimical to the primary need to make a profit. The public interest, he suggests, is also the corporate interest.

SCIENCE AND THE AMERICAN DREAM[1]

The most striking fact about the American economy is that it stopped growing a few years ago. Many economists are pessimistic about this development, and see it as the product of permanent weaknesses in American society. Depending on their point of view, they find the cause of the trouble to be that we spend too much on welfare (or too little); too much on defense (or too little); and government is too big (or too small). There is a general feeling that American labor costs are too high, capital investment is too low, and business hasn't been spending enough in recent years.

A look at the facts has convinced me the opposite is true. We're at the beginning of the biggest boom in American history—a period of unparalleled prosperity and economic growth. The reasons have a great deal to do with science and its first cousins, research and development.

Much of my work in science up to this point has been concerned with the cosmic mysteries: What is man's nature? How did he arrive on this planet? What is his relationship to the universe? Scientists have discovered very interesting answers to these questions. But there is another side to science just as interesting, and more practical. This is the ability of the scientist to create wealth by enhancing the productivity of human labor. The wealth created by science is real, just as real as gold taken out of the ground. If scientific experiments create new materials—strong, lightweight, easily worked—so that a worker can assemble two cars in a day instead of one, wealth has been created. The extra car is available for use by another person; it adds to his happiness and satisfaction, raises the standard of living by a small amount, and slightly increases the Gross National Product (the total value of all goods and services produced by a nation).

More important, it increases the Gross National Product per worker, the essence of what economists call *productivity*. Produc-

[1]Reprint of an article by the author Robert Jastrow, Professor of Earth Science at Dartmouth College and founder of NASA's Goddard Institute for Space Studies. *Science Digest* 91:46–8, Mr '83. Copyright © 1983 by Robert Jastrow. Reprinted by permission.

tivity is the key to the wealth of an industrialized nation like America. Arab wealth comes out of the ground and can run dry. American wealth comes out of the brains of people, and it is potentially inexhaustible.

Productivity is a magic word. It sounds like a dry term in economics, but it should conjure up visions of rubies, gold and diamonds. A country with a low productivity means a nation with open sewers, unpaved roads, barefoot children, hunger and misery. A country with a high productivity means a land of well-fed people with cars, homes, schools and a high standard of living. If the productivity of a country goes up steadily, more material wealth is available each year to be divided among its citizens, and life gets better all the time. People in such a country develop an optimistic view of life. That is the kind of world into which most Americans were born. It is the kind of world into which we like to bring our children.

Now we come to a disturbing fact: American productivity, after rising at a good average clip for many years, began to level off about 10 years ago, and in the last few years it has not grown at all on the average. But while America's productivity has increased very little in recent years, the productivity of certain other nations has been increasing at an extraordinary rate. In 1950, Japanese workers were one-sixth as productive as American workers, and Germans were one-half as productive as we were. Today, both nations have nearly caught up to the United States.

If we were alone on the planet, our zero growth in productivity would mean a constant—and relatively high—standard of living for Americans. In the real world, other nations exist and compete with us for business—especially Japan and Germany. When Japanese and German productivity goes up sharply compared with ours, the price of Japanese and German goods goes down, and these countries take away our customers. That is precisely what happened. The nations of the world are buying fewer American products because the price is better elsewhere.

When America loses customers for its goods, American plants close down, the GNP drops and unemployment rises. In the auto industry—the most famous case—imports captured 30 percent of the market in 1982. More than 250,000 auto workers have been laid off, largely as a result of Japanese competition.

Several million jobs have left America in the past 10 years as a result of business taken away by foreign nations.

Industrial productivity depends on technical innovations, engineering and general know-how—areas in which American prowess has been unchallenged. How is it possible that American productivity leveled off in the last 10 years, while the productivity of Japan and Germany increased rapidly? What happened? The experts have given many answers. They all sound convincing, but when I began to look into the situation I found that none passes the test of a comparison with the facts. Here are some frequently heard opinions on the causes of our decline, and the data that test their validity.

American labor has priced itself out of the market. The Japanese have captured our market with cheap labor.

True once but no longer. Japanese wages were pennies an hour in 1950, but factory wages in Japan are now about $10 an hour, nearly the same as in America. Steel and automobile workers in America make more than their counterparts in Japan but that is not true for industry across the board for the two countries.

We spend too much on social welfare, on defense, on government as a whole; the tax burden is oppressive.

The United States spends a smaller fraction of its GNP on social welfare than do its leading industrial competitors, Japan and West Germany. This item is surely not the main brake on American productivity.

And although we spend considerably more on defense than Japan and somewhat more than Germany, during the 1970s defense costs averaged only 5.5 percent of the American GNP—significant, but not large enough to slow down the whole economy.

In general, the United States spends approximately the same fraction of its GNP on government as Japan does—about 30 percent—and a considerably smaller fraction of GNP than West Germany spends.

Federal deficits are excessive; the federal debt has zoomed to astronomical levels.

Deficits in the federal budgets of our main competitors, Japan and Germany, are far greater than ours—three to four times larger as a fraction of GNP in recent years.

The federal debt in the United States has increased only 20 percent since 1954, when corrected for inflation. The astronomical zoom reflects inflated dollars.

Antipollution laws have increased the cost of doing business in America.

True, but no more so than in Japan, and less in some cases. In the steel industry, for example, although Japanese steel manufacturers spent nearly twice as much as we did on pollution control in the 1970s—$3.6 billion versus $1.9 billion between 1971 and 1977—they still had lower prices, and took away much of our market. In the automobile industry, Japanese restrictions on the emission of pollutants in automobile exhausts are far more stringent than the limits set by our own government, yet Japanese auto manufacturing costs are far lower.

American industry is not spending enough on R&D.

U.S. expenditures on industrial R&D are considerably higher than in Japan, as a fraction of GNP. The fraction of scientists and engineers engaged in R&D in industry is also higher. Furthermore, U.S. spending on industrial R&D increased throughout most of the '70s, during the period in which our economic growth was slowing down. This factor cannot explain the poor performance of the U.S. economy in the past decade.

The United States is not training enough engineers.

True; in recent years the Japanese have been turning out twice as many engineers as America in proportion to population. That growing pool of bright young engineers is a time bomb for America. Still, at the moment we lead the world in the number of scientists and engineers engaged in R&D in proportion to the size of the labor force, and we have done so throughout the recent period of slow economic growth in the United States.

Investment in plant and equipment is inadequate.

Total capital investment as a fraction of GNP is low in the United States compared with other countries. However, in the manufacturing industries—such as steel, autos, machine tools—investment in machinery and equipment increased nearly 40 percent as a fraction of total production between 1960 and 1978, just when industrial productivity growth was declining. Many economists favor this explanation, but it cannot be a major factor.

Business gets more help from the government in Japan than in the United States.

Differences between Japan and America in this respect are not as great as generally believed. U.S. government purchases of semiconductors, computers and aircraft for the defense and space agencies in the 1950s and 1960s nurtured the great growth industries in computing, semiconductors and aircraft, when they were weak and struggling, by paying a large part of their R&D costs and buying up most of their products. Between 1955 and 1967 the government bought 57 percent of all computers made in the United States, 40 percent of all semiconductors, and more than half of all aircraft. In America, as in Japan, these hi-tech industries prospered because of government support.

There is the puzzle: each explanation for our ailing productivity has its proponents, but none fits the facts. Yet the ailment is real; the economy is stagnating. What is killing our productivity? If we could identify the villain, we could cast him out.

I believe the System Dynamics Group at MIT, and a few scattered economists and business experts, have hit on the answer. There is no villain. The trauma we are passing through now is not a depression, but a natural interlude between two great waves of economic growth. American industry is shedding its skin, casting off old technologies and developing new ones. But the new skin has not yet hardened. Industries based on the new technologies—mainly computers and microelectronics but also robots, fiber optics, long-distance communications, biotechnology, and exotic new materials—are still young. They have not yet developed to the point where they can take up the slack in employment and industrial output created by the decline of the aging enterprises—the smokestack industries of steel, chemicals, autos, and so on.

Double Wallop

The potential for growth in the new hi-tech industries is mindboggling in terms of new jobs and new wealth. The computing industry alone is expected to grow from its current $50 bilion to at least $100 billion a year in 1986, making it the biggest business in America. The market in long-distance communications is about

$50 billion and growing at the rate of 18 percent a year. Robots, another major new industry, pack a double wallop. Not only do they increase industrial productivity, but the construction of robots itself is showing phenomenal growth, from $200 million in 1980 to a projected $2 billion in 1985.

Fiber optics is another rapidly growing technology. These light-pipes, made from glass fibers the thickness of a horsehair, can carry voices and data in a stream of tiny laser pulses at the rate of millions of pulses a second. AT&T plans to use a message-carrying light-pipe in a telephone cable between Boston and Richmond. The new cable would have taken 2 million pounds of copper with the old-fashioned wire technology.

There is little question that growth in the hi-tech industries will more than make up for the decline in the smokestack industries. Projected growth of $50 billion in the computing industry alone in the next four years is enough to offset the combined losses in the shrinking steel and auto industries. And new jobs go with the growth—easily sufficient to replace the jobs lost in the smokestack industries. Hewlett-Packard, one of the medium-size hi-tech companies, employs 57,000 people, Xerox more than 100,000. Two more Hewlett-Packards and a Xerox in the 1980s will make up for all the jobs lost in the auto industry.

Other countries will vie with us for a share in the wealth generated by the new technologies. Japan is the most formidable competitor. That nation graduated 87,000 engineers in 1980, compared with 63,000 in the United States, and is rapidly closing the gap in total numbers of scientists and engineers engaged in R&D in industry. The Japanese built their initial successes on technology borrowed from the United States, as we once borrowed our technology from Europe. Now, still following in our tracks, they are working very hard to acquire their own base of innovative research in semiconductors, computing, robotics, fiber optics, super-plastics and biotechnology.

I would bet my money on America in this competition. The Japanese have the advantages of long-range planning and very productive management of people. But their industrial organization tends to stifle initiative, especially youthful initiative. "The nail that stands up gets hammered down," says a Japanese proverb. Conformity and respect for elders are highly valued traits in Japan.

We Americans have the advantages of an open society and an upward mobility that gives free rein to the innovativeness and entrepreneurial energy of human beings. This is what counts most of all—human capital, and a society in which it is utilized to its maximum potential.

A small army of inventors and entrepreneurs is America's greatest asset. New businesses spring up like mushrooms; half a million were formed last year. Three out of 4 will fail in 5 years. The survivors are the great men of America. They create jobs, wealth, a bigger GNP, and a higher standard of living for everyone.

The business firms that make up the *Fortune* 500—mature firms like GE, DuPont and IBM—created essentially no new jobs from 1969 to 1976. Young, hi-tech companies like Digital Equipment and Data General, founded by inventors and entrepreneurs, generated new jobs at the astonishing rate of 40 percent a year in the same time period. The inventors and entrepreneurs also generate wealth.

In 1968, two engineers borrowed $2.5 million and formed Intel Corporation to manufacture semiconductors. Today, Intel's revenues are heading for a billion dollars a year. A billion dollars a year out of a few million! Where did that money come from? It didn't come out of the ground, but out of the brains and entrepreneurial energies of those men.

Another story, one of many. Kenneth Olsen, 31-year-old engineer, started Digital Equipment Corporation in 1956 in an abandoned textile mill. Today, Digital Equipment revenues are approximately $4 billion—a nice addition to the GNP. Still another example: the Xerox machine was invented by Chester Carlson, working in a little room behind a beauty parlor in Flushing, New York. Xerox revenues were $8.7 billion last year. Other examples abound. The list of modern innovations created by the solitary American inventor is impressive; not only Xerox but also the FM radio, Kodachrome, Polaroid, ballpoint pens, the zipper, cellophane, Bakelite and many others.

Why does the system work so well in America? Part of the answer is entrepreneurial zeal, fanned by the promise of huge profits. Nolan Bushnell started Atari on $500 and sold the business for $30 million. Part is the creative satisfaction to the inventor in seeing his brain-child make its way to the marketplace.

But creativity and the desire for wealth are found in other nations. The big difference in America is venture capital—money available to be invested at great risk in the testing of a crazy idea. The Japanese are our peers in technology and our superiors in education and industrial organization, but they lack venture capital and a system that could exploit it if it were available. Accordingly, they lack the army of entrepreneurial inventors that created America. The Japanese system funds innovations through the government and big business. It has no way of funding entrepreneurs and therefore it has none.

Capital Gains

The United States is awash in venture capital, thanks to a change in the tax laws in 1978 that lowered the tax on capital gains. Venture capital, which had been at the level of about a quarter of a billion dollars in previous years, doubled after the change in the capital gains tax, and then trebled and doubled again, reaching an extimated $6 billion in 1982. Venture capital, and the entrepreneurs it funds, are the secret weapon of America in the coming competition with Japan. The Japanese are aware of their weaknesses in this area, but they may not be able to do much about them, because the American way would go against the grain of their whole society. That is why I am betting on America.

HIGH HOPES FOR HIGH TECH[2]

Almost 300 leaders of America's high-technology companies gathered in Washington last week for two days of speeches, cheerleading and political lobbying. They came to discuss trade and tax policies more favorable to high-tech industries. But even as they buttonholed Reagan administration officials and Congress, the high-tech executives found themselves courted in turn by politicians who hoped the businessmen would create badly needed jobs for their constituents back home. Said Missouri Gov. Christopher Bond, serving as host at a cocktail party at the Shoreham Hotel: "Consider Missouri for your next high-tech profit center."

Among politicians, the term "high-tech" has become a kind of talisman. Mayors from Ft. Wayne, Ind., to San Antonio, Texas, are touting high tech as economic salvation. Michigan has pledged millions to make itself the robotics capital of the nation, and more than 30 states have established programs to lure these jobs. It seems like everyone wants to replicate the phenomenal success of California's Silicon Valley, or Route 128 outside Boston. "We're the Brooke Shields of the economy," says Howard Foley, chief lobbyist for the Massachusetts High Technology Council.

High tech's political appeal is understandable. Smokestack America is suffering. The steel, auto, glass and rubber industries limp along at half speed. In U.S. oilfields, falling crude prices have killed off the drilling boom of two years ago, leaving thousands of workers unemployed and about 2,000 rigs idle. Almost alone among major companies, high-technology concerns have survived relatively unscathed, raising hopes that it will usher in an age of economic prosperity. "As surely as America's pioneer spirit made us the industrial giant of the 20th century," Ronald Reagan declared in his State of the Union speech, "the same pioneer spirit of today is opening up another vast frontier of opportunity—the frontier of high technology."

[2]Reprint of an article by *Newsweek* reporters. *Newsweek* 101:61–2. F 14 '83. Copyright © 1983, by Newsweek, Inc. All rights reserved. Reprinted by permission.

The role of high-technology industries is at the center of a debate over future American industrial and economic policies. The so-called Atari Democrats—Sen. Bill Bradley and Reps. Richard Gephardt and Timothy Wirth, among others—are preaching economic salvation through high technology. But organized labor has been notably cool: "Those who urge us to concentrate on expanding high tech as a solution to our employment problems are barking up the wrong tree," says Howard Samuel, president of the AFL-CIO's Industrial Union Department.

But the country's fundamental shift away from heavy industries seems irreversible. High-technology industries—the semiconductor and computer manufacturers, telecommunications, robotics, aero-space, biotechnology firms and others—are the new frontier. Companies like Apple computer, born in a Palo Alto garage six years ago, have enjoyed meteoric growth, last year Apple reached $583 million in sales, and chairman Steve Jobs likes to boast that Apple's success has made about 300 employees millionaires. At the same time that Silicon Valley entrepreneurs have been getting rich, high-technology firms have had a big impact on the American economy: the more than $100 billion electronics industry, for instance, has been growing twice as fast as the economy as a whole, and in the past two years high-tech industries have run up a trade surplus of more than $60 billion.

Nonetheless, high-tech industries account for only a small portion of the overall economy—and can't singlehandedly lift the economy out of recession. "High technology is only the ninth largest industry," says John Young, president of Hewlett-Packard, one of the nation's premier high-technology companies. "If the eight above are sick, it obviously isn't going to offset the aggregate of all of them. It isn't magic." Moreover, there may never be enough high-tech firms to go around: some of the states now bidding to become high-tech centers are sure to be disappointed. "High tech isn't going to save the country," says Carnegie-Mellon University provost of science and technology Dan Berg, a former Westinghouse executive. "It's not going to take the 11 million unemployed now and give them new jobs in a year to two or even three. To wave a magic wand and say, 'High tech is our savior,' to an unemployed guy in Detroit is absurd."

High tech itself has other concerns, however: the threat of competition from Japan and Europe, and U.S. tax, trade and education policies. Last week Control Data chairman William C. Norris urged drastic action to protect American companies from the fierce competition they are now encountering from Japan, and he called for a ban preventing Japanese from studying in U.S. universities and research labs. "The first thing the government ought to do is shut them off—exclude them from the research labs," Norris said. But industry executives did not present a united front: David Packard, the co-founder of Hewlett-Packard, argued that the United States should work to lower trade barriers that now block U.S. exports to Japan.

Closer to home, high-tech executives urged changes in the current tax laws. Under the Reagan tax bill passed in 1981 high-tech industries wound up paying higher taxes while capital-intensive smokestack industries had their tax bills slashed. "We're really taxing the winners and subsidizing the losers," says John Albertine, the president of the American Business Conference, an industry group that represents many fast-growing, high-tech firms. Besides wanting more favorable tax laws, there is strong sentiment throughout high-tech industries to strengthen the U.S. educational system, beef up basic research-and-development funding—and prevent a crippling shortage of engineers and scientists in the late 1980s and 1990s. "In social terms it's unfortunate, but the kind of people we will need are not unemployed steelworkers," says Bill Wulf, president of Tartan Laboratories in Pittsburgh. "We're really talking more about the well-being of our children than (about) today's steelworkers."

In the meantime, there is some fear that the current political enthusiasm for high technology may endanger the industry's entrepreneurial independence. "We need to target the entrepreneurial process," says Don Gevirtz, chairman of The Foothill Group, a Los Angeles venture-capital firm, "and not any particular product, company or industry." Nolan Bushnell, who invented the video-game industry and founded Atari, is reportedly fond of telling friends that the "Atari Democrats" would never have targeted Atari because of its initial obscurity. Nor would a bureaucrat have found much promise in Apple Computer, when Steve Wozniak and Steve Jobs were hand-soldering circuit boards in a Palo Alto garage years ago.

A WORK REVOLUTION IN U.S. INDUSTRY[3]

A revolution in the way workers do their jobs is beginning to take hold throughout America's basic industries. Changes in work rules are moving the workplace away from rigid labor practices created by authoritarian management and institutionalized by narrowly focused unions. Instead, a more flexible structure is evolving that can adapt to advanced technology, provide new products at a competitive cost, and release the nation from the stranglehold of stagnant productivity. The movement is in its infancy, but the impact of international competition and deregulation is accelerating the trend.

Industrial America grew up and prospered with a work system that is rapidly becoming obsolete. At its foundation is "functional specialization"—pegging workers into narrowly defined jobs that required "arms and hands but no brainwork," as one steelworker puts it. The system also created a chasm between manager and worker that stymied cooperation and, in union settings, became a battleground between labor and management over contractual "rights."

Work rules are simply regulations that labor and management have set up to govern the workplace. And they have become restrictive largely because the system has, too. Now the recession—coupled with the declining ability of U.S. basic industries to compete in world markets—has given companies and unions a strong incentive to change these practices. "You can go back to almost any recession and find examples of unionized companies more aggressively going after work rules," says Thomas A. Kochan, a professor at Massachusetts Institute of Technology. "But you have to go back to the Depression to find as much of it as is going on now."

[3]Reprint of an article by the staff of *Business Week*. p. 100–110. M. 16, '83. Reprinted from the May 16, 1983 issue of *Business Week* by special permission. Copyright © 1983 by McGraw-Hill, Inc. All rights reserved.

Over the past two years airlines have persuaded their pilots to fly more hours for the same pay. Trucking companies have won the right to pay drivers on the basis of hours worked rather than by traditional, but outmoded, mileage formulas. Auto, rubber, and steel companies and oil refiners have overcome strong worker resistance—and what one oil executive calls "flat-out poor management"—to combine skilled maintenance trades such as millwright, welder, and boilermaker. In plants and offices—unionized and nonunion alike—work teams that increase productivity as well as job satisfaction are replacing the old, narrow production jobs.

The immediate payoff is improved productivity that will enable companies to make a profit at lower operating rates and compete more effectively in world markets. Changes in the rubber industry could boost productivity by at least 10%, says William K. Rusak, vice-president for labor relations at Firestone Tire & Rubber Co.'s World Tire Group. Oil refiners say work-rule changes have increased their output per worker by 10% to 15%. Jones & Laughlin Steel Corp. (J&L) has cut the man-hours required to make a ton of steel to three and a half, from six only five years ago.

Unions are not accepting all changes willingly. Several locals of the Oil, Chemical & Atomic Workers (OCAW) have mounted long and futile strikes against them in the oil industry. Lewie G. Anderson, vice-president in charge of meatpacking operations for the United Food & Commercial Workers, says that "if workers are kicked around at the work station, managers are making a grave mistake. They will breed and cultivate a militant work force."

Unlike many of the widely publicized wage concessions unions have made since 1980, however, "these changes appear permanent," says H.J. McClain, an OCAW official in Houston. Indeed, industries that have been deregulated, including airlines, railroads, and trucking—plus industries such as steel, autos, and rubber that have stiff foreign competition—may be forced to hold down costs for years.

Existing work rules reflect an industrial setting created a century ago. In the 1890s, Sidney and Beatrice Webb, British socialists and labor theorists, observed that early unions insisted on applying a "common rule" to groups of workers, in efforts to reduce competition over wages and working conditions. The early unions also wanted to restrict the numbers of workers in their trades—a practice that some building trades in the U.S. still try to maintain.

But the structure of work itself, especially in manufacturing, derives largely from the influence of such early 20th-century industrial engineers as Frederick W. Taylor, who used "scientific management" principles to organize work. Taylor advocated breaking down jobs into their simplest functions, to give employers maximun control over workers—mostly immigrants at the time. Most managements embraced job specialization, and eventually even organized labor accepted it. But people in both camps now disparge "Taylorism." "With scientific management," says Sam Camens, assistant to the president of the United Steelworkers, "the employer says to the worker, 'This is the only thing you're supposed to do. That's all we're going to train you for, and that's all we're going to pay you for.' There's no question it's all outdated."

Clark Kerr, president emeritus of the University of California and a labor economist, says the Webbs' common rule and scientific management merged into one concept that has dominated industrial life for most of this century. "Employers liked it because it simplified job assignments, and unions liked it because they could write down what the rules were and enforce them," Kerr says. "Now, with faster-changing technology and products changing quickly, that century of the common rule just doesn't fit any more."

Workers are better-educated and want more challenging jobs. Moreover, when industrial unions organized the mass-production industries in the 1930s, they demanded rules to turn job specialization to the workers' advantage. They won seniority rules to govern layoffs and promotions, "past-practice" provisions to make it harder for companies to expand jobs and reduce crews arbitrarily, and grievance procedures to protest management decisions.

The result was a "highly stylized system" that became the "dominant paradigm" for all U.S. industry, says Michael J. Piore, an economist at MIT. American labor's method of exercising job control is less accommodating to changing technology than the more flexible systems in Japan and West Germany, where unions or worker representatives participate in shop-floor decisions and thus do not need elaborate rules to protect the workers.

During good times, unions saw no reason to change the system, and management ignored growing competitive pressures. "We became accustomed to a certain level of affluence that maybe clouded our judgment," says Charles V. Jones, director of labor relations at B.F. Goodrich Co. Adds Kenneth W. Monfort, president of Monfort of Colorado Inc., a meatpacker: "About half the work rules arise through negotiations, and half you slip into as a result of bad practices. Once you do something for a year, that becomes a work rule." And few companies want to risk strikes for small annual increases in productivity.

In the past two years, however, employers and unions alike have been forced to change. Employers in the basic and deregulated industries have become convinced, like Goodrich's Jones, that "we're in a period of transition from affluence." Companies are giving workers the same ultimatum that has resulted in wage concessions: change work rules or see the plant close. "There has to be a heightened perception of a threat—a closing, a move, whatever," says Gerald Glassman, a Newark (N.J.) labor lawyer who represents employers.

In some instances, unions have extracted trade-offs. Kaiser Aluminum & Chemical Corp. and J&L are granting early retirement and $400 monthly pension supplements to workers as young as 50 whose jobs are eliminated. In Mansfield, Ohio, the United Auto Workers accepted work-rule changes that eliminated 145 jobs at General Motors Corp. But because the UAW's contract says that such changes cannot result in layoffs, the company "donated" 52 workers for whom there was no other work in the plant to local social service agencies. In return for changes made in early 1982 at its machining and forge plant in New Castle, Ind., Chrysler Corp. gave the UAW a written promise that the plant would stay open through 1985. But elsewhere, unions have not won quid pro quos. "They've got the hammer right now," says James E. Horn, president of United Rubber Workers Local 26 in Cumberland, Md., which recently accepted changes at the Kelly-Springfield Tire Co. subsidiary of Goodyear Tire & Rubber.

There are two major types of work-rule changes: those that leave the existing organization of work intact (but make it more efficient) and those that change the system itself, such as teamwork. Most changes so far are in the first category. And perhaps the most important of these is the combining of duties and elimination of superfluous jobs.

Many employers have managed to staff new plants as efficiently as possible. But most unions have resisted efforts to make the same changes in existing plants. United Steelworkers locals, for example, can file grievances objecting to such changes for existing units, and to win such a case in arbitration the company must show that the "underlying circumstances"—the technology or equipment—have changed. Over the years, this has resulted in bloated work crews at some plants.

But now, "we have begun to say to unions—and this is not a pleasant kind of discourse—'We're talking about doing the same amount of work with fewer people or more work with the same people'" says Goodrich's Jones. At its aircraft components operation in Cleveland, TRW Inc. has gone from more than 200 job classifications to less than 100, says Howard V. Knicely, vice-president for human relations. In talks last year, Goodyear and Firestone persuaded the United Rubber Workers to negotiate new work rules on a local basis, without interference from the international union or other URW locals at the company. Goodyear Chairman Robert E. Mercer calls this change "more important than the economics of the agreement."

Skilled craftsmen are often the most resistant to work-rule changes, partly because they are the highest-paid factory workers and consider themselves an elite group. But at Goodyear's largest tire plant, in Gadsden, Ala., the 420 craftsmen agreed last year to work outside their crafts up to 25% of the time. This can mean big savings. The cross-utilization of tradesmen at the Chrysler plant in Indiana helps save $2.8 million a year, a reduction of 30% in costs.

Gulf Oil Corp. negotiated a "universal equipment clause" with the OCAW in January, 1982. "If carpenters are building a scaffold, the pipefitters won't sit around and wait," says Merlin Breaux, Gulf's vice-president for labor relations. "They help." The clause requires skilled workers to learn seven other jobs. Operators of processing units, who once only monitored the refining process, now do minor maintenance, such as hooking up small pipes. After American Petrofina merged six classifications into two at its refinery in Port Arthur, Tex., it cut the work force by 25%, saving $4 million a year

The trend toward combining jobs is closely related to another change in work practices—altering job assignments. One aspect of this is simply cutting the size of work crews. Companies are doing this throughout the steel industry by analyzing production needs and combining jobs. U. S. Steel Corp. and Inland Steel Co., for example, are reducing their forces largely on a unilateral basis. They have that right, but local USW unions are filing grievances against the changes, and many complain that the grievance systems are becoming overloaded. By contrast, GM negotiated with UAW Local 549 in Mansfield, Ohio, before eliminating jobs such as machinists' "tool chaser." Machinists must now get their own tools. The job cuts and other changes raised productivity in the stamping plant by 26%, says George M. Ferguson, chairman of the local, who says tool chasers sometimes worked only two hours a day.

The Massachusetts Bay Transportation Authority—Boston's transit system—has reduced its work force by 10%, or 700 employees, since the state legislature passed a Management Rights Act in 1980, giving the authority the right to redesign jobs regardless of union objections. The MBTA now farms out the cleaning of buses and subway cars; staffs trains with an operator and just one doorman, instead of two doormen; and has hired 300 part-time bus drivers to fill in during peak traffic periods. Despite what James F. O'Leary, the MBTA's general manager, calls "a lot of confrontation" with workers over the changes, they have produced savings of $50 million since October, 1981.

The International Brotherhood of Teamsters made significant concessions last year when it agreed that long-haul drivers can make at least one stop per trip to deliver freight directly to a customer rather than unloading at a terminal, where a short-haul driver might have to backtrack to make the delivery. Many local contracts also require drivers to do some loading and unloading, a job previously reserved for dock workers. These and other changes, says one industry negotiator, may be enough at some carriers to offset the cost of the current 37-month contract.

Companies are cutting costs by altering work hours, too. For example, Swift Independent Corp., a meatpacker, has eliminated one of two 15-minute rest periods during a seven-hour workday, and rest periods are also being eliminiated throughout the auto and steel industries. But a more important change is the new freedom employers are winning to schedule work.

Many union contracts formerly called for time-and-a-half or double-time pay for weekend work. In the 1982 round of bargaining, however, some tiremakers won the right to pay straight-time wages for weekend work, as long as it is part of their regular 40-hour workweek—a change that trucking and textile companies won as well.

Employers are also aiming at the costs associated with seniority provisions, which were originally negotiated to eliminate favoritism as an element in promotions and job assignments. FDL Foods Inc., a meatpacker, has done away with seniority as a consideration for promoting workers, a move that the United Food & Commercial Workers has been trying to reverse in negotiations for several months.

More typical is a new arrangement at Goodyear's Lincoln (Neb.) plant, which reduces by 30% the number of employees who can be affected if slack work or a layoff causes a senior employee to be bumped down to a different job. Such a movement normally caused a chain reaction throughout the plant's job structure. But now, a senior employee will have to go much further down the job ladder before he can bump another worker. The aim is to reduce turmoil in the plant. Firestone's Rusak recalls that in one plant, under the old seniority provisions, filling 10 jobs required 93 moves. Goodyear has said that it costs $1,800 to train an employee who has been bumped to do a different job.

In some cases work-rule negotiations are changing overtime and incentive pay and ensuring that workers are not overpaid for the work they do. For instance, supplements to the national trucking contract were amended last year to do away with provisions that, among other things, guaranteed eight hours' pay for a trip from Cincinnati to Cleveland. This was based on the time the trip had taken years ago, even though today it takes only about five hours. If a driver were dispatched beyond Cleveland, the contract required that he be paid extra for the additional distance he traveled. With the change, truckers are paid only for the time they spend driving.

In another change, Swift pays workers only for the job they are doing, even if it is just temporary. In the past, for example, if a beef boner was pushed into a lower-paying loading dock job because there was no work at his station, he was paid at the higher rate. Now he is paid the rate for the second job.

The rubber industry is beginning to make major changes in its incentive pay system. In many plants, rubber workers are paid according to a "piece-rate" system that bases wages, to some extent, on how much they produce. Traditionally, these incentives have been changed only if employers brought in new equipment or altered the structure of a job. But workers have learned to produce as much in six hours as they were expected to do in eight when the incentives were designed.

So Goodyear is moving toward flat pay scales at many of its plants. Frank R. Tully, vice-president for industrial relations, says another goal is to get workers to make higher-quality tires. "Ten years ago the company tried to put everything on piecework, and they'd sell anything they built," says Allen Smith, vice-president of the United Rubber Workers local at Goodyear's Topeka (Kan.) plant. "Now the trend has just reversed."

Predictably, the effect of such changes is creating morale problems for some workers. The Boston transit system law "is so bad that even in a right-to-work state like Tennessee, a similar law didn't pass," complains Richard C. Branson, an official of the Boston Carmen's Union. And James F. Hammersmith, chairman of UAW Local 211 in Defiance, Ohio, is furious at UAW Local 653 in Pontiac, Mich., which has allowed GM to combine a number of jobs into one classification, among other changes. Complains Hammersmith: "They stole work from us that cost us 200 jobs."

But Goodrich, J&L, and Kaiser have made major changes without alienating the rank and file. In recent years, J&L has asked USW locals to negotiate work-force reductions instead of mandating them. "Threatening the workers and acting unilaterally is not constructive labor relations," says John H. Kirkwood, J&L's vice-president for industrial relations.

In 1982, says Thomas C. Graham, the former president of J&L who recently moved to U. S. Steel Corp. as vice-chairman, J&L saved $75 million, largely through "people programs" involving work-force cuts and worker suggestions. In lengthy talks at J&L's Aliquippa (Pa.) Works, the two sides agreed on staffing levels that would prevail if Aliquippa were a new, modern plant instead of 73 years old. The local agreed to combine jobs for a cost saving of $16 million a year, in return for early pensions for about 500 workers and increased pay for those who remain.

Kaiser followed essentially the same approach in winning work-rule changes for 5,700 USW members that it says could save $100 million a year by 1985 if production rebounds to prerecession levels. The key at Kaiser was shop-floor meetings in each department in eight plants, in which the company's managers solicited the suggestions—and objections—of workers. "It works when they (employees) help make the decisions and understand why it's done," says Harry Mayfield, the union's top negotiator at Kaiser. He adds: "I'm hopeful that this same procedure will be used to keep things updated."

Some companies are now trying to recombine the jobs that were fragmented many decades ago. They are moving increasingly to flexible systems that emphasize teamwork and worker participation in shop-floor decision-making. Harry Katz, an auto industry expert at MIT's Sloan School of Management, says such structural changes are most likely to be institutionalized in companies like GM and Ford Motor Co., where the effort to streamline work rules "overlaps and interacts with worker participation programs."

In the steel industry, J&L and the USW have set up 80 labor-management participation teams (LMPTs) to give workers a voice in decisions. Kirkwood says the company has found "less need for rules in areas where we have LMPTs." He adds: "When you walk into a department where the teams exist, you don't hear people talking about protecting jurisdictions and filing grievances."

J&L's LMPTs are problem-solving groups—in contrast to production teams, which are also coming into increasing use. Typically, each person on a team learns all the jobs on a production unit, giving the team flexibility in adapting to product changes and new technology. Japan and West Germany have developed this potential by using team assembly. The concept of teamwork in modern industry was first tested in British coal mines in the 1950s.

In the U. S., teamwork was rare and confined to a few nonunion companies. Hewlett-Packard Co. scrapped the moving conveyor belt for assembling small products in the 1950s, feeling that it was "disrespectful" of the employees to set their production pace. HP formalized the team concept in the 1960s, and now most of the 50 product divisions, each with 500 to 2,000 people, are using teams.

But teamwork has spread slowly in unionized companies in the U. S., largely because of work rules that grew out of Taylorism and that prohibit workers from moving from job to job. Recently, unions such as the USW, UAW, and URW have moved away from the old insistence on rigid job classifications and are permiting "pay-for-knowledge" systems like the one at GM's Livonia (Mich.) plant. J&L has set up such a team in a Youngstown (Ohio) mill, Ford is experimenting with the concept, and some rubber companies have work teams in place. "I think pay-for-knowledge will ultimately do more to break down the burden of narrow classifications than anything else," says Peter J. Pestillo, Ford's vice-president for labor relations.

GM's Packard Electric Div., which produces components for GM cars and other products, may well be the leader in applying the work-team concept in a unionized setting. With the cooperation of Local 717 of the International Union of Electrical Workers (IUE), it now has some 2,000 employees at four Warren (Ohio) area plants involved in work teams. "Productivity has imporved substantially," says A. Lee Crawford, director of Warren assembly operations, "because people believe in what they're doing.

They care for each other, they're interested in job security and cost reduction, and they work smarter." Adds Robert L. Sutton, shop chairman of Local 717: "It's the wave of the future. We should look at our people not only as dues-paying members, but we should use their minds and expand their horizons."

The degree to which these changes will actually alter the face of industrial America depends on the willingness of labor and management to put aside the old days of fighting for control of the shop floor. This calls for a revolution in attitudes. "If the unions give up the kind of rule-setting that limits flexibility, management will have to let them in on decision-making," says MIT's Piore. Increasingly, the experiments with team-work and worker participation demonstrate that this is not only possible, but imperative if the U. S. is to compete in the world market.

EIGHT SCENARIOS FOR WORK IN THE FUTURE[4]

Item on the TV news: The city's new Industrial Training Center has been inaugurated. Bugles are blown, ribbons are cut. Unemployed assembly-line workers are ready to enroll in droves. "I'll be a welder," one of them says. "Nowadays you have to have a skill." An official beams into the camera and hints that Americans are finally learning from the Japanese and Europeans, who have a long tradition of training their blue-collar workers with care.

A few days later, the news features an expert on robotics. "Anyone now in a training program for welders is learning an obsolete set of skills," he says. "Robots can and will weld much faster and better than human operators."

Who is right? More generally, what will the world of work— Daniel Bell's "techno-economic structure" and Karl Marx's "sphere of necessity"—look like 10 or 20 years from now?

[4]Reprint of an article by Martin Morf, associate professor of psychology at the University of Windsor, Ontario, Canada. *The Futurist* 17:24–9. Je '83. Copyright © 1983, by World Future Society, Bethesda, MD 20814–5089. Reprinted with permission.

Several issues will shape the future world of work, including: the rate of growth of technology, the degree to which future technology can be operated by the average worker, the amount of work generated by the economy, the kind of work (challenging or routine) generated by the economy, the degree to which workers are rewarded, the fairness with which work is distributed, the amount of make-work invented by the politicians, and the amount of informal work generated by personal needs that cannot be met with money from paying jobs.

We don't know the exact direction these issues will take, but we can use assumptions about them to create scenarios of what work might be like in the future. Some of these issues are closely related. For example, if the technological growth rate remains high, the economy might generate fewer jobs. Similarly, if the economy generates fewer jobs, the need for politically inspired make-work projects should increase. Because these issues affect each other, they generate a relatively small and manageable set of scenarios. The future may bring not one, but a combination of the scenarios explored here.

More Technology, Less Work

Among the more widely accepted scenarios of the future of work are those based on the assumption that technology will continue to grow exponentially. It has often been said, mainly to soothe nervous workers in the increasingly automated manufacturing sector, that technology creates as many jobs as it abolishes. But neither the empirical evidence nor common sense suggests that this is the case at present.

Unemployment is up in part because technology reduces the need for the kind of work most people do, and it is hard to imagine that the typical American manager will eagerly invest scarce capital in new machinery that will not save money on wages and salaries. What can we expect if technology continues to progress and to reduce the number of available jobs?

Scenario 1: Extreme Taylorism. Shortening the workweek has been the dream of utopians for ages. Work, after all, constitutes Marx's enslaving and alienating "sphere of necessity." Ironically, the capitalist Americans have been more successful in reducing the necessity for work than the communist societies. In 1881, American engineer Frederick Taylor timed and analyzed the motions of workers in Pittsburgh's Midvale Steel Plant, starting a quest for "scientific management" and efficiency that was considered uniquely American until Europeans and Japanese caught on with a vengeance in the 1960s and 1970s.

Taylorism reduces work to machine-tending that requires little training and effort and that maximizes productivity. It has two faces. We see its ugly face when it serves as the tool of short-sighted employers who replace motivated, proud, and self-respecting craftsmen with docile human robots, ignoring social costs such as unemployment and unbearably monotonous work. We see its attractive face in the work of Taylor himself. He saw scientific management as the means to increase productivity while reducing effort—the means to have one's cake and eat it, too.

To those who see Taylor's scientific management from the optimistic perspective, the extreme Taylorism scenario looks like the road to salvation and universal contentedness. Increased productivity makes most work superfluous and brings the 10-hour work-week within reach. Everyone serves on the economic front a few hours each day and everyone is entitled to a living wage.

Workers are liberated by machines, computers, and robots and can work less and live more; they spend their free time in productive pursuits in their vegetable patches, pursuing a liberal education, fixing their cars, helping their kids with the homework, traveling, and so on.

This scenario thus assumes that technology is user-friendly and that the economy generates less work, which is considered a mildly annoying duty one has to perform to be eligible for funds that society provides to those who have done their share. A basic income is assured and there is no need for make-work projects or for informal underground work activities on the fringes of the formal economy. Work is evenly distributed since most people have no desire to do more than their share.

But there is one telling objection to a future of extreme Taylorism, as French author Simone Weil writes: "No one would accept to be a slave for two hours a day." Indeed, if we spent all but two hours each day in the comfortable "sphere of liberty," we might find it difficult to change gears and adopt the values of punctuality, reliability, and diligence demanded by work. The prospect of doing chores at all might incite us to revolution.

Perhaps a more workable option is the three-and-a-half-day work-week suggested by author James Martin. A system of work shifts lasting eight hours on three days and four hours on the fourth would allow continuous operation of factories and offices. This system could be both efficient and beneficial to our quality of life as consumers of services. Such a solution would exploit fully the large capital investment in the complex technology that may characterize the workplace of the future, and it would provide services around the clock.

Scenario 2: Feudal unions. The news that available work may melt away like butter in the hot pan of technology is not greeted with joy by those who see work, or at least job-holding, as a desirable activity. Less work, or fewer jobs, raises the question of how work can be distributed among the many who, for one reason or another, want to do it.

One way would be to rely on powerful unions. In a bitter struggle against often greedy and brutal employers over the past century, labor has acquired a certain control over much of the work that needs to be done. Union leaders sometimes see themselves as entitled to distribute work, i.e., to decide who will work and for whom. They are also prepared to defend their turf vigorously, not only against employers and their technology but also against the unorganized work force, against other unions, and against politicians who venture into make-work projects that could, even indirectly, reduce the need for unionized workers. Thus in one jurisdiction the members of the school janitors' union may not fasten loose and dangerous seats to the floor because only the members of the carpenters' union may use the sacred instrument called the "screwdriver."

In a scenario of even greater union power, some current problems worsen. One problem is the effect of uncontestable job security on work motivation. When some grumpy bureaucrat barks at you, you know that he knows that next to nothing can separate him from his job.

A second problem is runaway wage rates. In the past, unions used strikes and the threat of strikes often and vigorously to extract an ever-larger piece from the economic pie. Wages outran productivity, a development that has already materially contributed to the present weak competitive position of the United States. With ever greater union power, runaway wage rates may be unbearable.

A final problem is unemployed youth. Seniority rather than skill or merit determines who will work, and one prospect facing many workers is that they will not be employed in the future unless they have supported the right union faithfully for a long time. This work allotment system shuts out the young from the job market to such an extent that many of them restlessly roam the streets, creating new jobs for themselves as drug dealers, hustlers, pimps, prostitutes, and muggers.

Scenario 3: Underground work. The feudal union scenario is thus quite compatible with an "underground work" scenario in which ever-greater segments of the work force operate outside the formal economy. High wages, complex jurisdictional rules, expensive fringe benefits, and the iron law of seniority encourage managers to operate with the smallest possible number of employees. The result is higher unemployment. But union-management contracts are only one factor among several that force many workers out into the cold where they are left to their own devices.

Government regulations reduce participation in the formal economy, no matter how good the intentions may be. For example, unfair or confusing income tax laws and excessively costly labor legislation spur workers to operate outside them and reinforce the tendency of manager to invest more in technology and less in people.

The complexity of technology can also contribute to this problem. In this scenario, technology is so complex that it can only be operated and serviced by highly trained workers. The requirement of union membership for job-holding is reinforced by qualifications beyond the grasp of many. Furthermore, the economy generates challenging jobs; intrinsically desirable work, added to a secure income, makes the lucky minority of job-holders even more eager to hang on to their jobs and to keep others from encroaching on them. The privileged job-holders, or even job-owners, are separated by an uncrossable chasm from the jobless. The jobless, with no "legitimate" income and little help from government, must look elsewhere—join the underground economy—to support themselves.

Scenario 4: Work coupons. The salient shared characteristic of the feudal union and underground work scenarios is an uneven distribution of the scarce, but essential and possibly interesting, commodity called a job. Both are depressing scenarios, with a large section of the population left to its own devices, and both go against the grain of American egalitarianism.

However, an equitable means of distributing work could be devised. Just as food was a scarce and essential commodity in many countries during the two world wars, work could be the most sought-after commodity of the future. Governments proved to be ingenious in devising systems based on ration coupons to distribute food, usually with reasonable fairness. A future of rationed "work coupons" could assure a fair distribution of limited employment opportunities to unlimited numbers of citizens eager to seize them

More Technology, More Work

The scenarios sketched so far assume that more technology means less work. But even if technology expands, there may be more work in the future than many people think.

New products and new services tend to create new needs, which in turn require new effort. The dishwashing machine may fulfill a housewife's dream, but it creates new needs for special soaps, water softeners, plumbers' services, and so on.

Even more important is the tendency of service work to increase exponentially with the number of people in a group or society. Whenever two people live on adjacent plots of land, some work is required to coordinate their activities. Today, huge office towers hum with the activity of millions of workers and managers checking, controlling, supervising, coordinating, expediting, and informing. The natural environment is also likely to require more work; nations will have to increase efforts to conserve and even rebuild the environment if populations continue to grow.

Scenario 5: Gods and clods. If the technology that society develops is impenetrable rather than accessible to the average person, there could arise, to an extent even more marked than today, a society made up of an extremely busy elite of professionals and a useless majority unable to manipulate the words and mathematical symbols of the information society: an elite of gods doing the work and a majority of clods merely getting in the way.

There might be much work, but few people would be qualified to do it. Managing the complex technology would require a high level of competence and long hours of work each day. The expert managers would have to work extremely hard, not only to meet the demand for their services but also to develop their skills and update their knowledge.

This gods and clods scenario raises the problem of how to keep the majority of the population occupied. The elite, the high priests of technology, would have a soft and a hard option for dealing with it.

The soft option might resemble the universities of the late 1960s, which were often described as "holding tanks," permissive and generally agreeable environments to keep restless and rebellious youths off the streets and away from crowded job markets. The soft option thus implies a liberal attitude toward sex and narcissistic self-expression, since both are time-consuming and mildly gratifying pursuits that keep the populace in a reasonably unrevolutionary state of mind.

But abundant leisure spent surfing, reading Playboy, and building tans may not be enough to prevent unrest. Thus, the hard option would make the majority work no matter what, either by selectively withholding technology or by creating make-work projects.

Straightforward make-work projects are not unknown today, but the form they might assume in the future is perhaps best depicted in Kurt Vonnegut's novel *Player Piano*. Vonnegut depicts a society of gods with Ph.D.'s in engineering and clods who have either joined the army or the "Reeks and Wrecks" (Reconstruction and Reclamation Corps). In the former, they stomp around in accordance with a sergeant's bellows; in the latter, they dig ditches and fill them up again.

Scenario 6: Shadow work. Even without formally created make-work, the future may bring more "shadow work." The phrase shadow work, coined by Ivan Illich, refers to activity that does not contribute to subsistence but is a necessary complement to the production of goods and services in an industrial society. Much of this activity will be necessary (for example, children will probably continue to be raised in the home). But much of it might not be necessary; much of it could be make-work informally created by "the system."

Consider the time spent getting to and from work. The average person commutes by car; usually there is no alternative. This means that a car must be maintained, and this car generates the ample unpaid work of taking it to the garage and back and learning enough about how it works so that we can vaguely follow the mechanic's scribbles on our substantial bills. It also means fighting traffic into and out of the city and, when there are accidents, visits to hospitals and insurance companies.

Much of this make-work will be generated by unnecessary service consumption. We need the services of accountants to follow the regulations of the Internal Revenue Service and to straighten out its errors. We need lawyers to defend us against nuisance suits and to help us buy a house.

Productive technology may well increase such informally created make-work in the future. "By the end of the century," Ivan Illich writes, "the productive worker will be the exception." Rising productivity will generate unemployment and an "increasing need to diagnose ever more people for shadow work."

In the future foreseen by Illich, most people work as hard as ever—but not in traditional jobs. They are engaged in shadow work generated inadvertently by a highly technologized environment that gives rise to many artificial personal needs that must be attended to.

In this scenario, there is no need for formal make-work projects. The shadow work is distributed unfairly: The rich and powerful hire agents to stand in line for them and to fly them to the workplace.

Technology is mystifying; effort and time are required to locate someone who knows what is going on, who can press the right buttons and call the right programs to find the missing file. The lucky minority employed in the formal economy may find their work unchallenging, but since these people are powerful, they see to it that they are well paid.

Scenario 7: The electronic cottage. Two decades ago, only the specially trained worked with computers, which were demanding, unforgiving, and temperamental beasts with flashing lights and rumbling moving parts. Today, home computers grace many a den, and high-level programming languages, essentially simple and standardized combinations of basic English and elementary mathematics, have already placed the awesome potential of computers at the fingertips of the office worker and the hobbyist.

In the "electronic cottage" future, technology is pervasive and accessible to all. The high economic growth rate generages challenging and profitable work, and the work is distributed fairly. Electronic networking replaces the need for much informal and shadow work, such as doing the shopping, standing in line at the bank, waiting in the doctor's office to ask a question, or fulfilling other personal needs.

In this scenario, there is plenty of work for home workers engaged in both routine tasks and highly creative and specialized ones. Workers are needed to create and update data banks containing vast amounts of standardized and easily accessed legal, medical, economic, and scientific information. Specialists write counseling programs that generate diagnostic questions to assess the needs of people inquiring about medical symptoms and psychological problems.

Working in the electronic cottage could bridge the gap between the world of work and the culture in which we live—that sphere of liberty encompassing everything from disco dancing and banal commercial TV entertainment to family relations and obligations, higher education, and hobbies. Futurist Alvin Toffler even surmises that the shift from the central workplace to the home could revive the nuclear family and bring about a future of more closely knit relationships contrasting sharply with our present cold society of apathetic bystanders.

Working with Less Technology

Scenario 8: Subsistence work: While all eight scenarios in this article are prsented as heuristic tools designed to stimulate thought on the future of work, the subsistence work scenario plays a particularly important role because it challenges a basic assumption of the other seven: the assumption that the future will bring more of the same as far as technology is concerned.

But the future is not necessarily more of the same. Not only are people consuming available resources voraciously, but society is also only as rich as its most limited vital resources permit it to be. If, for example, new supplies of cheap fossil fuels were to become available in the United States, the country might be poorer than before because vigorous energy and industrial production would accelerate the depletion of the really limited resources: clean air, clean water, and clean land. It is thus by no means clear that the technology-intensive scenarios are more plausible than the view that the future may bring less wealth-producing machinery.

Resource limits mean that people will have to lower their expectations. The attitudes and optimistic hopes of the resource-rich ages of colonization and industrial expansion are not likely to serve us well in the future. Terms like "expectations" and "attitudes" suggest that people should approach work not only from the economic but also from the psychological point of view. Perhaps Americans are beginning to question the creation of artificial needs by relentless advertising and to examine which needs are real and worthwhile.

This radical scenario demands a reversal of our ulcer-producing path toward ever-greater consumption, material wealth, and physical comfort, back to earlier methods of production that are more labor intensive and more clearly linked to the important and meaningful business of subsistence.

According to this scenario, the future could bring a society in which more people roller-skate, cycle, and jog to productive jobs and live in smaller houses, apartments, and niches, compensating for crowdedness and thinner walls by being considerate enough to turn down the volume on electronic boom boxes and TV sets.

Lowered demands reduce the importance of productivity and transform work from a large-scale campaign against nature to what Illich calls "subsistence work."

Americans may not become meditating and fasting Buddhist monks living on a daily glass of spring water or a properly peeled orange, but they may cease to be hogs rummaging through supermarket aisles loading their carts with mountains of junk food. Workers may learn to execute with care and competence the meaningful work required for subsistence.

This scenario suggests that the quality of life may be higher in the future even in case of economic decline. The quality of life has much to do with the balance between what people need and want and what their environment can provide. Lower expectations could thus increase satisfaction with the quality of life.

The quality of life depends on the quality of work done by the many people around us on whom we depend. The technical meaning of "quality of work" is good or bad working conditions, the degree to which workers can use their skills and develop new ones, the degree to which they find their work meaningful and are in a position to make decisions about how it should be executed. Few people seem to use the term *quality of work* in the more obvious sense of the superb, adequate, or poor way in which work has been done. The notion that workers can be competent on the job and do work of high quality is deemed outdated in an age of complex work organizations that consist not only of people but also of machinery, regulations, plans, and goals. But it may have been discarded too soon. The individual may matter once again in a resource-poor future trying to optimize the quality of life.

Demise of Work Greatly Exaggerated

The future may bring more work than most people think. The immediate environments of individuals are likely to generate as much work as ever. People will always feel a need to repair their houses and to pull weeds from their flower beds. They will always farm out some of this work to the neighbor's kids and to small entrepreneurs offering specialized services. Perhaps communal work will increase as the bureaucracies of governments and multinational corporations grow more immense, more distant, and more ineffective. There may be more cooperative efforts to maintain neighborhoods, to look after the very old and the very young, and to provide training programs tailored to local needs.

Under some conditions, the amount of work generated by the formal economy may decrease. But under most conditions it is likely to stay at present levels. If technology is severely constrained by the lack of natural resources, the economy could even produce more work than it does now. Labor-intensive methods of getting things done might replace capital-intensive ones.

Even if technology continues to grow at a rapid rate, there need not be a dearth of formal work. It seems premature to think of a 10-hour workweek while inner cities need large-scale refurbishing, while the buses run only sporadically, and while many freeways are deteriorating and sport dangerous potholes.

As we saw earlier, a growing population makes social relationships ever more complex, requiring greater efforts of coordination and regulation. A few dozen settlers in the Old West were able to function with a marshal, a station master, and a preacher; a thousand urbanites today require hundreds of workers providing essential services ranging from pest control to heart transplants.

There will probably be work not only for an elite of the technologically astute, but also for the average person. Microcomputers have already become user-friendly and raise the possibility of a thriving electronic cottage industry. And if we stop looking only at quantitative economic indices, we see that the quality of life depends as much on character, patience, and motivation as it does on exceptional brains. In fact, the helpful cab driver, the caring and knowledgeable gardener, and the dutiful train conductor may have a more direct impact than the technological elite on the quality of daily life.

NOW, HONG KONG ON THE HUDSON?[5]

The South Bronx, 1988: The old neighborhood hardly looks the same anymore. Long-abandoned industrial buildings along Jackson Avenue have lost their coats of rust and are suddenly shiny and alive, in use again as factories and warehouses. Scattered among them are some new, low, windowless structures crowned with antennae—the signatures of the high-tech industries inside. A few blocks away, not far from the Bruckner Expressway, several Fortune 500 companies have built large plants on burned-out tracts of land.

The jobs and money these businesses throw off have encouraged landlords to spruce up the eight-story elevator buildings and old-law tenements that line many South Bronx streets. Shopping has also picked up as the Hub comes back and the Third Avenue strip welcomes an influx of new stores for the first time in years. The heart of the area's revival, however, is a busy shopping center anchored by Sears and crammed with a bevy of smaller stores. This monument to enterprise has sprouted from the rubble on the Charlotte Street lot where Jimmy Carter and Ronald Reagan both promised a bright future to the South Bronx.

This seemingly farfetched urban fantasy is the offspring of two of the stranger bedfellows in modern politics, Congressmen Jack Kemp and Robert Garcia. Kemp, the Republican ex-football player from Buffalo who quarterbacks Ronald Reagan's supply-siders on Capitol Hill, has traditionally opposed almost everything dear to Democrat Garcia, a South Bronx Puerto Rican leader with a liberal's faith in the power of government to help the poor.

But for more than two years, these two have been huddling together to find a way to attract business and jobs to slum neighborhoooods. The device they came up with—the so-called urban enterprise zone—has now been adopted by the Reagan administration and turned into the centerpiece of its decidedly skimpy list

[5]Reprint of an article by Harvey D. Shapiro. *New York* magazine. 15:35–7. Ap. 26, '82. Copyright © 1983 by News Group Publications, Inc. Reprinted with the permission of *New York* Magazine.

of domestic proposals. With Kemp and Garcia on hand last month, President Reagan told a Rose Garden gathering, "Enterprise zones offer a bold new means of invigorating economically crippled communities and improving the lives of some of our most disadvantaged citizens." He proposed to create 75 of them.

The concept is simple: Taxes and regulations are slashed in designated needy areas to encourage businesses to invest there and create jobs. True to supplyside theory, the administration hopes to harness the market to pull blighted neighborhoods out of distress.

"Enterprise zones are the Model Cities movie run backwards," says Steve Savas, an official in the Department of Housing and Urban Development. "Model Cities was an effort to create and cram as many government programs as possible into one geographic area. The idea of enterprise zones is to remove as many government programs as possible from an area." Savas, a former Columbia University professor who drafted much of the administration's proposal, says unleashing the private sector would help create a "Hong Kong on the Hudson."

Indeed, the South Bronx is clearly a leading candidate to get the Hong Kong blessing if Congress goes along with the Reagan proposal. It's in Bob Garcia's district and Jack Kemp's home state. It's where the president's putative friend Ed Koch has said he'd like to see an enterprise zone. And, says one administration official, it's also "the paradigm for urban blight. It's the place where you wring your hands and express concern about the plight of the urban poor. And so it's the place where you try to work your wonders as well."

Though a lot of people question just what wonders, if any, these zones will work, the concept has picked up a surprisingly broad coalition of support among liberals, conservatives, minority leaders, and urban officials. This coalition may prove fragile, however. Despite the Kemp-Garcia entente, liberals see enterprise zones as one more way to help the cities, while many conservatives view the idea as a substitute for costlier, centrally directed programs.

In New York City, the Koch administration has supported the zone concept—in part because it's the only bone being tossed the cities by Washington these days. But Karen Gerard, deputy mayor for economic policy and development, says, "We cannot meet economic-development goals by stimulating investment in an enterprise zone while we let other vital programs lapse."

The curious bi-polar appeal of enterprise zones extends back to the idea's origins in Great Britain five years ago. Peter Hall, a city planner and former chairman of the socialist Fabian Society, had concluded that the bureaucracy was stifling the entrepreneurs who had once generated inner-city jobs. His solution: an experiment in "fairly shameless free enterprise."

The idea appealed to the Tories, and after Margaret Thatcher took office, she established eleven zones. The results have been mixed. The British zones are located mainly on vacant or abandoned land outside the cities. Tax concessions have lured businesses, but it's turned out to be mostly warehousing that doesn't employ many people. Thus, though the zones have proved attractive to some established companies looking to expand, they haven't helped solve Britain's unemployment problem.

Meanwhile, however, the Heritage Foundation, a New Right think tank in Washington, got wind of the idea from England and inspired Jack Kemp to begin developing an American version. When his ideas received favorable notice from the Washington *Post*'s black op-ed columnist, William Raspberry, Bob Garcia's interest was spurred.

At the time, Garcia says, "I didn't know [Kemp]. I don't think I ever spoke two words to him." But Kemp asked Garcia to work with him in developing an enterprise-zone bill, and a Jack-and-Bobby team for the eighties was born.

A rudimentary Kemp-Garcia Urban Jobs and Enterprise Zone Act was introduced in June 1980, offering certain impoverished neighborhoods a package of business-tax cuts if the local community made some deep tax cuts itself. A refined version of the bill was introduced a year later. While the bills sat in committee, Kemp and Garcia were busy preaching to their respective congregations. They quickly found believers. In 1980, Kemp says, "I put enterprise zones in the Republican platform; Bob got it in the Democratic platform."

Kemp, however, also had the ear of presidential candidate Ronald Reagan, and when Reagan made his requisite pilgrimage to the South Bronx site Jimmy Carter had promised and failed to redeem, he talked of enterprise zones. In his State of the Union message, last January 26, President Ronald Reagan was still promising them. The proposal he finally unveiled on March 23 had taken nearly a year to draft.

"There was a big debate in the White House," Kemp says, between "the libertarian side, which wanted the Britain idea or nothing," and "the more pragmatic side," which wanted something that could make it through Congress in an election year. The only thing that kept the process moving, says one administration official, was that "the president really wanted this."

Under Reagan's proposal, 25 areas would be selected annually for the next three years and designated enterprise zones. For up to twenty years, any new or expanded business activities in these zones would qualify for such benefits as: a 3 to 5 percent investment tax credit for capital spending; a 10 percent property-tax credit for industrial and residential construction projects; a 10 percent tax credit for wages paid to an expanded labor force; and a tax credit for hiring disadvantaged people that starts at 50 percent of the wages paid and winds down over seven years.

The proposal would also give employees a tax credit equal to 5 percent of wages earned in the zone; eliminate any capital-gains taxes; guarantee access to low-cost industrial revenue bonds if this controversial tax-exempt financing device is discontinued elsewhere; and extend the tax-loss- and tax-credit-carryover periods throught the life of the zone, so that benefits unusable in one year could be stored up and used late.

The Treasury Department estimates that if each zone employed 10,000 people, the tax benefits handed out would amount to $12.4 million per zone, or $310 million in the first year. The total would increase as zone activity expanded.

So much for the federal-tax cupboard. There's another side to enterprise-zone largess that's put considerably more strain on the left-right coalition. The original notion called for the elimination of "burdensome" federal regulations in the zones. That plan has been largely toned down in the Reagan bill, which talks about easing regulations—but only if state and local officials request it and federal regulators agree. Moreover, rules on discrimination, minimum wages, and occupational health and safety can't be relaxed.

"It's come a long way from the original laissez-faire talk," says an aide to one Democratic congressman. Savas, of HUD, and several White House aides fought hard for lowering the minimum wage in the zones, but ideas like that are political suicide on Capitol Hill. "Bill Gray [Democrat, Pennsylvania], Bob Garcia, and I helped get that out," says Kemp.

In addition to soft-pedaling deregulation, the Reagan plan—though designed to encourage neighborhood participation—also blurs the local contributions. The first Kemp-Garcia bill required local-tax cuts. Mayors of financially pressed cities blanched at that, so the president adopted a New Federalism version of the Metropolitan Museum's admission policy: To get a zone, state and local governments can contribute what they want, but they must contribute something. Suggestions include targeting federal revenue-sharing funds to the zone, improving services there, and simplifying local regulations.

That, then, is the administration's offer to the business community—a smorgasbord of tax benefits, deregulation, local contributions, and neighborhood involvement. What kinds of businesses are expected to respond?

So far, no one seems to agree. Says Kemp, "The proposal is aimed at the entrepreneur more than the big corporation." Says Garcia, "We're hoping we can get big businesses as well as local entrepreneurs." His model is the suburban shopping mall, where "you have big national department stores like Sears and Macy's as anchors, and in between are tons of small shops—entrepreneurs, local people."

Clint Hoch, executive vice-president of Fantus, a corporate-relocation consulting firm, is less sanguine. "We suspect most of the activity [in the enterprise zones] will be among companies who are already in these zones and want to expand," he says.

At HUD, Savas insists the bill is neutral regarding the size of a company. But he says it's been designed—in response to criticisms of earlier versions—to favor labor-intensive industries over capital-intensive ones.

Of course, some people wonder whether any business at all will be eager to take up the administration offer. Roger Vaughan, deputy director of the New York State Office of Development Planning, says, "Trying to influence business-location decisions or expansion decisions through the tax code at this time is a misplaced emphasis." Since last year's tax cut, Vaughan argues, "any business making substantial investments does not have any taxable income." Moreover, he adds, "most studies have shown that federal taxes do not significantly influence location decisions or expansion decisions."

Herman Starobin, research director of the International Ladies Garment Workers Union, worries that a South Bronx zone would attract "nickel-and-dime guys, and it just means they'll close their operations in Manhattan."

While the debate on the concept was getting louder around the country, former New York City budget director David A. Grossman tried to figure out what would happen if the South Bronx got enterprise-zoned. Grossman's Nova Institute examined the second version of the Kemp-Garcia bill and assumed it would increase employment 5 percent in the Bronx south of Fordham Road. Grossman calculated that if 4,000 jobs were generated, they would bring $10 million in benefits annually to the South Bronx—which is meanwhile losing nearly $50 million in federal aid this year and next because of budget cuts.

"One large enterprise zone does not appear likely to do more than make a useful dent in the economic problems of the South Bronx, much less the rest of New York City," Grossman says.

Kemp concedes that the strongest criticism of the plan is a criticism of the national economy—that it will be hard to get anything started until interest rates come down and other financial signs perk up. But he insists the tax incentives will attract business.

Garcia has tried to restrain expectations and put some distance between himself and the administration. He says things like "What I'm trying to do is get the debate started," or "This is just a small part of what I consider to be important in rebuilding American cities." But he also makes it clear that he thinks the zones are worth a try. "I believe it can work. And nothing else has worked. There is nothing else in the wings."

One reason for the idea's broad appeal, of course, is that it offers benefits in an era of cutbacks. Although the administration is asking for 75 zones, Steve Savas is concerned that "you con't do anything here except in multiples of 435 [the number of congressional districts]."

"I would hope that we would earmark this so that the concentration would go to hard-pressed areas of the Northeast," Garcia says. But he points out that the federal Economic Development Administration (E.D.A.), when it first "became an agency under Commerce, was only designed for a small portion of the country; by the time we finished with E.D.A., 90 percent of the country was E.D.A. eligible."

Similarly, New York City will probably find it difficult to choose among potential zone sites. Under the Model Cities program, Lyndon Johnson required the city to designate a single area for benefits. Rather than make such a politically charged decision, the city demanded—and was given—three Model Cities neighborhoods: the South Bronx, parts of Harlem, and Bedford-Stuyvesant.

"Make the whole country an enterprise zone—I'd love it," Jack Kemp says with a laugh. But liberals in Congress are also eager to reshape the proposal. Bob Garcia is concerned about ensuring community participation in the zones. Others believe the Reagan plan needs a mechanism to help finance new ventures. The embattled federal bureaucracy is also looking for a role.

"It's this year's Christmas-tree bill," warns one Democrat. And for just that reason, Roger Vaughan says, "we'll probably have some form of enterprise zone this year." However, Ronald Reagan's supply-side curves have frequently gotten bent by the realities of government as well as economics. This supply-side urban program may ultimately find itself not only moderated but wrapped up in regulations, set-asides, inter-agency coordinating committees, annual plans, and various compromises.

In order to maintain the odd alliance that has propelled enterprise zones this far, for better or worse the "fairly shameless free enterprise" Peter Hall envisioned is likely to remain an interesting theory. What may emerge instead is a vaguely business-oriented collection of goodies, bland enough to be palatable, but not quite

satisfying to either liberals or conservatives. A vast array of interests in Washington have already gone to work carving their ini-
tials on the enterprise-zone proposal. As Bob Garcia says, in
urban policy "it's the only game in town right now."

CORPORATE SOCIAL RESPONSIBILITY IN THE REAGAN ERA AND BEYOND[6]

If we are to gain a proper insight into the issues of corporate
social responsibility during the 1980s, it will be necessary to view
them as an extension of the social issues and problems of the
1950s, 1960s, and 1970s. "Corporate social responsibility" —the
idea that business firms have an obligation to act for the social
good, even if in so doing they may pursue activities not normally
in the business domain, possibly lowering their economic profits
in the process—is an idea that has been vigorously debated in the
United States since the early 1950s. The philosophical belief that
those in power should be called to account for their power by those
subject to it extends far back into human history. The application
of this principle to the contemporary business corporation was
first observed in the early years of the twentieth century. Allowing
for the vicissitudes of depressions and warfare, the idea has gathered strength as the corporation became America's primary vehicle for organizing business operations.

A Social Responsibility Agenda

The debate on the role of business in society has generated an
agenda of social issues and problems that many accept as a proper
focus for socially responsible business actions.

Environmental pollution arising directly or indirectly from industrial operations and from the use and disposal of items produced.

[6]Reprint of an article from *California Management Review* adapted from a paper delivered at the University of Santa Clara, May 20, 1982 by William C. Frederick. *California Management Review* vol. 25, no.
3, Spring 1983. Copyright © 1983, The Regents of the University of California.

Discrimination in employment and other business opportunities on account of race, sex, ethnic group or national origin, physical or mental handicap, age, religion, and other characteristics.

Consumer abuses in the marketplace, including price gouging; misleading advertising claims; sale of ineffective, unreliable, and unsafe products; difficulty in obtaining satisfaction after purchase of faulty items; sponsorship of advertising and sale of products offensive to good taste, risky to human health, and projective of negative cultural sterotypes.

Threats to the safety and health of employees while at work or due to work processes and materials. Some business firms have exhibited reckless and negligent attitudes toward the physical and mental welfare of their employees, as well as a defensive posture when risks are revealed through independent studies.

Minimal concern for the quality of work life, particularly for those employees performing repetitive, low-skill tasks over long periods of time. Authoritarian, nonparticipative, hierarchical organizational procedures modeled along military lines are typical of most business firms, excluding significant involvement of employees in determining the conditions under which work is performed.

Economic, social, familial, and psychological dislocations attendant upon business decisions to terminate or relocate industrial and commercial operations.

Massive deterioration in the quality of urban life and in physical characteristics of urban communities, especially in the central core of major metropolitan areas. Business has contributed directly in some cases and indirectly—by neglect or disavowal of responsibility—in others to the decline of the city.

Questionable or abusive practices by multinational corporations, including the payment of bribes and other questionable outlays for securing contracts not otherwise obtainable; explicit and tacit cooperation with and toleration of governments that are repressive of basic human rights; foreign exchange speculation in contravention of the needs of parent and host nations; disregard of the basic economic needs and national policies of parent and host nations; observance of lower standards of public welfare in foreign sales of risky goods, in the safety of foreign industrial workers, and in pollutants generated by industrial production and mineral extraction in foreign nations; and shifting or threatening to shift production to the lowest-cost, and especially the lowest-wage, areas as a means of maximizing profits to the firm.

Uncritical support of and direct gain from national defense policies that advocate high levels of military preparedness, perpetuate a global arms race, support repressive political regimes through sales of weapons, and lead to general preparation for nuclear confrontation among major powers.

Still other items could be added to the agenda: issues of corporate governance; unfair treatment of corporation stockholders by management; business advocacy of favorable tax treatment by local, state, and federal authorities; business acceptance of government subsidies and other forms of support denied to nonbusiness groups; illegal corporate contributions to political candidates; and many of the commonplace, day-to-day ethical excesses encountered in business, such as embezzlement, contract rigging, use of insider information for the purchase or sale of stock, delivering products and services that do not meet contract specifications, and bribery and kickbacks associated with the purchase of supplies and raw materials used in production.

Two evaluative comments about the agenda are in order. First, the disruptions of the social, ethical, and legal fabric are a function of the business system itself, rather than nonbusiness phenomena imposed on the business order from the outside. Left to its own devices and inclinations, business operating in an unregulated market system produces these effects in the communities in which it operates. The issues and problems that have been at the heart of the social responsibility debate are a natural consequence of the institutionalized quest for profits normally sought through the free market. They represent the raw edge of business values rubbing against the social values of human communities and the eco-systems that sustain those communities.

At first, this charge might seem a shockingly harsh judgment, unjustified by the common sense and humanitarian inclinations that all recognize to be a part of business character. Would the typical businessperson consciously and deliberately be so callous, so intent on the Almighty Dollar or the greater glory of The Company, as to create for society this list of grievances? While most would prefer to answer this question negatively, a realistic response reveals that individual actions are often a function of organizational imperatives.

The core values of the business system—economic and organizational growth, the preservation of power, the quest for profits, the rational calculation of gain, the expedient and pragmatic perspective, and loyalty to the ideological spirit that pervades the system—drive all business firms to a social end that is perhaps no part of the intention of the individual businessperson caught in the system's toils. Unless we are willing to acknowledge that the problem of corporate social responsibility lies deep within the business order itself—within the central values that activate and sustain the whole—there is little prospect of finding a way out of present difficulties.

The issues agenda also reveals how woefully inadequate the "free" market is as a mechanism for approaching and resolving such problems. That mechanism gives full rein to the very values and inclinations that have contributed to the problems in the first place. How can the patient be made well by administering large doses of the toxin itself?

Society has long recognized the dangers inherent in an unfettered business and commercial system. From ancient times the money changer, the peddler, and the merchant have been on society's list of prime suspects. (A recent Gallup poll revealed that only 19 percent of the U.S. public believe business executives rank high in honesty and ethical standards.) No society in human history has been willing to entrust its fate to the uncontrolled values of business and commerce, for the simple reason that business values, when taken out of social context, will soon eliminate or denigrate those features of community life whose worth cannot be calculated in monetary terms. Humanity's response to this challenge has long been an imposition of social controls—religious, political, governmental, ethical, or ethnic. The market has never been free of social controls.

Corporate Social Responsibility: The State of the Art

What can be said about the current status of corporate social responsibility after nearly three decades of scholarly debate and trial-and-error experimentation by business? A first observation is that many business leaders have accepted the idea of corporate social responsibility. A relatively small, elite group of business executives has been in the forefront of the social responsibility movement from its beginnings in the early twentieth century, speaking of the need to curb corporate power and turn it to broader ends than mere profit taking. Today, the two-hundred-member Committee for Economic Development, the two-hundred-member Business Roundtable, and chief executive officers of many of the larger corporations are on record favoring the broad principles of social responsibility. Just how widely their views are shared by the business community is not known.

Secondly, a small wedge of corporations have put theory into practice by adopting some of the tools of corporate social responsiveness—which differs from corporate social responsibility. A responsive corporation responds pragmatically and defensively to social pressures. If a minority group complains about lack of job opportunities in the inner city, the corporation responds by constructing a ghetto plant which is staffed by minorities. When abnormal mortality rates are recorded by employees working with an exotic chemical compound, the company adopts safeguards to reduce exposure to the chemical agent. A socially responsive company does not pause long to consider whether these pragmatic actions are ideologically proper; it acts as if they are. It accepts a responsiblity for acts that create negative social consequences. In its more advanced form, corporate social responsiveness may be anticipatory. A company may employ environmental scanning, value trend analysis, socio-political forecasting, social auditing, social responsibility committees composed of board members or top-level managers, comprehensive public affairs programs, and various other social innovations intended to enhance the organization's ability to respond to present, and to anticipate future, social pressures.

Just how far this trend toward social responsiveness has progressed is not known. Newgren and Carroll, in a 1975 study, found that 42 percent of 183 large corporations had formally adopted social forcasting, and 69 percent expected to increase their use of the technique of corporate social responsiveness in the future. If these ratios were applied to the Fortune list of the one thousand largest firms, one could reasonably expect to find from four hundred to five hundred socially responsive corporations.

Thirdly, corporate philanthropy has flourished over the years. Corporate contributions for charitable and similiar purposes were $2.7 billion in 1980. Without these funds, many fragile and humanitarian institutions would die: health care for the poor and needy, basic medical research on rare diseases, artistic activities in many fields, educational opportunities for youth, recreational programs for the elderly, family support programs, and many other such undertakings benefit from corporate largesse. Critics have pointed out that corporations have never approached the limits of giving encouraged by Internal Revenue Service rules, which until 1981 permitted the deduction of such contributions up to 5 percent of pretax income and now allow up to 10 percent of pretax income. The national average for corporations hovers around 1 percent. Nor do many, including some influential business groups themselves, believe that corporate philanthropy has the answers to most of the problems and issues on the social responsibility agenda.

Fourthly, some socially innovative ideas have emerged from the social responsibility movement. Control Data, Levi Strauss, and Xerox Corporation have shown what might be done when corporate talent is focused on society's problems and needs. But few will know of or remember those innovative deeds because such social initiatives tend to be smothered by the dominant economic and financial values of the business system. As a result, social wheels are frequently reinvented by business.

More important than all the foregoing insights into the present status of the corporate social responsibility movement are the basic limits that constrain corporate enterprise as it moves into the social domain. Corporations excel in organizing and directing resources—capital, natural, and human—for the purpose of producing and distributing goods and services, in the hope of making a profit and remaining in business. Their managers and employees are trained for this basic purpose. Performance measures, while imprecise, are well understood and accepted by all. A legal system embodies the principles necessary to sustain and protect the contractual requirements of those engaged in trade. An overarching ideology of free enterprise rationalizes and justifies the pursuit of profit as being not just essential to society but wholly beneficent in its long-run consequences for material welfare, human freedom, and (in some versions) spiritual expression.

Beyond this most formidable system of thought and action, no individual firm or executive can venture without suffering penalties more severe than most are willing to accept. Neil Chamberlain of Columbia University has argued persuasively that corporations are captives of values and motives that drive them to seek profits above all else and are hostage to society's consumption ethic. It is not just business but also society that places limits on corporate and regulatory social initiatives through fear that costly social reforms will threaten jobs, increase prices and taxes, and ultimately reduce the economic effectivenes of the corporate cornucopia from which flow all material blessings.

David Vogel of the University of California, Berkeley, came to the same general conclusion in his study of the social protest movements of the 1960s and 1970s. These movements demanded little of business, and they accomplished few of their aims. Corporate authority, though challenged, was not directly diminished. The ability to change corporate behavior directly and substantively proved marginal. The reasons, according to Vogel, are traceable to the economic traits of the private business corporation.

As long as corporations remain dependent on private capital markets, there are real limits on their capability to consider nonprecuniary values in their decisions. . . . The most important decisions made by any firm are out of the control of those who govern it; they are dictated by the imperatives of the market economy. . . . The extent to which business executives could actually change the basic orientation of their companies is severely limited: corporate accountability is fundamentally limited by the inability of a privately owned firm to pursue objectives that are incompatible with long run profit maximization, however loosely that objective is defined: a politically [and socially] accountable corporation in a capitalist system is a contradiction in terms.

This much we can conclude about the corporate social responsibility movement in the United States: both external and internal advocates of corporate social actions have been, and remain, highly constrained in what can be accomplished through the corporate structure. Corporate philanthropy, while part of a life support system for many important community activities, cannot begin to serve many of the community's most urgent social needs. Corporate social responsiveness appears mainly as a defensive tactic utilized by an elite group of socially aware companies; it is not generally perceived or treated as a broad-scale societal strategy capable of leading humanity to a resolution of its most severe problems.

Social Responsiveness and Reagan

What are the prospects for corporate social responsibility in the Reagan era? Can, or should, we expect business to become more—or less—active in the social arena? If the federal government is to do less in the way of social problem solving, should or will the private sector do more?

It is useful to distinguish between voluntary and coerced social responsibility. Over the years business has undertaken a great many socially responsible activities on its own initiative: making charitable contributions, lending executives to a variety of community projects, advising governments on a whole host of national and local problems. These voluntarily assumed social responsibilities stand in contrast to those mandated by government regulations: pollution controls on production processes and on products such as automobiles; equal employment opportunity guidelines; industrial safety and health requirements; consumer protection measures; trade union recognition and wage-and-hour guidelines.

In the voluntary sphere, what reason is there to expect business to be either more or less responsible than previously? The basic business values, goals, and practices that presently constrain social reforms in and by business are still in place. The same basic strains of decency and social conscience that motivate some business leaders to be alert to social needs are not likely to disappear overnight, or at all, for that matter. The greed that some observers have remarked upon may be countered, at least in spirit, by a greater generosity on the part of others.

One should not be misled by politically inspired talk about business and the private sector "filling the void" left in social programming as government devotes fewer resources to these tasks. First of all, the dollar gap is very large when compared with current business outlays for social purposes. Figures are slippery but most sources have estimated that the combination of tax changes and budget reductions will deprive individuals and nonprofit organizations of perhaps forty to forty-five billion dollars of federal support through 1984. Corporations and private foundations in recent years have contributed a total of about five billion dollars annually for charitable and educational purposes.

The Conference Board reported in a survey of 427 companies that 60 percent were planning to increase charitable contributions in 1982 but nine out of ten of these were not doing so in response to federal budget cuts. Nor did the companies have plans to shift contributions to the social programs most affected by budget restrictions, such as job training. Only one-fifth of the corporations headquartered in major cities were planning increases in financial aid to urban programs. Moreover, corporate contributions historically are closely correlated with corporate profits, and the prolonged recession of 1981-82 threatens voluntary contributions. Tax cuts also discouraged greater giving by removing one of the incentives for these tax deductible contributions.

Business leaders have repeatedly said that business cannot and should not be expected to fill the gap. The comment of David Roderick, chief executive officer of the United States Steel Corporation, is typical: "There is a feeling in this country—wrongly so—that corporations are to step up and fill the void . . . but it should be obvious that we can't do it all." Another executive remarked, "Our company supported the president because we believed in the elimination of a number of these programs. Naturally, we're not too enthused about continuing the programs and shifting the burden to the corporate sector."

For all these reasons, it is quite unrealistic to expect significant modifications in the level of business's voluntarily assumed social responsibilties, so far as they are represented by corporate contributions. What about business's other social responsibilities—those mandated by government and enforced by regulatory agencies? Will a clean environment, safe work places, consumer protections, and equal employment opportunities be pursued in the 1980s with the same degree of success as during the 1960s and 1970s? Here, there is good news and bad news.

First, the bad news. President Reagan came into office having promised to "get government off our backs," a code phrase meaning less government regulation and fewer social initiatives. In this respect, he was continuing and perhaps accelerating a policy trend that was set in motion by President Ford and endorsed by President Carter. *Deregulation* became the watchword of the late 1970s, as business learned to be more effective in countering what it believed were the excessive social demands and social legislation of the 1960s and early 1970s.

"Getting government off our backs" has led to a partial dismantling and overall weakening of the federal regulatory structure. Budgets of the agencies have been reduced, drastically in some cases (30 percent or more at the Environmental Protection Agency and over 70 percent at the Council on Environmental Quality). Staff cuts have been deep, hampering enforcement efforts in some agencies: coal miners have complained bitterly that the Mine Safety and Health Administration has reduced the number of inspectors sent into mines.

Selective appointments—a normal part of the political spoils system—have been made to various agencies, with the apparent aim of shifting regulatory administration to a softer phase. Secretary of Interior James Watt is the most notable example of a public servant determined to loosen the regulatory hold on mineral exploration of public lands and offshore drilling opportunities. James Miller III, head of the Federal Trade Commission wants to reduce the agency's powers to protect consumers, a goal in which he has been aided by a Reagan-inspired congressional veto power over FTC rules. Thorne Auchter, who now heads the Occupational Safety and Health Administration, has made it tougher for the agency to issue new rules to protect workers. And two appointments to the National Labor Relations Board are, according to *Business Week,* "tilting the NLRB sharply toward management" and eventually "will make it harder for unions to organize workers."

Among the policy changes advocated or already accomplished are: the Civil Aeronautics Board's proposal to abolish rules requiring air travelers with reserved seats to be reimbursed when bumped from an overbooked flight; the Federal Trade Commission's hint that it may discard its rule requiring advertisers to substantiate their claims; Secretary Watt's policy of opening up vast offshore areas for leasing by oil companies; a softening of administration policies toward school desegregation that would, according to the U.S. Civil Rights Commission "threaten to reverse more than a generation of progress toward equal opportunity education"; the Labor Department's proposal to exempt 75 percent of business employers from submitting written affirmative action plans for hiring and promoting minorities and women; and a proposal to drop required annual inspections of nursing homes, drop follow-up checks on noncomplying facilities, and turn accreditation of these health care institutions for the elderly over to a private commission.

All of these changes are usually defended as being cost effective, or as putting regulation in the hands of those who understand business requirements better than their predecessor, or as freeing business decision makers from burdensome bureaucratic routines. These defenses may be justifiable; but the problem is that the changes also may lessen adherence to mandated social responsibility goals.

Business often has charged that government regulations have pushed them "too far." One might reasonably ask: Are workers "too safe" from job hazards? Are women and blacks "too highly paid" relative to men and whites? Are consumers "too well protected" from marketplace fraud and deception? Are the air and water "too clean" for public health? There are many persons, in business and outside of it, who believe that government regulation is essential to the successful pursuit of these and other social goals. If they are even partly correct, then we can expect a lower level of mandated socially responsible actions to be taken by business during the Reagan era.

But—as Gabriel Heatter, a 1940s radio commentator, used to say—"There's good news tonight." Although it may be seriously weakened, social responsibility will not fade away, for two reasons. First of all, business has learned during the 1960s and 1970s that social responsibility benefits business. It projects a good and caring image of an otherwise monolithic organization. It dampens down the fires of social upheaval and revolution. It produces a more satisfied and perhaps a more politically stable environment in which to conduct business. It may offset further inroads into business decision making by government or dissident social groups. It may be consistent with long-run profit goals. There are gains worth preserving and many business leaders are well aware of the positive impact of social responsibility on business.

In the second place, the habits of social responsibility are increasingly embedded in the practices and policies of large corporations. These habits are not likely to fade away, even with less government pressure being exerted. Many social functions have become institutionalized in the corporation: whites and blacks have learned to accept and work with each other; men, with perhaps more difficulty, are learning that women can manage a business or use a jackhammer; marketing professionals realize that placid consumers can turn into raging consumer activists if treated unfairly; production engineers know that social grievances can be avoided by designing low-polluting, safe industrial equipment; and even Detroit seems finally to have caught on that U.S. car buyers prefer small, safe, fuel efficient, nonpolluting automobiles. Abandoning these socially congenial practices would not be in the interest of business, whose executives might well shudder at the prospect of reactivating the social tensions of the 1960s.

Putting the good news and the bad news together gives this result: voluntary social responsibilities, which by themselves have never significantly addressed society's major social problems, may be expected to remain at present levels; mandated social responsibilities, which have produced the greatest social gains, will be weakened as government relaxes its regulatory purview. If the business community finds itself the target once again of a disaffected and aroused public claiming that business is irresponsible and should be curbed or penalized for social transgressions, business will have brought these charges upon itself. The corporate community favored the election of Reagan and congressional conservatives, supported White House deregulatory initiatives, and, in April 1982, almost two-thirds of them believed Reaganomics was working just fine. To put the matter plainly, the business community seems to favor a government policy whose effect is to exacerbate—rather than ameliorate—social problems and pressures. Under these conditions, there is every prospect that social tensions will increase, public criticism of business will mount, and the agenda of unresolved social issues will grow longer.

A Cooperative Framework for Social Responsibility

What would it take to move beyond this bleak prospect and to make a genuine advance in the art of social responsiblity? It would take a development that we are not likely to witness in today's political climate. Those basic business values that have continued so centrally to the present agenda of social problems and issues would have to be deflected from their natural course and either be replaced (an unlikely occurrence) or supplemented by nonbusiness values that would drive society in more fruitful directions. Enough is known about the dynamics of social change for us to conclude that fundamental value shifts of this order simply do not occur, even when a society undergoes radical revolution. *Plus ça change, plus c'est la même chose.*

But alternative values do exist and they continue to find expression. What is lacking is a comprehensive institutional structure to which these values can be attached and through which they can find full expression in the business arena. By contrast, the modern business corporation is a powerful institution vehicle giving life vigorously and enthusiastically to the values of business and commerce. A deeply embedded business value system finds itself unable to respond fully and adequately to the social challenges of our times, while nonbusiness values more compatible with the needs of the populace simmer beneath the surface without institutional structure.

What would such an institutional structure be? Some have imagined that business itself is the institutional shell into which alternative values could be infused, as new, young leaders whose own personal values are more compatible with social demands occupy positions of power and influence in the corporate system. This hope is a vain one, for the contest between established organizational values and contrary personal values is always uneven, and normally reaches a foreordained conclusion: Goliath wins. Organizations, especially business corporations, reject "misfits" or those who do not exhibit organizational loyalty; in no case are such persons entrusted with significant power over policy or important decisions. One's intended values are far less influential in organizational life than one's adopted values—those that are accepted as appropriate for getting the (organizational) job done. After long years of socialization to the dominant values of the business system, those who have struggled the hardest and reached the highest levels will hardly wish to abandon the system and the values that have made them what they have become.

The institutional structure needed to revivify corporate social responsibility cannot be based exclusively within the business order, for it would then become a captive of the very values from which relief is sought. Nor can it be formed from those external groups whose values would be likely to smother the business system under a blanket of punitive social controls. The social critics of the corporation face compromise and accommodation.

The essence of the new institutional system will have to be cooperation, collaboration, and coordination among organizations whose goals, purposes, and values may differ greatly. For want of a better term, it will be useful to call these associations social partnerships or social coalitions. Neither capitalist nor socialist, such partnerships would be more than pluralism but less than social cartels. Government, business, labor, church groups, the university, social activist groups, professional organizations, and other organizational units constitute the raw material for these social coalitions.

Many, perhaps most, of the successes scored thus far on the social responsibility front are the work of social partnerships—coalitions established among groups whose values are sharply different but who found ways to achieve sufficient harmony among themselves to address serious problems without abandoning their central values in the process. Business has yielded autonomy over pollution control, employment discrimination, job safety, and other matters to coalitions of government agencies, environmentalists, labor unions, and civil rights groups. In doing so, it has not lessened, and perhaps has strengthened, its status as our society's central institution. Nor have the competing members of these coalitions gained all they desired. The nation's air and water remain considerably contaminated with industrial by-products, women and minorities continue to suffer discrimination, preventable industrial accidents still occur. What has happened is tangible movement toward resolving some of society's major problems. In all these cases, business values have yielded to social values, but social values have not been allowed to overwhelm the essential economic mission of business. Surely, the future of corporate social responsibility lies in these directions. Social partnerships are the institutional device to which vital social values can be linked, modifying but not destroying business values, and permitting business to participate fully as one member of a coalition serving broader goals and purposes than those of business alone.

Over a decade ago, one group of business leaders rather courageously advocated the formation of a "government-business partnership for social progress." They understood well that society's problems were too complex and too large to be tackled by business alone. They also feared increased government initiatives in the social arena if business did not act promptly and voluntarily to address society's problems, and these fears were subsequently realized. They believed that the answer to the problem of corporate social responsibility was to be found through a coalition of interests in which both government and business would play central, complementary roles. With the passage of time, that social vision and belief in a social partnership has faded among those executives and has been replaced with a renewed faith in the "free" market.

But the notion of social partnerships for resolving social problems is a powerful idea. Its time may not yet have arrived. But like one of those comets that sweeps by the earth at periodic intervals, look for its reappearance when both business and society tire of the current fascination with free market approaches to social problems. Sooner or later, if corporate social responsibility is to have genuine and enduring meaning in society, a new way must be found to link social values with business purposes. The social partnership offers that prospect.

BIBLIOGRAPHY

An asterisk (*) preceding a reference indicates that the article or part of it has been reprinted in this book.

Books and Pamphlets

Ackerman, Robert W. and Bauer, Raymond A. Corporate social responsiveness: The modern dilema. Reston. '76.

Becker, W. H. The dynamics of business-government relations. University of Chicago Press. '82

Buckholz, R. A. Business environment and public poliy. Prentice-Hall. '82.

Buck, T. Comparative industrial systems. St. Martin's Press. '82

Carrington, J. C. and Edwards, G. T. Reversing economic decline. St. Martin's Press. '81.

Chamberlain, Neil W. The limits of corporate responsibility. Basic Books. '73.

Chamberlain, N. W. Social strategy and corporate structure. Macmillan. '82; Collier Macmillan (W. Drayton).

Collins, R. M. The business response to Keynes, 1929–1964. Columbia University Press. '81.

Dewar, Margaret ed. Industry vitalization; toward a national industrial policy. Pergamon Press. '82. Papers presented at a conference held at the Hubert H. Humphrey Institute of Public Affairs, Ap. 1981.

Dewar, Margaret. Industry in trouble; the federal government and the New England fisheries. Temple University Press. '83.

Diebold, J. The role of business in society. AMACOM. '82

Edwards, C. D. Big business and the policy of competition. Greenwood Press. '80.

Fine, B. Theories of the capitalist economy. Arnold, E. '82.

Giebelhaus, A. W. Business and government in the oil industry. JAI Press. '80.

Hayes, R.S. How to finance your small business with government money. 2nd ed. Wiley. '83.

Heilbroner, Robert L. and Thurow, Lester C. Economics explained. Prentice-Hall. '82.

Herman, Edward S. Corporate control, corporate power; a Twentieth Century Fund study. Cambridge University Press (Cambridge). '81. Available in USA from American office of Cambridge University Press.

Hitchcock, T. S. American business: the last hurrah? Dow Jones-Irwin. '82.

Freeman, Harold. Toward socialism in America. 2nd ed. Schenkman. '82.

McQuid, K. Big business and presidential power. Morrow. '82.

Maddison, A. Phases of capitalist development. Oxford University Press (Oxford). '82.

Magaziner, Ira C. and Reich, Robert B. Minding America's business; the decline and rise of the American economy. Vintage Books. '83.

Nelson, Richard R. ed. Government and technical progress; a cross-industry analysis. Pergamon Press. '82.

Novak, Michael. The spirit of democratic capitalism. Simon and Schuster. '82.

Peterson, H. C. Business and government. Harper & Row. '81.

Reisman, D. A. Tawney, Galbraith, and Adam Smith. St. Martin's Press. '82.

Rothwell, R. Industrial innovation and public policy. Greenwood Press. '81.

Steiner, G. A. and J. F. Casebook for business, government and society. 3rd ed. Random House. '80.

Thurow, Lester C. Dangerous currents; the state of economics. Random House. '83.

Vogel, David. Lobbying the corporation: Citizen challenges to business authority. Basic Books. '78.

Walker, David F. ed. Planning industrial development. Wiley. '80.

Wilson, R. W. and others. Innovation, competition, and government policy in the semi-conductor industry. Heath (Lexington) '80.

PERIODICALS

*Atlantic. 251:43–58. Mr. '83. The Next American Frontier. Robert Reich.

Business Week. p 8. Jl. 26, '82. The majority view: let companies sink or swim [corporate bail outs].

*Business Week. p 37. S. 13, '82. Bendix can only profit from its Marietta bid.

Business Week. p 15+. O. 25, '82. A plea to prop up basic industries. M. Hopkins.

Business Week. P 10. Ja. 17, '83. The search for a new engine of growth. J. Bowles.

Business Week. p 88. Ja. 31, '83. How strong a recovery?

Business Week. p 133-36. F. 14, '83. Can Chrysler keep its comeback rolling?

Business Week. p 106. Mr. 21, '83. Why the recovery may skip the farm belt.

Business Week. p 84-8+. Mr. 28, '83. America rushes to high tech for growth [special report].

Business Week. p 18. Ap 18, '83. Executives split on saving smokestack industries [Business Week/Harris Poll].

*Business Week. p 100-110. My 16, '83. A work revolution in U.S. industry.

Business Week. p 74-5. My. 30, '83. A bipartisan swing back to more regulation.

Business Week. p 59-60. Je. 6, '83. An industry plea for the freedom to compete.

*Business Week. p 54-62. Jl. 4, '83. Industrial policy: Is it the answer?

Business Week. p 23-4. Jl. 25, '83. The point man for industrial policy [J. A. Young].

*California Management Review. 25:145-57. Spring '83. Corporate social responsibility in the Reagan era and beyond. William C. Frederick.

Current. 250:3-15. F. '83. The future of capitalism [interview with R. L. Heilbroner].

Current. 252:27-37. My. '83. Increasing productivity in the U.S. R. M. Kans.

Current. 253:15-22. Je. '83 America and high tech.

*Forbes. 130:62+. A. 30, '82. So, what's wrong with a service economy? James Cook.

Forbes. 131:82-4. Je. 20, '83. The argument for plant closing legislation [interview with B. Bluestone].

Forbes. 132:30-1. Jl. 18, '83. Do-it-yourself industrial policy-making [Hyster Co. call for state and foreign subsidies to offset effects of Japanese imports]. M. Cieply.

Foreign Affairs. 60:836-51. S. '82. Trade, investment and deindustrialization: myth and reality. S. C. Chaikin.

Foreign Affairs. bibliography. 60:852-81. S. '82. Making industrial policy. R. Reich.

Foreign Affairs. 61:773–804. Spring '83. Beyond free trade. R. Reich.

Fortune. 105:42+. Ja. 11, '82 Eight questions for conservatives. Herbert Stein.

Fortune. 107:22–3. Ja. 10, '83. The dynamic duo of Atari democracy [views of I. Magaziner and R. Reich].

Fortune. 107:70–82+. Mr. 21, '83. How to foil protectionism [aiding healthy industries]. W. Guzzardi, Jr.

*The Futurist. 17:24–9. Je. '83. Eight scenarios for work in the future. Martin Morf.

Harper's 264:6–8. Je. '82. Reagan's industrial tonic. M. Kinsley.

*Harper's 266:17–22. F. '83. Can (creeping) socialism cure (creaking) capitalism? Robert M. Kans.

The Nation. 234: 163–4. 167–88. F. 13, '82. The selling of Japan [special issue; with editorial comment].

The Nation. 235:199+. S. 11, '82. Plan for people—not profits [excerpt from The deindustrialization of America]. B. Bluestone and B. Harrison.

The Nation. 235:395–7. O. 23, '82. Federal aid for worker on ownership [excerpt from The fight against shut-downs]. S. Lynd.

*The Nation. 236:687+. Je. 4, '83. Industrial policy—now the bad news. Samuel Boules, David M. Gordon and Thomas E. Weisskopf.

The Nation. 237:108–10. Ag. 6–13, '83. Strategies for a new economy [discussion of June 4, 1983 article, industrial policy—now the bad news]. S. Bowles and others.

*Nation's Business. 71:28–9. My. '83 How U.S. automakers are fighting back. Seth Kantor.

New Leader. 65:8–13. D. 27, '82. Overcoming capitalism's death wish. G. Tyler.

New Republic. 186:28–31. Mr. 31, '82. Industrial policy. R. B. Reich.

New Republic. 187:11+. O. 18, '82. Urban enterprise fraud. James Traub.

*New York. 15:35+. Ap. 26, '82. Now, Hong Kong on the Hudson? Harvey D. Shapiro.

New York Times. 1+. My. 8, '83. The Twilight of smokestack America. Peter T. Kilborn.

*New York Times Magazine. p. 20+. Ag. 15, '82. The future of capitalism. Robert L. Heilbroner.

Newsweek. 99:53–4. Je. 21, '83. The battle over bailouts. D. Pauly.

*Newsweek. 101:61–2. F. 14, '83. High hopes for high tech.

Newsweek. 101:56–7 F. 28, '83. GM and Toyota cut a deal. D. Pauly

Newsweek. 101:63. Ap. 25, '83. The road to lemon socialism. L. C. Thurow.

Progressive. 46:25–33. Jl. '82. Remaking the motor city—and America [views of J. Russell and D. Luria; symposium]. J. Wylie and L. Walsh.

Reader's Digest. 122:158–60. Je. '83. Cutting the ties that bind. M. Frazier and D. Cowden.

Scholastic Update. 116:11–12. S. 2, '83. Pressure for an industrial game plan.

Science. 217:781. Ag. 27, '82. The high-technology fix [methods of attracting industry]. B. C. Derry.

*Science Digest. 91:46–48. Mr. '83 Science and the American dream. Dr. Robert Jastrow.

Science News. 121:374. Je. 5, '82. Ill health still plagues nuclear industry. J. Raloff.

Society. 19:44–47. Jl./Ag. '82. Industry-growth sweepstakes. Bradley R. Schiller.

Society. 19:33–38. Jl./Ag. '82. Reaganomics, reindustrialization and regionalism.

Society. 20:59–63. N./D. '82. America's identity crisis. R. J. Whalen.

Successful Farming. 80:22. My. '82. White House threatens to shake up farm credit system.

Technology Review. 85:38–47. O. '82. Is the nuclear industry worth saving? R. K. Lester.

Technology Review. 85:48–57. N./D. '82. Reindustrialization past and present. R. Williams.

Time. 117:46–48. Je. 15, '81. Outlook brightens.

*Time. 121:50–9. Mr. 21, '83. Iacocca's tightrope act.

Time. 121:54. Mr. 21, '83. Was the bailout a blunder? [Chrysler Corp.]

U.S.A. Today. 110:22–3. My. '82. Rebuilding America [Machinists Union economic program]. W. W. Winpisinger.

U.S. News & World Report. 90:18–19. F. 23, '81 Turn for the better?

U.S. News & World Report. 92:43–6. Ap. 26, '82. The ever present hand of government.

U.S. News & World Report. 93:42–3. Ag. 9, '82. When business comes to cities' rescue. J. M. Hildreth.

*U.S. News & World Report. 93:89. D. 13, '82. U.S. business leaders "Are out of touch with society."

U.S. News & World Report. 94:66–71. Ja. 31, '83. How to get the country moving again.

U.S. News & World Report. 94:68. F. 14, '83. Chrysler: Classic turn-around in U.S. industry.

U.S. News & World Report. 94:51-2. My. 2, '83. How to turn recovery into long-term prosperity [interview with E. Jefferson].

U.S. News & World Report. 94:45-6. My. 16, '83. Why U.S. needs a new industrial policy [interview with R. Reich].

*U.S. News & World Report. 95:45-6. S. 12, '83. There's still life in smokestack America. Manuel Schiffres.

*Vital Speeches of the Day. 48:316-20. Mr. 1, '82. Productivity and American world competitiveness. William Van Dusen Wishard.

*Vital Speeches of the Day. 49:73-79. N. 15, '82. Gotterdammerung of the giant corporations? Arthur Burck.

Vital Speeches of the Day. 49:203-6. F. 15, '83 Getting our basic industries back on track. W. P. Tippett.

*Vital Speeches of the Day. 49:517-21. Je. 15, '83. Are farmers on the way out? Seeley G. Lodwick.

Vital Speeches of the Day. 49:670-2. Ag. 15, '83. Individual liberty and the free market system. W. S. Johnson.

Vital Speeches of the Day. 49:124-8. D. 1, '83. American strategies for productivity and profitability. T. J. Murrin.